Drinkers, Drummers, and Decent Folk

Drinkers, Drummers, and Decent Folk

Ethnographic Narratives
of Village Trinidad

JOHN O. STEWART

State University of New York Press

Published by
State University of New York Press, Albany

© 1989   State University of New York

Printed in the United States of America

For information, address State University of New York
Press, State University Plaza, Albany, N.Y., 12246

Library of Congress Cataloging in Publication Data

Stewart, John O.
    Drinkers, drummers, and decent folk.

    Bibliography: p.
    Includes index.
    1. Ethnology — Trinidad. 2. Trinidad — Social life
and customs. I. Title.
GN564.T7S74   1988   306'.097298'3   87-33632
ISBN 0-88706-829-4   Rev.
ISBN 0-88706-830-8 (pbk.)

10 9 8 7 6 5 4 3 2 1

To the Neighbors of Naggee Road, Moruga Road,
and Sixth Company

whose immeasurable patience, hospitality, and
co-operation were essential to the fieldwork
on which these narratives are based

Contents

Contents

Acknowledgments

I am indebted to Clifford Geertz and James Fernandez for various ideas which have been stimulating in my approach to writing ethnography. I acknowledge, also, my former colleagues in anthropology at the University of Illinois, Urbana for their support. For direct comments on this work, my thanks to Dan Rose, University of Pennsylvania, William Merrill, Smithsonian Institution, and Earl Lyons.

Earlier versions of "Small Victories" have appeared in *Tapia*, and *Black Scholar*, Vol. 9, No. 5, January/February 1978.

"Shadows in the Moonlight" was first printed in *Chant of Saints*, Michael S. Harper and Robert B. Stepto (eds.), University of Illinois Press, Urbana 1979.

"The Community Center" was first printed in *TriQuarterly 58*, Evanston, Fall 1983.

Foreword: Hermeneutics and the Anthropology of Fiction

ROBERT A. MANNERS

John Stewart's warrant to record and delineate life in rural Trinidad was established initially by birth and direct experience, later confirmed, elaborated and contextualized through years of postgraduate study and anthropological field work in the area. The format he has designed for this collection represents his desire to enrich ethnographic exposition by joining it to storytelling without either blurring or concealing the line of demarcation between the two. Thus the notes and commentaries (Who's Speaking Here?, etc.) have been designed to draw attention to the "general concerns of the work, and the process of its construction" (from Stewart's Abstract). Although fictional techniques and the "selected field notes and commentaries" cohabit within the covers of this stunning volume, each retains its own formal identity as it offers telling testimony to the value of the symbiosis. Other ethnographers before Stewart have told stories, either as recounted to them by informants or as experienced by them personally. But the latter have sometimes been so ruthlessly blended into the general ethnographic account that one cannot know where interpretive projection and imagination let off and so-called positivism/empiricism begins.

The artistry of Stewart's "invention" is that it allows him to tell us something about Caribbean "realities" as his life, training, talent and creativity reveal these "realities" to him. But he does not offer the stories as factual history, only as the product of insights permitted him by his gifts and his experience. The anthropological cement that helps to explain and is in turn explained by his fictions is supplied in the aforementioned fieldnotes and commentaries.

In the best of all possible worlds the anthropologist and the writer of fiction are one, *but write as two*. In his role as anthropologist he may make the leap that carries him through and beyond his ethnographic data to the creation of an hypothesis or a theory. He may not, however, invent either the ethnography or the characters portrayed, for this is a privilege reserved to the writer of fiction.

During the past ten or twenty years, anthropology and its variously certified practitioners have been marching off in many different directions. Democracy of interpretation — in all likelihood the genetically disordered offspring of cultural relativism — is the current mode. Expertise is not only irrelevant, it has become a hindrance to the free exercise of imagination. Any opinion, perception, analysis, interpretation or explanation of cultural phenomena, as Raymond Firth has observed, is about as good as any other.[1]

However, for anthropologists outside this adventurous company

> Social Anthropology is not just an exercise in speculative reasoning. It is about the actions and thoughts of people. . . . So when any statement is made about such actions and thoughts, a very proper question is, what is the nature of the evidence? . . . I think it of prime importance that generalizations about thought and behavior should clearly indicate the evidence on which they are based in 'empirical' terms, with attention to source, frequency, systematic distribution and logical coherence . . . generalizations must relate at some point to *what* who said and did where, when and how. (Firth, Ibid., emphasis in original).

While all generalization involves a creative leap from observed data to synthesis/hypothesis/theory, many of the new ethnographers have discovered that their data may impose unwelcome restraints on creativity. And since they are undeterred by any compulsion to let us know how they got to here from there, they leap over tall buildings at a single bound, allowing falsifiability to take unassailable refuge inside their heads. Adherents of Karl Popper may shudder, but the poetic exercise of explanation by intuition and the esoteric manipulation of symbols multiplies. Sometimes it makes for fun reading, but to many anthropologists the Popperian touchstone still seems to matter.

It may be that the most reasonable explanation for this frenzied departure from the more traditional kinds of hypothesizing has to do with the long-apparent inadequacy of monocausal or other simplistic kinds of explanation. Or, to put it another way, to the near infinitude of variables, of somatic and extrasomatic influences at work in the making, unmaking and preserving of cultural forms and institutions.

Or, on the other hand, as suggested approvingly by Richard Shweder (*New York Times Book Review*, September 21, 1936), the ethnographer-home-from-the-field must "figure out which point of view will have the greatest impact on [his/her] audience. . . . That is why the retelling is often better than the original experience. Unburdened of the small truths of positive science, the tale grows tall. The idea is that the best way to write a compelling ethnography is to lose your field notes." Better, perhaps, one might add, not to take any field notes. And if one should be so carelessly conventional as to have done so, still better to destroy them before one sits down to write. After all, every ethnography, no matter how scrupulously researched, organized and presented, is in some respects inexact. Now, it seems, inexactitude may be self-consciously elevated to new heights in the creation of ethnographies of imagination. "I've got to come back and tell a consistent and entertaining story about what the 'whoevers' are like and everything they do had better fit this one story." (Paul Kay, as "semi-seriously" quoted by Shweder).

Paul Rabinow ("Humanism as Nihilism: The Bracketing of Truth and Seriousness in American Cultural Anthropology," in *Social Science as Moral Inquiry*, N. Hahn, R. Bellah, P. Rabinow and W. Sullivan, eds., New York, Columbia University Press. 1983.p.66), citing Clifford Geertz, notes that: "'The essential vocation of interpretive anthropology is not to answer our deepest questions but to make available to us answers that others . . . have given and thus to include them in the consultable record of what man has said.'" Nothing new here. Rabinow adds: "The point is to enter into the imaginative universe of others, to *construct fictions* about these cultures and thereby extend the range of human discourse. The task of anthropology is to . . . return home and construct an account, to preserve their culture for the historical record" (Emphasis added).

Or, one might add, to trade whatever feeble claims to science our discipline may have for an ethnographic Tower of Babel. What kind of "historical record" would be preserved? Thus, Albert Spaulding remarks somewhat apprehensively that the "recent interest in explicitly nonscientific humanistic anthropology, including . . . hermeneutics, reflexive and critical anthropology" threatens to leave only "prehistoric archaeology as the sole relic of traditional scientific anthropology." (*Anthropology Newsletter*, October, 1987).

The irony is that in all of the flood of post-modernist, deconstructionist, anything-goes accounts there is an obvious attempt to compensate for the generally dessicated character of ordinary field ethnographies. Unfortunately for the rest of us and for that part of the reading public who are drawn to the product by the enchanting payoff — how the so-and-so people *really* are, packaged in a "good read" — these free-swinging efforts to provide "deeper understandings, insights and explanations" get validated by the professional credentials of their creators. In short, while many of the new ethnographers may be appropriately modest in their claims, they do speak and write as *anthropologists*. Consequently, their exegeses, no matter how detached these may be from "evidence," gain a measure of scientific respectability through their structured inclusion in "an anthropological study."

On the other hand, the writer of fiction observes only the constraints imposed upon him by his imagination and his determination either to create, embellish or adhere to the truth as he sees it. He, unlike the anthropologist in the field, can indeed get inside the minds of his creations. For they are his mind. In short, the anthropologist must be guided to his conclusions by the evidence, constrained by his observations and his disciplined deductions from these observations. When he leaps from these into the minds of his *real people*, he is trespassing on the territory of the writers of fiction — but willy-nilly sheathed in the exalted mantle of "science."

The novelist or writer of short stories may invent both setting and character. Verisimilitude constrains him only to the degree that he wishes his fictive universe to be as real, as internally consistent or believable as the story demands. Even those anthropologists who write science fiction are generally careful to maintain "believability" and "internal consistency" in their work. When they are not dabbling in the future or mucking around in some remote galaxy, they will try to yoke a familiar habitat to characters and situations synthesized from fact and fancy. When they get inside the heads and hearts of their creations, they have, as it were, permission to do so, a permission granted by their role as writer of fiction. Were they to commit the same kind of intrusion in a fieldwork monograph, we would be justified in saying: "How do you know?" While such untoward intrusions may provide sharp and even compelling insights, it is the guise or framework in which they are offered that triggers one's resistance.

In his essay on "Post-Modernism and the Fictive Mode," Stewart wrestles with the central problem of "incompleteness" in the traditional ethnographic monograph. He tells us that he paid his debt to his examiners and to the anthropological part of his being when he wrote and submitted his thesis for the degree. Since then, he says: "I write stories."

But it is our good fortune that Stewart's background and talent have lodged him (rather comfortably, I trust) between the two schools: ethnography and fiction. For while he does indeed "write stories," he has in this volume offered us hope for a resolution of the dilemma posed by the desire to humanize the cultural study of "the other" without betraying the Firthian injunction against simple "assertion." "Inner structures must be demonstrated, they cannot be invented." And conclusions must be supported "by some body of evidence" (Firth).

Stewart asks: "If entering the 'native' subjective world is desirable, and standard ethnographic texts do not take us there, why not the literary text based on as thorough a knowledge of 'native' culture as field-work makes possible?" He answers the question in this volume. And in the process he demonstrates that the "literary text," written with wit, humor and a special kind of poignancy that comes from immersion *cum* controlled detachment, can be very satisfying indeed. But can one who has the skills do more?[2]

Because Stewart, like some of the rest of us, is concerned about the trend towards the fictionalization of ethnography, he has, in the present collection, provided us with a work that could prove a model for the mutual enrichment of both: ethnography and fiction grounded in fieldwork. Thus the volume includes history, biography and other kinds of descriptive and factual data normally presented as part of an ethnographic study. Since much material of this kind may not be appropriate for inclusion in the stories but does provide a context of time and place that increases our understanding, he presents it separately. These data come in the sections he has titled: Who's Speaking Here, In the Field, At the Desk and At the Second Desk.

The combination works. It is a device that reminds one somewhat of the format used so effectively by John Dos Passos some sixty years ago. And it works because neither the stories nor the carefully demarcated sections tries to be the other. The very form of his presentation emphasizes the logic and the necessity of the disjunction. "The individual engaged in solving problems, transcending, understanding, or interpreting them in a personal way," he tells us, "plays a major role in how I think culture happens. One could write about this, but *one could not present it in the formal ethnography*. One could in the literary form which allows exploration of the interior world of thought and feeling" (Emphasis added).

Citing Bradd Shore, Stewart writes: "'It is a common mistake to assume that the web of mysteries, minor and major, that constitute an alien culture may be resolved by careful observation alone. Even the most painstaking and perceptive observer eventually discovers that the key to many of the most intriguing and significant aspects of culture lies within the minds of those he observes.'" How to get there, however, will discourage the more conscientious seekers-after-the-whole-truth, for they must know they cannot achieve that epiphany. But determination seems often to overcome good sense. Consequently, many of the "new anthropologists" are engaged in an endless and inevitably frustrating (if not to them, at least to those of us who read the results) manipulation of signs, symbols, rituals, myths and concrete behavior in their attempt to enter the minds of their subjects/objects, and then, as it were, to smuggle their projections directly into the body of their ethnographies.

What Stewart has managed to do in his juxtaposition of fiction and "ethnography" is to demonstrate that the two should not try to be one. Enclosed within a single volume but dramatically distinguished in tone, typography and substance, each of the genres embellishes the other and enhances our appreciation and understanding of the whole.

John Stewart writes stories. And he writes interstitial ethnography. There are ethnography and imagination in his stories, but the notes and commentaries stick to what, for want of a better word, we call facts. One need not be an intransigent empiricist or positivist to stress the difficulties of translating field data into individual thought processes. Nor even to raise questions about the reliability of information on thought processes imparted to the ethnographer by the informant. There is only one way to get into "the other's" head. That is to imagine yourself there. And that, of course, is a lot riskier and should be more intimidating than measuring the dimensions of a yam garden or recording a couple of generations of clan begats.

We don't need a new genre to get at the exciting world of "the other's" inner life. Such a genre already exists in the form of fiction. And that is where some of the sharpest insights into the humanity of "the other" may be found — in short stories and novels, creations in which the author need feel no self-consciousness about mind probing nor about his license to explore the interior world of his fictional characters.

While it is possible, as this collection demonstrates, for good fiction to supplement or even in part to supplant ethnography in revealing important aspects of the culture of the "other," (Good fiction is often acutely ethnographic.), ethnography, because it must submit to reasonable tests of reliability if it is to be useful, must not make knowledge claims it cannot verify.

Because Stewart knows this, and because he writes from his background as a Trinidadian and an anthropologist, without confabulation, the stories instruct and inform us subtly about the inner world of his "others" and, in part, about the outer against which the small or large dramas of their lives are being played out. Thus the fictions in this volume are unobtrusive though incomplete ethnographies of a special kind. Many of the residual but more traditional kinds of ethnographic data are skillfully supplied by Who's Speaking Here? and the other notes and commentaries. Stewart does not, of course, maintain that what he does is all of ethnography. But he does, it seems to me, demonstrate conclusively and to our great pleasure and profit, that there may be a format in which the anthropologist *cum* writer-of-talent can fill in those revealing dimensions of the "other's" humanity and at the same time give us a cultural document that does not violate suitable limits of ethnographic conjecture.

A few friends tell me that some day the goal of multidimensional analysis now being pursued by the new ethnographers will be encompassed within a single work in which creativity and the presentation of "fact" are so cunningly blended and so convincingly demonstrated that even the cautious post-positivists will find the result agreeable. Perhaps. But until that day comes, and unless something like the model demonstrated in this volume gains wide acceptance, we may have to be content with carefully detailed and occasionally soporific ethnographies *and* fully separate but richly informative works of imagination. Meanwhile we are most fortunate to have among us an anthropologist who combines a proper regard for evidentiary norms along with singular talent as a creative writer.

Notes

1. "There is a sloppy notion abroad that since all perception is subjectively organized there are no 'facts' to which appeal can be made; any interpretation of social reality is as good as any other"(Raymond Firth, "An Appraisal of Modern Social Anthropology," in *Annual Review of Anthropology*, 1975. Bernard Siegel, Ed.

2. "[Loren] Eiseley himself clearly understood the different purposes of the scholarly and the literary scientific essays. *He never confused the two*, and there are some cogent and valuable defenses of the literary essay in these pages." (Review of Eiseley's *Lost Notebooks*, New York Times, 9/14/87. Emphasis added.)

Introduction

I. Post-Modern Ethnography and the Fictive Mode

(i)

A revisionist impulse in professional anthropology has surfaced from time to time in the past, but not with the sustained intensity of recent years. From Hymes' omnibus critique (1974) to Goldschmidt's warning that fissiparous tendencies among anthropologists are an imminent threat (1986), there has been a steady voicing of concern over the future of institutional anthropology. Without some revision of its methods and objectives, critics say, the discipline is likely to be the agent of its own disappearance. The written ethnography which is the most notable and enduring product in anthroplogy is at the center of much of the revisionist critique, with direct aim being taken against both form and substance in the standard ethnographic monograph (Marcus & Cushman 1982; Clifford & Marcus 1986).

The formal ethnographic monograph, as it developed, was not assumed to represent the totality of the field research which underpinned it. Anthropology, Levi-Strauss reminded, is an impassioned afair, "the outcome of a historical process which has made the larger part of mankind subservient to the other," and which has seen one part of mankind treat the other "as an object." (1966) The asserted intention of orthodox ethnography is to understand "the other" from an objective, value-free perspective and to document such understanding for a neutral and accurate record. Such an approach was quite in keeping with the strategy of carrying out field research

1

in the "exotic" societies of the world, which were seen as being at a great remove historically, aesthetically, and structurally from the world of researchers. It helped too, that many of these societies were either dying physically, or facing the circumstance of massive de-culturation: "In the 1850s and after, one could be objective about the Indian as one could not have been ten, twenty, or thirty years before; one could be objective about a creature who had been reduced to the status of a specimen picked up on a field trip. One could move toward scientific analysis and away from pity and censure" (Pearce, quoted in Hymes 1974).

From a superordinate remove, anthropologists could approach their work as tantamount to collecting and analysing the detritus of a passing, or passed, era — fertile ground for the development of a museum-oriented mentality. Along with the artifacts of a given culture, written accounts would serve to fix, objectively, the social and cultural features of given groups. The written ethnography was consciously depersonalized. Any "native" sensibility was thoroughly subordinated to the elucidation of abstract structures which purportedly evidenced evolutionary or other significant patterns. Formal metaphors in language that translated field experience into data were developed. And as anthropology became a firmly institutionalized discipline, the development of scientifically oriented theories, designed to refine our understanding of the abstract formalities that govern peoples' lives, took precedence over communication of the living experience itself. Ethnographers went after truth of an aggregate and supra-personal order.

On balance, it must be noted that the scientific orientation was adopted in ethnography somewhat in reaction against an earlier approach, which was marked by questionable research procedures, blatantly ethnocentric speculation, and standards of rhetoric and interpretaion that were borrowed from the study and practice of literature. Transcending these limitations, which were often of a colonial-imperialist cast, and arriving at value-free interpretations grounded in fact and the discovery of natural laws, was seen as the difference between an anthropology that was overly given to imaginative fantasy, and one that was directly descriptive of the real world. Separation between the workings of the imagination, especially as expressed in literary form, and anthropology as scientifically grounded truth became a disciplinary priority particularly during the Boasian era.

Boas' students were required, it is said, to hide their literary efforts from the master. Yet, while literary forms of expression were falling into disrepute among anthropologists as a way of presenting their serious work, the literary impulse itself was not altogether neutralised. Some of Boas' most famous students — Margaret Mcad, Edward Sapir, Ruth Benedict — struggled against the invalidation of artistic literature as a serious form for anthropologists by cultivating joint identities as both literary artists and anthropologists (Clifford & Marcus 1986). By others it was on occasion found that literary form and technique made up for deficiencies to which the formal monograph was subject. As early as 1890 Adolf Bandelier had published *The Delight Makers*, an ethnography of the Southwest pueblo dwellers, in the orthodox form of a novel. About his choice of form he explained, "I was prompted to perform the work by a conviction that however scientific works may tell the truth about the Indian, they exercise always a limited influence upon the general public, and to that public, in our country as well as abroad, the Indian has remained as good as unknown. By clothing sober facts in the garb of romance I have hoped to make the 'Truth about the Pueblo Indians' more accessible and perhaps more acceptable to the public in general." (1918:v).

Alfred Kroeber later articulated a rationale for anthropological adoption of the fictional form which relates to, but is not identical with, that of Bandelier's. Noting that the stories in *American Indian Life*, (Parsons 1967), sprung from the same intensive studies out of which scientific monographs were issued, Kroeber then marked certain limitaitons of the monograph:

> "The monographs have a way of sticking pretty closely to the objective facts recorded. The mental workings of the people whose customs are described, are subjective, and therefore much more charily put into print. The result is that every American anthropologist with field experience, holds in his memory many interpretations, many convictions as to how his Indians feel, why they act as they do in a given situation, what goes on inside of them. This psychology of the Indian is often expressed by the fron-

tiersman, the missionary and trader, by the man of the city, even.
But it has been very little formulated by the very men who know
most, who have each given a large block of their lives to acquiring
intensive and exact information about the Indian and his culture,
(Parsons 1967: 13.).

The fictional form, on the other hand, allowed for "a freedom in
depicting or suggesting the thoughts and feelings of the Indian, such
as is impossible in a formal, scientific report," (p. 13). Not only did
the fictional mode allow for a certain depiction of "native" thought
and feeling, it forced the anthropologists to realize "how little we
knew of the workings of the Indian mind on some sides, how much
on others, (p. 13).

The scientifically objective monograph may be flawless in a certain sense, but lacking in others. It did not captivate a wide enough
audience; it excluded the essential arenas of thought and feeling; and
did not encourage the ethnographer's comprehension of the boundaries beyond which his or her acquired knowledge did not go, or
what this might mean. By 1947 Clyde Kluckhohn could comment:
"Until anthropologists can deal rigorously with the 'subjective factors' in the lives of 'primitives' their work will be flat and insubstantial. Unless they can learn to delineate the emotional structure of
societies, serious persons who wish to learn about the life of human
beings in groups will properly continue to turn to literature rather
than to science for enlightenment. (quoted in Borenstein 1978:131).
The intense pursuit of legitimacy as scientists, however, functioned
as a formidable barrier among ethnographers to the comfortably
open practice of any writing which could be characterized as literary.

Kluckhohn could see that the emotional structure of societies
had to be integrated into the domain covered by anthropology and
that imaginative writers had already found a successful way to deal
with this. But his recommended techniques for an improved anthropology did not include practising what imaginative writers do.
Instead, he emphasized improvements in range and completeness of
objectively observable data, and comprehensive recording techniques. More of the same. Through the 1950s several anthropologists who considered themselves mainstream professionals, and who
published literary works, did so under pseudonyms, or with the
public understanding that such work was not to be considered with

the same seriousness as their scientific publications. In spite of certain notable efforts, such as that of Joseph Casagrande's *In The Company of Man* (1964), the textual form of the monograph, in which consciousness of the subjective factor is held at a minimum, or ignored altogether, remained entrenched as the legitimate form for ethnographic presentation.

A serious concern with the subjective factor in anthropology did not emerge again until the late sixties, and once again focus was on its constraining rather than its liberating properties. With the work of Charles & Betty Lou Valentine, and others who saw anthropology as a serious contributor to the continued oppression of dominated peoples, a sharp scrutiny of the aims and achievement of the profession was renewed. Emotional and subjective factors widely assumed to have been eliminated through adoption of the objective scientific mode were found to be very present, nevertheless, particularly in the form of ethnocentric biases which anthropologists either endorsed or failed to recognize in themselves and their work. It became clear that the pursuit of a value-free anthropology had not been, and probably could not be successful. In the new, politically aware criticism, it was charged quite openly that anthropology was guilty of "scientific racism," and that it had — wittingly or unwittingly — contributed to the dehumanization of those people whose social and cultural systems were the objects of its research. (Jones 1970, Valentine 1972, Asad 1973, Lewis 1973, Willis 1974).

As a systematic, objective record, anthropology had served well the colonial systems (internal and external) which had sponsored it. Could it serve as well those whose lives and histories comprised its data? Should anthropologists be advocates in the liberation struggles of subject people? Do anthropologists have a responsibility to make up for past wrongs to which the discipline had contributed? Could anthropology actually fulfil its promise as an undertaking on behalf of all humankind? These and similar questions led to the eruption of a "critical anthropology," which took aim at various errors and weaknesses that inhibit anthropology from reaching its full potential as a science of culture and society. An early response to this criticism focused on encouraging "native" participation in the construction of the ethnographic text (see Betty Lou Valentine's *Hustling and Other Hard Work*), but this practice has not been widely adopted. Concern for the authenticity with which published ethnography presents the

fieldwork upon which it is based also led to the publication of what
some call "confessional" texts. These texts (Rabinow 1977 and
Dumont 1978 are examples) are critical of both the standard training
received by young ethnographers, and the established conventions
which govern the form and substance of published ethnography.

With the political sensitivities of the sixties and seventies now
in decline, the welfare of those subject to ethnographic research and
the ethnographer's responsibilities to the field are no longer sharply
focused issues. The contribution of anthropology to the modern
world is seen once again primarily in philosophical, rather than in
political or social terms. Institutional fossilization is a serious concern, as is the search for a refreshing theoretical charter. This is
reflected in the current experimentation in ethnographic writing
which, as noted by Marcus and Cushman (1982), is of a consciously
philosophical nature. Central to the new experiments is a perception
that ethnography is as much a literary as a scientific undertaking,
and that more careful attention should be given to understanding
and exploiting the literary dimensions: "Anthropologists have finally
begun to give explicit attention to the writing of ethnographic texts
[and the experimentation in writing] may not just be altering the
traditional nature of ethnography; it may also mark the beginning
of a profound reshaping of the theoretical ambitions and research
practices." (Marcus and Cushman (1982:25).

Among the experimental ethnographies of note cited by Marcus
(1986), [Dumont (1978), Crapanzano (1980), Rosaldo (1980), Willis
(1981), Shore (1982), and others], there is some difference in the
literary features emphasized. In general, however, story-telling, in
various degrees of completeness, is integrated directly into the
ethnographic text, primarily for dramatic effect. The anthropologist-
writer is still most comfortably at home in the discursive field of
"technical ethnography." Consequently, although certain features
borrowed from the practice of imaginative writing are used to bring
to the text a more intimate experience of the field, texts are separated
into a dramatic presentational part, and a philosophical part. The
dramatized section gives substance to the assertions and arguments
of the philosophical section. The latter explains.

As Clifford (1986) correctly notes, there is as yet no discernible
trend to current experimental ethnographic writing. But in addition

to the general division of texts into dramatic and philosophical sections, certain other tendencies may be observed. There is a common
attitude that the ethnographic experience is an encounter with the
different, and that this encounter stimulates a dramatic awareness of
the indeterminacy against which society and culture are creative
ventures. There is a self-conscious awareness of the active participation of the ethnographer in creating the meanings that find their way
into the text; and a concern with text-building as a contextured exercise in constructing the representation of social-philosophical structures of varying degrees of completeness and power. There is, finally,
a return to the notion that the problems and answers sought in
ethnographic research are imbedded in integrated subjective strata.
The following observation by Willis (1981: 122) echoes that made by
Kroeber over sixty years ago: "Direct and explicit consciousness may
in some senses be our least rational guide. It may well reflect only
the final stages of cultural processes and the mystified and contradictory forms which basic insights take as they are lived out." Shore
(p.127) extends the echo: "It is a common mistake to assume that the
web of mysteries, minor and major that constitute an alien culture
may be resolved by careful observation alone. Even the most
painstaking and perceptive observer eventually discovers that the key
to many of the most intriguing and significant aspects of a culture
lies within the minds of those he observes."

There is a clear recognition of something about culture which
cannot be broached directly. But the problem of getting at that
something, while it may focus on the written work, is couched less
as a problem in writing than as a philosophical or investigatory problem. The appropriated literary techniques — direct speech
(dialogue), plot construction, internal characterization, multiple
points of view, etc. — constrained as they are by an expository intention, succeed more as transparencies through which the intellectual
struggles of the ethnographer are revealed, than as presentations that
effect intersubjective communication. Among modern experimental
ethnographers, the task of integrating literary elements into the
ethnographic work, so that they would function as more than
embellishment for the philosophising of the ethnographer, and be
productive in their own right, remains to be done. Alongside them,
however, are others who seek to transcend the tension between

technique and intention by presenting their work as ethnographi-
cally informed literature, or the literary work that is substantively
ethnographic.

Accounts by Adolf Bandelier — some honor him as founder of
this minor tradition — and Elsie Clews Parsons have already been
mentioned. Among other writers in this vein are Oliver LaFarge,
Hilda Kuper, Juan Pozas, Peter Matthiessen, Carter Wilson, and
Nan Salerno/Rosamond Vanderburgh. Some underlying assump-
tions in the work of these and other writers who have adopted the
literary ethnographic approach are that (a) science and communication are distinct categories, (b) the results of ethnographic enquiry
may be communicated in different ways and need not be restricted
only to scientific terms; and (c) through the techniques of literary fiction ethnographic knowledge and experience can be evoked sufficiently, so that readers may to some extent participate in the interior
world of an ethnographic situation. Though not widely used, the
term "ethnographic fiction" has been coined to describe works that
evince this approach. There are some unresolved problems with the
defining limitations of this term. But there can be no question that
literary techniques are ideal for plumbing the subjective, and that by
calling forward sensations through which much of the world is experienced, literary techniques also effectively energize intersubjective
communication.

At its best, artistic literature, or imaginative writing, compels
the total attention of its audience, as it moves toward subjective comprehension. It anticipates already the "post-modern" work which
Stephen Tyler (1986) foresees in the future of ethnographic writing:
"A post-modern ethnography is a cooperatively evolved text con-
sisting of fragments of discourse intended to evoke . . . an emergent
. . . world of commonsense reality, and . . . provoke an aesthetic
integration that will have a therapeutic effect. It is in a word, poetry
. . . in its return to the original context and function of poetry, which
. . . evoked memories of the ethos of the community and thereby
hearers to act ethically." (pp. 125–6). In this statement Tyler has
made central to the "post-modern" ethnography two characteristics
that already give the literary its compelling and transcendent quality
— an aesthetic and a communal dimension.

Tyler also emphasizes the textual objective of "evoking" (ellipses,
indirection, metaphorical association, etc.) rather than "represent-

ing" — "The whole point of "evoking" rather than "representing" is that it frees ethnography from mimesis and the inappropriate mode of scientific rhetoric that entails "objects," "facts," "descriptions," "induction," "generalization," "verification," "experiment," "truth," and like concepts that, except as empty invocations, have no parallels either in the experience of ethnographic fieldwork or in the writing of ethnographies" (p. 130). The process of evoking experience is an elemental one in the practice of imaginative writing. Integration of the aesthetic, the communal, and the evocative is regularly achieved not only in poetry but in the best fiction (literary genre) as well. Consequently, if Tyler's foresight may be accepted as a guide, modern ethnographers in their struggle to produce more vivid and comprehensive writing, might appropriately reconsider the earlier positions taken by Bandelier, Kroeber, and the other contributors to the *American Indian Life* volume. Concurrently with the actual process of writing, however, is another circumstance at which the new experimental texts take tangential aim, but which is not developed fully — that is, the communal and aesthetic relationship between fieldworkers and the people they study. This relationship has a definite impact on, and remains central to, whatever is achieved in written ethnoraphy.

(ii)

In both traditional and recent ethnography the people of the field are regarded mainly as "strangers," "others," "natives," and are brought into the published discourse not so much as palpable beings in their own right, but as severely edited and generalized versions of themselves, which may be manipulated for intellectual purposes. The writing is neither to them, nor for them. Anthropologists do many useful things for the people they study. They often provide basic amenities and are frequently ready to provide representation in courts or before government offices. But, as a rule, anthropologists do not write for the people they study. (Bandelier's novel explained the Indian for the benefit of the public at large; but what explained himself — or more importantly, the white man — to the Indian?)

This writing, which in an essential way stands for the difference between "savage" and "civilized" — or however else the hierarchy may be stylized — which, finally, is what separates anthropologists from field people, stands as a privileged performance which "natives" are left to acquire on their own. Writing brings the world under control, subjectively, for both writer and reader. A compact on the subjective level makes this possible. Such a compact is exactly the one resisted by anthropologists in their relations with "natives." And the dilemma remains how to get (without the subjective engagement) our "natives" — defined as strange and not comfortably predictable — into the controlled discourse that is written ethnography, not only as social-cultural virtuosos whose repertoires we finally come to comprehend, but also as authors engaged in a prior discourse (conceptualized as culture, or society) which we all share.

One way to address this dilemma would be for ethnographers to apply the same kind of investigatory lens to themselves as they apply to the "natives" of their studies. Instead of agonizing over negated subjectivities in the difference between research and writing, let us examine ourselves along with all others as member objects in the field of study. A move in this direction was made by Dumont (1978), but it can be carried further. Such a move would focus attention on another inchoate and related dilemma cited by Levi-Strauss some twenty years ago — that the culture of the ethnographic populations of Africa, Asia, and elsewhere "is resembling more and more that of the Western World. Like the latter, it tends to fall outside the field of anthropology." (p. 25).

If Levi-Strauss was correct, and there is every reason to believe that he was, (in fact, "modernization" in the non-Western World is a high priority activity) it would seem that in continuing to emphasize the difference of field people, ethnographers avoid the opportunity to study the international culture in which they share, in favour of studying some version of a foreign past. The highlighting of difference suggests either a contrived naivete, or a romantic endorsement of the anthropologists' own preferred difference. Yet, the apparently unassailable gap between anthropologist and "native," interposed by the unmodified assertion of difference, need not preclude the "native" being integrated into ethnographic texts as more than a rhetorical device in support of the ethnographer's intellectual arguments.

In the study of literature, we used to learn that at a general level people are more alike than they are different from each other and that difference is the more insubstantial (though by no means unimportant) part, or that part most susceptible to change: " . . . if literature has any social justification or use it is that readers can identify the common humanity in, and can therefore identify with, characters vastly different from themselves in century, geography, gender, culture, and belief . . . " (Burroway 1982: 69). Literature achieves this "social" function largely through the rule of metaphor in which difference and sameness can be integrated. Ideal practice is to capture oppositions (difference/sameness, simplicity/complexity, etc.) as coexisting conditions reflected as aspects of each other. If ethnographers are to achieve the effect of poetry in their written texts, then mastering the application of metaphor, and acquiring the craft of poetic composition — not just verse, but finely wrought prose as well — becomes a necessity. A starting point in the acquisition of craft is the undertanding that the writer works in the service of the subject. The subject is not unrelievedly dominated by the writer, the way it is in most traditional ethnography.

(iii)

Ethnographers habitually acquire skills in native speech, cuisine, horticulture, technology, etc. to better understand the cultures they research. It is also fashionable to cultivate a second or third discipline for the enhancement of analytical skills. Statistics, linguistics, ecology, literary criticism, psychology, political science, psychiatry, are among the disciplines favored by ethnographers. Imaginative writing, as discipline or craft, is seldom chosen. Perhaps this is because according to academic folklore imagination, as an individually inherited gift, is adisciplinary, and imaginative writing — or anything to do with the imagination, really — less the result of discipline than of some unconstrained talent whose sole purpose is to mesmerize. But, as is clear from a number of texts on the subject, imaginative writing involves a good deal of discipline and craft skills. There are, as a matter of fact, certain conventions to be mastered, and these may well be put to use in the interest of a vivid ethnography.

Craftsmanship in imaginative writing involves choosing significant details, presenting them as events, or the description, action, vocalization, and inner life of distinct personalities, and linking them within a plot so that they derive meaning through juxtaposition. All of this being subject to a concern for plausibility, since, given the liberation from external means of verification, the legitimacy of detail in imaginative work is adjudged in accordance with what may be plausible within the overall terms of the work itself. This does not mean that the composition has to follow from totally invented, or fantastic, situations: "The fictional form of presentation . . . has definite merit. It allows a freedom in depicting or suggesting the thoughts and feelings of the Indian, such as is impossible in a formal, scientific report . . . At the same time the customs depicted are never invented." (Parsons 1967: 13) Invention is an important facit of imaginative writing; but not everything about the imaginative work has to be — nor indeed can be — invented. In fact, much of the substratum of fiction is never invented, but is simply based on the writer's reserve of acquired experience. The defeating danger occurs when texts too thoroughtly rely on the other texts for their authenticity — a problem which occurs in just about every genre, and one which is very much the case with ethnographic writing. A problem, most likely, too, with this introduction.

What I want simply to say is that I see most current ethnographic writing — traditional and experimental — as deficient in dealing with the inner lives of people: that ethnography would be a more complete and productive artifact if it undertook to present this interior universe. (Armstrong 1971). Such presentation cannot be done through abstract chatter, or any series of direct expository statements. Indirection has to be the mode. What I want to say is that this presentation can be done by drawing on certain conventions (character, plot, metaphor, display, etc.) that are already well developed, and innovations that have already been anticipated in imaginative writing. Even the innovative presentation of the divided page, [for which Price (1983) is highly praised by Marcus] was anticipated by Gabriel Josipovici's story, "Mobius the Stripper" (1972). If this raises the concern that borrowing such powerful and well established conventions will too fully eclipse the genre distinctions between ethnography and artistic literature, that possibility, it seems to me, is more than balanced by the literalness in ethnography that is grounded in the historical time, place, and conduct of research. What I must say, too, is that my perception of all this follows from my training and practice as both anthropologist and writer.

Ethnography that embraces the subjective need not be seen as displacing objective ethnography. Rather, it should be recognized as standing some place between, perhaps functioning as a link, some continuity, between objective ethnography and imaginative literature.

In an ethnography of the outside, that objective field to which most ethnographers are still grounded, social and cultural "structures" are the central concern. Not people. In an anthropology of the inside, how people fashion such "structures," how they manipulate, manage or are controlled by them, become the focus. It is a dramatic relationship, involving people in dialogue with themselves, other people, the things and events which give order and meaning to everyday life. Even where there is no insufficiency of material or social resources, how people feel about things, events, other people, themselves, carries a great deal of power in the transactions that comprise everyday living. This makes the affective world, "The world of feeling, imagination, and intuition" (Armstrong 1974), an extremely important gateway to ethnographic understanding, if we will know people the way they experience themselves. In an ethnography of the inside, the ethnographer cannot be hero.

II. Native and Anthropologist in the Field

(i)

When I first entered college many years ago, I signed myself up to major in anthropology as we went through the gymnasium during registration. It was what I wanted to do. I had never met an anthropologist before. I had read and heard a little about Egypt, and I was egotistical enough to believe I deserved to undertake 'the study of man.' In my first class, however, a clear-sighted professor in the discipline kindly suggested that anthropology was not for people like me. Why not try P.E., he said. I didn't know what P.E. was. We had no such thing in my school in Trinidad, and I had never heard of it. I ended up as an English major instead.

Some years later when I was about to pass out of a graduate English program, one of the genteel professors puzzled, but what will you do with this degree? It was not easy being a Black graduate in those days. Or being a Black anything else. One endured. One drifted back into another graduate program, in Creative Writing. One wrote. And wrote. And saw the first publication. Then stayed in the academy as a professor.

In the mid-sixties I was called upon to provide leadership on behalf of some Black and Chicano students who were "in revolt." While working with them, and searching for my own meanings as member of a "revolting" ethnic category myself, (those were the days when identity and consciousness were foregrounded issues) I was led up to a confrontation with how much there was to know about the real world outside my personal life, and the discipline in which I was making a career. I went into anthropology at this point (to make a long story short) because it seemed to offer the best opportunity for me to learn about this larger reality in an experiential way, while at the same time discovering how I fitted into it more fully.

As a student in anthropology, I read all the ethnographic descriptions I could find that dealt with Afro-American and Caribbean societies and cultures. In those days they weren't that many. But two things happened in response to this reading: (a) I discovered that although I was born and raised in Trinidad, there were many details about the culture (which I still claimed as mine) that were foreign to me. There were hidden and unusual things, which some foreign researchers had come there and uncovered. How was it I didn't know that so many people worshipped Shango seriously? That Spiritual Baptists were an illegal bunch even during my childhood? That Black Americans had settled those villages which from mine we regarded as on the other side of primitive? That carnival was a French tradition? That Barrackpore was an Indian name? That I had been born and bred in a plural society? And (b) I had the peculiar sense, when reading ethnographic descriptions of particular places and situations I had known, that these descriptions were artificial and incomplete. I didn't believe all that I read about this "plural society."

When the time came for me to do my own fieldwork/ethnography, it seemed quite natural to return to my culture of origin to see for myself if all that I read could really be true. And, of course, to put the lie where it belongs — do a job of research beyond what any foreigners could do.

As my wife, infant son, and myself moved into the small village so that I could do fieldwork, the intellectual parameters for this research were reasonably clear. They had to do with testing certain premises which underlay the plural society thesis, a major one being: How do people who mix but not mingle truly get along in an intimate peasant village? Or, Is it correct that these people (some of whom I used to know when a child) mix but do not mingle? Or, What would mixing be in this context? How does it occur? Are social and cultural groups in this "plural society" isolated from each other as the theory and model implied? If so, how is the space between them negotiated? These were some of the questions which comprised an intellectual intention behind fieldwork. But there were other questions as well which involved not only doing, but using anthropology in a personal way.

Some ethnographers have been steered into the field by their desire to encounter the primitive "other" — an alternate form of beingness from that of themselves. This paradoxical "other," to whom we are linked biologically but from whom we are differentiated culturally and socially serves, we are told, to reveal essential knowledge bout the cultures of both. I have never been quite clear on how this works. What did Bronislaw Malinowski learn about his native culture from living among his savages? (Joseph Conrad's Marlowe came to see the Thames in a different light after contemplating his extraordinary journey up the Congo.) How about Franz Boas? And Margaret Mead? Or my academic advisers? What did they learn about their culture, themselves, from their fieldwork? And did it make a difference? During all my training, this aspect of the encounter was never discussed. American culture was never discussed: not in terms equivalent to those used in the discussion of "native" cultures, anyway.

For myself, fieldwork was not to be an encounter with any primitive, or yet again, even foreigners. The "other" in my field was heavily constituted out of a tension between my own memory of an earlier time, and the recognizable changes of my return: out of the memory of how I used to be, and the inadequacy of my new cultural reflexes. I was not truly foreign to Trinidad. But I had lived in the U.S.A. for many years, during which time I had come to identify as Black American. And, also, I had come to experience Trinidad from an external point of view. As student of anthropology, and expatriate, I had a certain angle on things which was unfamiliar to those who had spent their entire lives there. I returned, then, not as a true foreigner but as a partial stranger, carrying a sense of belonging to a larger world of which Trinidad could only be a part.

I couldn't work in that single village only, I could see how it contrasted with the one in which I had been born: how it was similar in some ways, but different too, from other villages in the county. People there knew the differences too, and were most often content to live within the boundaries that marked them. But not me. I wanted equal access and participation in the whole society. Having intellectually conceptualized Trinidad as a "society," a "culture," I kept wanting to appropriate all of it, and have my awareness be a common property. Of course, I couldn't. As visiting researcher I could travel where my village neighbors could not. I could challenge situations that wouldn't cost me much but could cost them their jobs, or other deadly important necessities. I was one among them, but I was a different one among them, even though I wanted them all to be like me.

I wrote the usual ethnography for my dissertation: I have yet to write a standard ethnography for publication. And, no doubt, much of what I have written in the first part of this introduction has to do with explaining that to myself. Why have I not written a standard ethnography? I go back to those accounts which I read in my early student days that seemed so artificial and incomplete. If I wrote an ethnography in the traditional style, mine wouldn't be much different. The cultural and social structures are there. But what strikes me as more interesting are the idiosyncracies (small things sometimes) that people take on and guard in their drive to compose themselves as unique individuals, within the framework of their ethnic memberships. The structures permit that, because they are neither indigenous, nor chartered by a powerful history. The individual, engaged in solving problems, transcending, understanding, or interpreting them in a personal way, plays a major role in how I think culture happens. One could write about this, but one could not present it, in the formal ethnography as one could in the literary form which allows exploration of the interior world of thought and feeling. I write stories.

Interestingly enough, the villagers among whom I lived, and whom I observed closely knew almost nothing of what had been written about them, or about other villagers in Trinidad. One pastor remembered a White fellow from long ago who came to his house

to ask questions about ceremonial things. But no foreign Whites —
except the itinerant missionaries — had ever lived in the village.
Who had lived in the village, and within a short time before my
arrival, were two Black anthropologists: one from Africa, the other
from a neighboring island. The villagers made comparisons: the
African was a good man. He worked. The other fellow had others
do his work. To my face they said I compared well: I worked. Of
course, I worked. I was driven.

Since that stint I have done fieldwork in other Caribbean
societies — Belize, Puerto Rico, Jamaica, Dominica — and in
Georgia, U.S.A., but in between I kept (keep I should say) going
back to Trinidad. I have some unfinished business with that place,
or my understanding of it. How is one carrying out, and how is one
understood as, being a stranger and a familiar at the same time?

(ii)

In all the years since I was a first-semester freshman I have never run
across that first anthropologist who had directed me away from the
discipline. There have been moments, though, when I thought he
had been correct — even if unknowingly — in his assessment that
anthropology was not for people like me.

Such moments were most intense in the sixties when one
learned that certain anthropologists had played a willing role in the
colonization of African peoples, and the disappearance of others in
the Pacific; that in certain instances the anthropological record was
purposely glossed and incomplete; that certain anthropologists were
responsible for the expropriation of vital artifacts from among native
peoples, and defended still the hoarding of these artifacts in western
museums against the protests of their original owners; that some
anthropologists firmly believed racial determinism was a justified
policy in the U.S.A.; that anthropologists were divided on just about
every social and political issue; and that no matter how they divided
up on social and political issues, anthropologists were generally
united in the professional goal of maintaining the psychological
distinctions between themselves and their "natives."

How could they talk about themselves as legitimate guardians
of the knowledge of humankind when they were so confused, and
inconclusive about what constitutes essential knowledge? Anthro-

pology was a survival game, not a growth game. And anthropologists
were makers as much as anybody else, groping for the toe-holds, the
hand-holds, the lines which they themselves must produce. Not
uncover. That was a useful discovery. Anthropology is not a system
of junctures where the timeless and the universal have already been
immutably fixed. It is artifice, at the heart of which is ethnography
— a staged encounter with the "other." Out of this staging come the
personal experiences that we examine in order to comprehend and
explain what it is we teach ourselves through the masquerade.
Ethnography is a system of discovery and inscription. And it is all
right if one's not going to be the hero. Inscription on behalf of others
is certainly at this time a useful undertaking.

(iii)

There is a well-established and growing complement of literary texts
in which various aspects of Trinidadian culture are richly presented.
Novels by C. L. R. James, Samuel Selvon, Vidia Naipaul, Merle
Hodge, Michael Anthony, and Earl Lovelace are among the more
widely read.

By comparison, the published works in anthropology are few.
Trinidad Village (Herskovits & Herskovits, 1947) was the first published full-length ethnography on Trinidad. The research for that
work was carried out during an extremely brief stint in 1939, when
the Herskovitses were busily in search of ethnographic proof of his
thesis that the retention of an African provenience was central to the
culture of Blacks in the New World. The work includes much useful
information on how Blacks lived in the remote village research site
at that time. It also includes a good deal of esoterica but fails to present effectively the process by which the villagers were actively
'creating themselves.' African origins and the experience of slavery
are identified as the significant cultural determinants, modified
somewhat by pecularities in the economic system and the size of the
carrying population.

The Herskovitses might have weighted their variables incor-
rectly. Fuller attention to what people were doing, rather than to
what chosen informants said, might have resulted in more carefully
thought out conclusions. What was considered to be "disordered
orientation" — "in northeastern Trinidad, the life of the Negroes

presents such an adjustment, one that may be thought of as a kind of disordered orientation" (p.4) — might have been more usefully recognized as the struggle to integrate multiple traditions. And the absence of an efflorescing Shango cult in the village ("in rural settlements, there are not enough people and not enough resources to support cult-groups of this kind." p. 174) might have been understood as the result of complexities of social ecology, and the absence of a strong enough charismatic leadership. In the Southeast area of the island, quite as rural as the Northeast, Shango flourished under the leadership of a papa who remains legendary for his power to make things happen.

The village highlighted in the Herskovitses text, because of its location — sandwiched between the base of a coastal range and a notoriously rough sea — was not a prime area where plantation slavery and its concomitants would have been the basis for entrenched traditions. That was more the case in the Naparima and Caroni plains, and the lowlands of the sheltered Northwest. Toco was an outpost, a place where freedom and independence probably carried much greater value than the maintenance of any inherited tradition. Emergence of that body of religious worshippers whom the Herskovitses found in Toco — they called them "The Shouters" but these worshippers call themselves "Spiritual Baptists" — is known to coincide elsewhere with very strong assertions of personal independence. Indifference to African roots, and the relative weakness of African cultural survivals — which the Herskovitses also found — while indicating a certain loss on one hand might just as readily have been evidence of fresh elaborations on the other.

Following Herskovits, the major publicatios based on anthropological fieldwork continued to focus on the problem of cultural retention. Both Morton Klass, (1961) and Arthur and Juanita Niehoff, (1960) published works on the persistence of Indian culture among descendants of the indentureds who were brought to Trinidad. And, as would be expected, given the research focus, neither paid much attention to processes of indigenization. Barton Schwartz, (1963), also wrote a dissertation on Indian culture, but unlike Klass he saw "the cultures of the multiple ethnic groups . . . moving in the direction of establishing a common culture which cuts across ethnic lines." J. D. Elder, (1969), and George Simpson, (1965), carried forward the concern with African retentions, and the emergence of syncritized folk expressions. Frances Henry published some short papers on folk psychology and healing practices. But Daniel Crowley, (1957), was one of the earliest anthropologists to join the sociologist Lloyd Brathwaite, (1953), in showing an interest in structure and process. Ivar Oxaal, (1965), dealt with the problem of postindependence nationalism, and suggested that the process of significance was not cultural but social. He coined the phrase "plural dissociation" as a term for that process

In the last several years two full-length works have been published, *Lower-Class Families: The Culture of Poverty in Negro Trinidad* by Hyman Rodman (1971), and *Street Scenes: Afro-American Culture in Urban Trinidad* by Michael Lieber (1981). Both texts focus on the defeat and distress of lower class Blacks who suffer from the historical destruction of African culture in the West, and from racial and class discrimination in an exploitative economic system. Both works note that Trinidad is a migrant and therefore nonindigenous society. But neither treats the struggle to establish indigeneity as a significant problem.

There can be no denying that many Blacks are the victims of poverty and class oppression in Trinidad. But I don't think either condition is to be explained solely by ancestry — cultural or otherwise — among Blacks themselves. To claim that Chinese, Indians, and Syrians have been more successful than Blacks as entrepreneurs because they were able to retain traditional family ties and modes of corporate behavior whereas under slavery Blacks were unable to do so does not take us very far. (Why, for instance, have these same Asiatic groups outdone local Africans as entrepreneurs in Africa?) Such assertions as "There has never been a viable black peasantry as there has been an Indian one . . . " or "The social consequences of slavery generated a role for the Afro-American limited to wage labor at menial work . . . " (Lieber 94) show either a misrepresentation or a heavy-handed reduction of Trinidadian history. The roots of a Black peasantry in Trinidad go back at least to the early nineteenth century, and its ranks grew significantly following emancipation in the 1830s. While Indians were still for the most part indentureds, Blacks grew and marketed produce in most regions of the country. For a long time, as a matter of fact, Blacks and others would not eat food sold or prepared by Indians because the latter were regarded as unclean and the carriers of chronic diseases.

The development of the oil industry from the 1920s onward, and the massive amount of high-wage labor created by the American presence during World War II drew many Blacks away from the land and encouraged development of a negative attitude toward it. The years during and following World War II were the years of greatest acquisition of land among Indians. They also were years when Trinidadian Indians were forced to recognize that they could no longer think of India as "home," and that they should give their energies to making "home" where they were. But more to the point, poverty and class oppression are not the special province of Blacks alone. Significant numbers of Indian families and individuals also live in poverty. Perhaps this goes unrecognized because among scholars poverty is mostly understood as an urban problem. In Trinidad, though not an entirely new pattern, urbanization among Indians has had its greatest surge with the last generation. In urban centers Indians are freshly and glaringly present as entrepreneurial and professional successes. They leave their poor behind in the villages. Blacks, on the other hand, are known for sending their young, unemployed poor to the city.

A characteristic which distinguished Black from Indian on the question of poverty has to do with separate traditional attitudes toward the acquisition of material wealth. Typically, Blacks tended to distinguish between material wealth and true wealth — understood as a combined social and spiritual state in which the individual exists in benign harmony with neighbors and the deity. Indians, on the other hand, integrated the acquisistion of material wealth with spiritual attainment, so that to amass materially facilitated passage through the spiritual realm. Indians could find deep satisfaction in the pursuit of material well-being; for Blacks it was, though necessary, an encumberment. At the village level, to be "Indian" means, in certain instances, to be aggressively and unceasingly concerned with material acquisition, whereas to be "creole" (Black) means to be open-handed, generous. In practice, neither group has a hegemony on either form of behavior, but the typology is used in people's assessment of each other. Increasingly, these "typical" behaviors are seen less as ethnic properties than as strategies that may be employed in appropriate situations. This pattern is true for much that could be identified as specific ethnic culture at particular moments in the history of the society, and lies close to the core of what I refer to as a process of indigenization.

We are all faced with the task of creating ourselves in the places in which we find ourselves. The stories in this volume are an effort to show how the villagers among whom I lived, whom I observed and questioned, did so. Some were taken by the constraints they faced in the external world, others were more aware of clamors in the interior worlds inside them. As people elsewhere, they arranged and rearranged the details of their everyday lives, sometimes in an indulgence of whimsy, sometimes in calculated efforts to attain control over contradictory claims they could not avoid. They do not regard themselves as engaged in acculturation, indigenization, or any of the other processes by which anthropologists characterize cultural development.

They make a living in various ways, but most earn income by working outside of the villages. They are craftspeople, mechanics, carpenters, factory attendants, woodsmen, field-laborers, taxi-drivers, clerks, or policemen. A few women work as domestics. Some work for the sugar company which cultivates extensive fields within walking distance and operates a factory a short taxi ride away. Others work for the oil companies, at refinery or drilling sites all of which are within commuting distance. Employment with the government, either in public works, schools, or clerical departments also occasion travelling out for villagers.

Those who make their living at home usually are gardeners. Gardening is a ubiquitous activity. Ground-breaking is usually man's work, but beyond that men and women work at gardening with equal competence. Horticultural knowledge, hard work, and an intangible known locally as 'having a good hand' are critical to success in gardening. The family, generally, is the unit which maintains the best gardens. One of the elder daughters in a successful gardening family has been a consistent winner in the annual national gardening contest. Locally, one of her brothers is known as probably the best gardener in the area. Root crops, sugar-cane (which must be sold to the company), corn, rice, vegetables, and ornamental plants are cultivated. A few villagers grow enough to operate produce stands in the town markets. Most households, and in several cases, householders, earn or supplement income from a combination of activities. Some do things that are officially illegal. Grocery stores and drinking places are mostly owned and operated by Indian families. There is one combined grocery store and rum shop that is owned and operated by a Korean family, but most of the smaller 'parlours' which sell home-made food and two popular inns are owned by Black families.

The supernatural world is important to everybody, but villagers worship in several ways. These villages were the first Baptist communities in Trinidad, settled by Blacks from America who had served in the British Colonial Marines. Mostly from Georgia and the Carolinas, these Blacks in taking a stand against slavery had fought with the British in the war of 1812. After being demobilized in 1815, they and their dependents were granted small holdings in the then virgin forests of Southeast Trinidad. Among these settlers were some of the earliest converts to the Baptist faith among Blacks in America, and they were able to establish their church as the dominant moral, educational, and socializing force in the new communities. The majority of Blacks in the villages remain true to the faith. Other Christian faiths — Anglican, Catholic, Methodist, Pentecostal — are also observed in the villages.

Indians, who were first brought into the area as laborers on a family-owned (White) sugar estate during the late 19th century remain mostly Hindu. They have no temples in the villages, but pujas and bhagwats are frequently observed in individual homes. Marriage and funeral ceremonies are also carried out in the home. The few Muslims who live in the villages must travel outside too, when they wish to worship at a mosque. In the past, Indians seldom attended the Baptist church, but increasing numbers have recently begun to adopt the faith. Their conversion to Pentecostalism is also growing. Blacks seldom attend Hindu ceremonies, except as an expression of friendship with particular Indian families, and few know much of anything about the Ramayana or the Bhagavad Gita. On the other hand, many Indians know something of the Christian Bible, and it often serves as a common moral reference among both Christians and non-Christians. Shango survives as a minor tradition, but an animist sensibility is pervasive. Both Blacks and Indians subscribe to a system of magic that integrates scraps of belief and formulas from Christian, animist, Hindu, and Islamic traditions.

There is a strong disposition toward sharing and egalitarianism among villagers, and a cutting — if at times surreptitious — displeasure for those who glaringly fly in the face of such an ideal.

At the same time there is open criticism for those who fail to take advantage of opportunities to achieve, and admiration for those who achieve without becoming bombastic. The balancing of these and other oppositions sometimes takes revealing turns. Distinction and balance between the moral and the practical is appropriately negotiable.

The stories which follow cover a period from the days of World War II to the late seventies. The physical landscape has undergone some change during that period, as has the availability of utilities and services. The estate barracks no longer exist, and cane is hauled by motor trucks and tractors as well as animal-drawn carts. Few people ride bicycles, and they don't walk as much as they used to because improved roads and individual entrepreneurship now make taxi service available. There are no longer any white families in the area. The only resident whites are the occasional priest sent out by the London Baptist Mission or the Anglican church.

Change has, however, not been total. The "old-time" and the new, the backward and the innovative often co-exist alongside each other, and hopefully the stories capture this. They are not meant to be understood as an exhaustive presentation of all the things villagers do. Instead, they are distillations from field notes — and other less objective forms of information — of the values, relationships, and performances which seem to me pertinent to an undertanding of the ways in which villagers create or refresh meanings in their lives. Although I am very present in the texts, as an ethnographer necessarily must be — selecting, juxtaposing, emphasizing — I hope that I have managed to let the villagers speak and present themselves sufficiently, and in their own engaging way. Being among them taught me a great deal about everything. It would be enough if these stories showed them a little something about themselves.

Small Victories

There are wars going on all over Africa. And I am not in one of them. I spend many nights wondering how this will be justified to my son when he questions. I was not born in Africa. But the milk of herself runs so full in my face I have no choice about the guilt which washes me for being so safely here, while others, most certainly my brothers, are there fighting, risking, losing their lives. How will I convince my son that the guilt I carry is a small price to pay for survival? Or that the big price, those buckets full of blood thrown on the line each day in Mozambique, Angola, will buy no greater meaning? And who knows? I may have already done a share against the brothers of those Portuguese in Africa. Not with guns, grenades, and the like, but with weapons that perhaps burn in more serious places.

When I was a child the Portuguese shop-owner brought a wife to our village. He bought her a motor-car. And it wasn't long before she managed to terrorize us daily with the roar of her engine which, when she was on the road, could be heard a mile or so away like some ill-tempered tiger growling its way between the fields. The road would empty then. Grown-ups carrying water or garden baskets on their heads stepped off into the grass. And we snatched our marbles and tops, our bat and ball, and stepped off into the grass too, although not as far away as the grown-ups because we wanted to boast that we stood nearest to danger as she passed by. It was not that cars were strange to our village. The manager of the plantation and some of his staff had cars, and there was a doctor who came from town once every two weeks who also drove his own motor-car. The priest had a car which we used to help Tommy the chauffeur shine on Saturdays. But none of these had ever drawn blood in the village.

The Portuguese wife was different. By the time she was with us a month her car had killed several dogs and chickens had broken Ma Trumble's hip when she didn't step off into the grass deep enough, and, worst, had run over one of my infant cousins who had crept from the house into the road unnoticed.

Were it a boy-child, I believe some quick retaliation would have taken place. But Min-min was a girl. And even though neighbors wailed over how the car rolled the child into a pulp then spread her along the road, no one drew a weapon on the Portuguese that day, no fire was set to the shop that night.

Tante insisted that even though Min-min never lived with us the wake should be kept at our house. Tante, however, was known in the family as the one who loved children. Having rejected marriage to take care of Grandpa when she was young, she never had a child of her own. But I was example of her affection for young ones. She had taken me from her sister after the old man died, and I was raised the same as her son. I was the only one who lived with her, but Tante kept Grandpa's place open to all the children in the family, and the day Min-min was run over several of us were at play in the yard. I still find it strange that none of us either missed Min-min, or left our play to run to the front of the yard to watch the motor-car passing as we usually did. It was only when we heard the screams that we ran out, and Tante was there before us. She neither screamed nor cried. Her face looked dried and hard as they picked Min-min up from the dust, and she showed no change all through the night as people gave consoling words during the wake to herself and the child's mother. The Portuguese shop-owner brought several bottles of rum to the wake. He also brought a brown paper bag full of cheese, biscuits, and coffee. I didn't see him talk to Tante or the older women, but he slapped the men on their backs, sat and played a few hands of cards with them, then went home.

If I were older I might have paid deeper attention to Tante's feelings that night. I might have been curious as to what was taking place in her mind. But I had never all up through that time thought of Tante as being subject to unseen pain.

It was not as if Gomez was a stranger in our house. Tante had no husband, and before he brought the wife Gomez used to be her regular visitor. He never came during daylight, but after darkness fell he would slip in, not fearful but furtive like a lord consorting among lesser subjects. Many times I spied him passing our gap along the empty road, going past once or twice, then materializing out of the dim like a shadow melting into the house. In those days when London was under the blitz and we lived with regular air-raid blackouts, Tante kept all the windows and jalousies closed at night, and I was never permitted to remain in the front room once Gomez arrived. But from the other side of the wall I could hear their voices — not those of shopkeep and customer — with something softened in Gomez's hovering over Tante's submissive whispers.

When it was dark-night and no other boys outside to play I would be alone on the front steps until sleeping time when Tante opened the door and called me in softly. And sometimes there was Gomez, when I went in, formally posed in his green silk shirt and plaid pants — we villagers understood that Portuguese had little taste in clothes — his arms folded in the rocker. Other times he sat wearing not a shirt but a sleeveless singlet rocked back with arms behind his head, his soft, hanging chest slobbing out of the over-sized armholes. Yet I was never asked once to acknowledge or respect his presence. When he was there on moonlight nights I would find other boys to play with and would be gone for hours, exploring shadows in our neighbors' backyards, or even in the pasture, or village burial ground. And one night in the pasture after we had stolen oranges and sat at an urchin's feast a boy asked, "Why that Potagee Gomez always at your house for?"

"I don't know."

"He at your house every night and you don't know what he come for?"

I could recall even now how still the night grew around me then.

"What he does be bringing in that brown paper bag?" the boy asked, challenging me with his voice to give a contrary answer.

"I don't know."

"You're playing stupid. What he does be doing with your Tante then? You know that?"

To which, of course, I could make no answer.

"Talk! You don't know?"

And I was ready to go crazy, and fight. But another boy said, "What Cyril care? He eating rice and have salt-meat to go with it every day, oui."

"But what his Tante do to get all that food?"

Rudy was my best friend in those days, and in the sing-song voice we used to beg pardon before the schoolmaster he said, "She only does wash his clothes."

Everybody broke up laughing.

If I was really smart then I wouldn't have laughed with them. Tante and I weren't the only ones to eat from what Gomez brought in his brown paper bags. Several of her friends used to share in what she got, particularly if they had children. The war was making it hard to get many things in the village, and Gomez was the only one who knew how to go to town and come back with a load of goods. Further, when not even the police could get Gomez to give them a ration of flour, rice, or oil, Tante usually had enough of these things to share with the very mothers of some of my laughing friends. But I was young, and not only did I laugh with them, I went along as we collected old bottles and stones and then, hiding in the deep grass across the road, fired barrage after barrage onto the tin roof of Tante's house, waiting after each to see whether she or Gomez would appear. But the house remained shut and silent, and they gave no sign if we ever disturbed them.

To this day I have no idea if Tante knew I was one of the boys who stoned our house. But the stoning didn't stop Gomez from coming. In fact, he was a regular visitor right up to a few days before his wife appeared in the village. But after she came, we seldom saw him out of the shop anymore. We never once saw him behind the wheel of the car. She was the one who trafficked back and forth to town. And it might have been coincidence, but almost simultaneously with her coming rationing got even worse than before, and some items as condensed milk and arrowroot on which babies were weaned disappeared from the shop shelves altogether. Sugar got scarcer too, and some days the shop never opened at all. It wasn't rare to see villagers hanging around Gomez's door, their mouths turning white, banging on the door without getting an answer. And sometimes in the middle of their waiting, the wife would march out, get in her motor-car, and take off with a roar. And so while many villagers vilified Gomez, in their minds he still carried less blame than the wife, since it was clear she encouraged him to hide more goods than he usually did, and particularly since she was the reckless one with the motor-car. For Tante though, they were two of the same, and this became clear to me the day after Min-min was buried.

The policeman came and left. He wanted to know who was responsible for letting Min-min go into the road, and Tante, the child's mother, Cousin Ambrose and his wife had stood around in our front room while the policeman asked questions and wrote in his black leather book. Then after warning us severely about letting children play in the road he left, and Min-min's mother began to cry. Tante said, "Ever since Gomez bring that nasty woman in this village it have people crying and lamenting about some loss or the other. But she gon get what she looking for."

Cousin Ambrose laughed. He was a hard man. He had big teeth and was well known as a hunter. His teeth were yellow. He laughed his yellow-teeth laugh and said, "That Gomez, he a very smart Potagee."

"What so smart in him bringing that woman here?" Tante flared back. "This village was a decent place till he bring she. You could send children to the shop, or go yourself, and know you didn't have to fight up with all the riff-raff men this village have barring the counter to see she cock up."

"That's the truth," Ma Ambrose added. "Them nasty nigger-men hang around that shop thicker than flies ever since he bring that woman there."

"You women too funny," Cousin Ambrose laughed again. "You too funny, oui! You looking at one side and yuh getting hot. There's two sides to everything, you know."

"What two side?" Tante's voice was in a decent rage. "What two side, tell me! All yuh men too nasty. Potagee, nigger-men, you all the same. That woman ain't nothing but a ho. I don't care what two side you talking about. A ring down generation ho, and she shouldn't be in no shop where children have to go."

"Well if you feel so bad about she, why yuh ain't buy somewhere else?"

"Where? You want me to walk to town every time I want a penny lard?"

Cousin Ambrose skinned his teeth, but didn't laugh out loud. "That Gomez too smart," he said.

"Smart if he smart," Ma Ambrose said. "But she gon get what she looking for, and she gon do for he too in the bargain."

"You women too funny. If was a young fella he did bring to sell in the shop all yuh wouldn't've had one complaint to make. But rum making more money than rice and sugar these days, and Gomez know that. I bet since she there he selling three times as much rum as before."

And you mean to say, a man would bring a woman in his house just for that?" Tante's indignation was not loud, but it was hot.

"Why not?"

"What Ambrose say making sense, you know," Ma Ambrose chirped, as though she had just had a revelation. She would disagree with him, but it was again comfortable to know he was never far from being master. "Them nigger-men run to spend their money in the shop, but all they getting is a see. Besides, she behind the counter, and let one of them try to cross it and Gomez pulling out his gun. All they getting is a see, but they spending plenty money to get that."

"Then is not she alone who nasty," Tante said. "He nasty too. And if that so, is time he clear out of this village for good. Any man who so nasty he let people see his wife bottom for a few shillings . . . "

"Tante, you too hostile," Ma Ambrose cut her off. "You ain't ever feel you want to hice your petticoat and put up your foot sometimes too? What in that? We don't do it, but what in that?"

"It nasty. It stinking. People who do it ain' have no bringing up. That's why we don't do it."

"But times we would like to."

"I don't care. We don't do it because it uncivilize. And you Ambrose, you sitting there laughing at me — would you let people come peep at Ma's bottom for a shilling or a dollar or two?"

Which made Cousin Ambrose laugh louder still while saying, "I don't got no shop. . . . "

It made a funny picture all told, the idea of Ma Ambrose's bottom beneath all her skirts and double petticoats. The Portuguese wife never wore much. She never talked much either, no more than to ask what you wanted, and to tell you how much you owed, but her eyes were black in white and fierce, and the hair bunched on her head bristled always like a hawk's feathers. Took nerve to face her. Especially since among us boys it was understood she was a temptress. A direct descendant of Delilah, some said. But from our side of the counter we boys used to sneak our share of helpless peeking as the wife went back and forth fetching things. Her bottom swung three ways independently as she walked, and her loosely hung breasts had a way of falling out of her clothes when she reached into the bins for rice or flour. In the section where the men crowded around the counter drinking she propped her feet on a high stool when she took a rest, so that her skirt fell away, and the rubbery banks of her white thighs were bare up to her underclothes sometimes. She was a temptress, who gave us hot dreams within which to imagine the realization of our coming manhood. But the idea of Ma Ambrose was only funny, so I laughed too. And Tante, remembering my presence, thundered, "What you doing in here boy? Don't you see big people talking?"

I had to leave the room then. But not to go far. And from beneath my favourite window I could hear Cuz Ambrose saying " . . . I don't got no shop. But that Potagee too smart. You see how he didn't take nobody from the village?"

"Nobody here nasty like she," Tante shot back.

"That how they does live," Cuz Ambrose went on without hearing her. "You did think he was gon put you behind that counter? Potagee, Chinee, Indian — all of them too smart. They come, play around, and they get around, but when it come time to make partners concering money or anything else they does find their own kind. Is only we black people who don't do that."

"I hear he send quite overseas for she," Ma Ambrose said. "That place where Christmas wine does come from . . . and that is his country? He send quite there for she, they say."

"That not what I hear," Tante said.

"Just like the Chinee fella have the shop in Petit Morne," Cuz Ambrose said. "He make children here and there in the village, but when he get ready for wife he send back to Hong Kong. That the way they does do business."

"That not what I hear," Tante said. "That piece of saltfish Gomez pick up ain't from no Madeira. I hear she used to taking sailors around the wharf in town. She nothing but a piece of rotten saltfish — and you only have to look at how she get on in the shop to know."

"I still say Gomez put she in the car and not no woman from the village," Cuz Ambrose said.

"She and that blasted motor-car. . . . the devil gon do for she in that blasted motor-car," Tante said.

"Tante you're talking disrespectful," Ma Ambrose said.

"Who got to respect she? What she got for me to respect?"

"She don't care," Cousin Ambrose said, "whether you respect she or not. You can't touch she, and if you get in the way she gon put she motor-car on you."

"You're disrespecting against yourself," Ma Ambrose said.

"I know God doesn't like ugly." Tante couldn't let it rest. "But if is one time I'll dirty my hands is to get rid of she and Gomez and all the nastiness they bringing here in this village."

"Tante, you better be careful now. You talk like a woman want vengeance. But vengeance a very dangerous thing. It strike the very one who call it." Cousin Ambrose had quickly turned quite solemn.

"Let it strike," Tante said. "The Lord knows who's wicked of heart and who isn't. And somebody got to start cleaning or else this whole village gon rotten down like a old latrine."

"Village ain't never been clean, ain't never gon be clean. Whe whe, whapee, dice, cockfight, hoing — this village little but it have everything. Look at them rich white people living on the estate . . . and Granny Alberta who could still recall you what slaving days was like. It have high church and low church, and people who don't go to neither one. What I saying is it have everything here. But if you keep your eye too hard on rottenness the very thing you don't want bound to bring you down. And if enough people like you, then the whole place bound to tumble down. Leave vengeance where it is, I say."

Talking, Cousin Ambrose, almost like a preacher, and it affected Tante in a most strange way. Her face did not soften, even as tears came down, and she made no sign to acknowledge them. Defiance, and a certain intense hardness where she stood, chin erect, her arms folded beneath her breasts. "You know how much I do for that man?" she said. Her voice quietly filling the room, her eyes focused much beyond it. "You know how much?"

"Forgive and forget," Cousin Ambrose said.

"I give him my best. I used to stand hours over the coalpot ironing his shirts, and if they wasn't starched right, washing them out again . . . "

"That time pass, girl," Ma Ambrose consoled. "That water gone the other side of the bridge."

"I used to cook for him. Anything he bring — chicken, beef, pork, I used to cook for him all hours of the night . . . "

"Forgive and forget," Cuz Ambrose said. "The worse you could sin against yourself is hard-heartedness."

"Everything in the Lord hand, girl," Ma Ambrose said. "And wherever a door shut he does make another one open."

"When he come here tired I used to make him take off his shoes and clothes and rub him down head to foot. He used to say, "You creole, you're the best woman God put on this earth. . . . "

"Forget all that," Cuz Ambrose said. "The world already old but it still getting newer every day. . . . "

" . . . Ah, Emelda, he used to say, you the best woman God put on this earth. How I gon ever live without you. . . . "

"Tante, Tante! Control yourself, girl."

" . . . And all the time I know what people thinking behind my back. But it was alright. Even with them young vagabonds stoning this house at night, it was alright. And then for Gomez to throw that nasty woman in mi face and turn his back like he ent ever know me! Well who I is, dog?"

"You're doing a wrong thing, I tell you," Cousin Ambrose was very stern himself. "Stop the remembering. Is tomorrow you should worry about, not yesterday."

"I don't want to hear nothing," she said. "I gon get mi chance. I gon get it, I gon get it. If is the last thing I do, am gon get mi chance."

Tante's voice frightened me. Terse as nails, yet sad. And I had never seen her cry before. Had had no idea she carried such wounds which in a moment could come to be my own, and I couldn't help myself crying too where I stooped outside the window.

A few people came to the house to set up with us that second night. They sang slow hymns, and the women gave consoling words again to Min-min's mother —

". . . What you gon do when the Lord calls?. . . ."

". . . the little lamb's been called home, child. . . ."

". . . But by the grace of the Lord. . . ."

". . . Not to fret child. Your womb will flower again. . . ."

And on this second night Tante did not serve the coffee and biscuits. She let the women go to the kitchen for themselves. She sat mostly still in her straight-backed chair thinking what nobody knew, whether of Min-min or Gomez, but definitely not crying, and somewhere now removed from the sadness that was in her voice the earlier hours.

I fell asleep right after the midnight cock crowed, and don't know what time the neighbors finally left Tante alone, but she was up early the following morning. She got me up too, and in the chilly dawn took us on a journey from our village to the outskirts of Penal where an Indian sadhu lived.

She spoke only twice the entire way, once when as we were taking a short-cut through an overgrown field I accidentally put my foot in a hole and twisted my ankle. She made me sit down in the grass and bandaged my ankle with strips from her headtie. When she was finished she asked, "It still hurting plenty?" and I said no. "It gon be alright," she said.

And later as we went uphill through a short stretch of forest she asked was I smelling snakes. I wasn't, but a few paces ahead we came on a boa constrictor coiled in the middle of the path. Tante immediately dropped to her knees in silent prayer, and before long the snake uncoiled and disappeared into the roadside bushes. Tante was a marvel. She was a wonder. There were depths to her none of my friends or I had ever guessed.

The sadhu's yard was dim and damp. His thatched hut was surrounded by overhanging trees, with moss dangling from some branches. The dampest spots on the ground were green. After Tante called, the sadhu came to meet us at the roadside. He was a thin man wearing nothing but a dhoti. Long curling hairs grew from his chest and arms, but his head was clean shaved. He had the kindest eyes I had ever seen.

"Neighbor, you reach," he said. As though he had witnessed the beginning of our journey. Then he made me stand behind Tante and did something with her hands in his before leading us up to his hut.

They made me sit outside while they two went in. Then after a while Tante came out and asked me to let her have my cap. I gave it to her. Again, shortly afterwards, they both came out, and the sadhu replaced the cap on my head. "You a good boy," he said, placing both hands on my shoulders. "Do as your Tante says and God will bless you." He had the kindest eyes, and when I glanced at Tante she wasn't smiling but the hardness was gone from her face.

On the way home we saw no snakes. And although my ankle

was swollen, Tante walked slowly enough so that with a little limping I could stay beside her. When we came to the forested part of the road she broke me a stick and showed me how to use it so that I could even run on the swollen foot if I had to. And Tante was in a much better mood. We talked about school, and she seemed to enjoy telling what it used to be like when she was a girl. There were no Portuguese in the village then, and no shop either. Other places already had their shops, but not ours. When villagers wanted flour, saltfish, oil, and other things that are sold in shops they walked to town, or rode in hansoms. Grandfather had a hansom. No motor-cars in those days. Only gigs and hansoms, and a tall black carriage or two that had to be drawn by pairs of horses.

"But I imagine there'll be many more motor-cars by the time you grow up," she said.

"And I'll have one to drive you to town," I took the liberty of saying.

Tante only smiled. Then after a long spell with only the sound of our feet along the road, said, "By the time you grow up I won't be needing any way of getting to town."

I wanted to ask her what she meant. But something in the tone of her voice warned that the words came from still another layer of her that was new to me. One that maybe I didn't know enough to ask about.

By the time we got back to the head of our village it was mid-afternoon. I was very hungry, and would have hurried my limp to get to the house for something to eat, but Tante definitely refused to quicken her pace. Instead, for the first time that I could remember she put her arm around my shoulders, letting me nudge against her as we walked. She called out to several neighbors who hailed back, and as one or the other came to their gaps with refreshed consolations on the death of Min-min, she held them in chat for what seemed unbearably long periods. Our progress toward the house went unhappily slow for me, and Tante came to show another change. She continued with her arm about me, but I could feel her growing tight and distant. Once when I glanced at her face there was no smile in her eye. If she wasn't sweating from the heat her face would have looked dried and hard the way it did when they were getting Min-min from the dust.

Two bends before our home I heard the familiar sound of the

motor-car coming from behind us, and almost reflexively said, "The Potagee wife coming."

"I hear," Tante said, but she didn't move toward the grass although I pressed in that direction. We heard the car coming, getting nearer and nearer, and Tante gave a little, edged closer to the grass bank at the side of the road. We could hear the car coming, and by the time it was around the bend where we could see it we were at the edge of the road, but a strange thing happened. We did not back off into the deep grass. And when the car was almost abreast of us a stranger thing happened. I raised my stick and jumped out, striking at the shiny black bonnet. A totally erratic act, for which up to now I have no explanation. I felt no pain. I recall myself rolling through the dust and getting dirt in my mouth, but I plainly heard the noise as the car skidded into the opposite grass bank and crashed into Mr. Francis' cedar tree. It made a big noise like a house falling down. Then everything was silent.

My mouth was full of grit and dust, and when I tried to stand up I couldn't do it. My right leg had no feeling, and I fell back to the ground again. Tante rushed over to where I sat without wanting to in the dust, and the first thing she did was put the cap back on my head. As she bent down to grab me under the arms she pushed her eyes into mine and said almost fiercely, "Don't cry. Don't you cry!"

I didn't cry. Neither did the Portuguese wife. For as soon as the neighbors were able to dowse the small fire and get her out of the car, she struck out down the road without a word to anyone. If she had spoken, the first thing out of her mouth would have been curses, they said. But she didn't say a word to anyone. Soon the policeman came and Tante told the story. I was too lame to jump out of the woman's way and it was only after her car hit me that she veered, and lost control of the vehicle. The villagers clucked and shook their heads, and the policeman wrote in his book, then went back to the station.

Later that night while I lay on the floor behind my leg strapped between two flat pieces of board and bandaged, a huge fire lit up the village. It was Gomez's shop. Nobody knew how the fire started, but people immediately ran out with their buckets, and emptied their rain barrels on the blaze. That didn't stop it. The fire spread. It burned the shop, then took several buildings, as it made a path to

the canefields where it roared away like a living streak to curve back
through the burial ground and threaten the high church. But there
it petered out. Tante helped me up to a chair and sat beside me looking through our window at all the commotion, with men running up
to take our water and dash out of the yard again, and voices yelling,
and some people crying for the loss of all they ever owned. The police
station was partly burned too, and though no one was found dead,
when the blaze finally ended it left heaps of charred rubble and ashes
where the shop and the other buildings used to be.

The next day when Gomez and his wife left our village with
nothing but the clothes on their backs, some were glad to see them
go. And later when a man came with two horses and hitching them
to the broken motor-car started hauling it toward town, some
villagers, in spite of their own trauma followed behind, as though
someone was keeping a funeral. Tante propped me up in the window
to see the procession. And though her face was neither soft nor set,
she seemed saddened somewhere inside by the show and finally
dropped out "Niggers! Just like niggers. Look at them!" Then she
went back to putting out what clothes we could spare, and dishes, for
those who had nothing left after the fire.

I had no idea what she saw to make her say 'just like niggers,'
but perhaps I was still to taken with my own pain. On top of my
sprained ankle I came out of the crash with a broken knee.
Although, thanks to the skill of the senior village midwife and Tante's
hovering care, my leg soon mended. I never asked her what it was
she saw to make her say something like that either, but once before
I was well enough to walk again I did ask "Tante, what made me
jump in front of the motor-car like that?"

"The Lord moves in mysterious ways," she said. And no more.

Sometimes I wish I were as good as she was with sayings. Particularly when my son teases me now because I have to have every
pair of pants I buy altered to accommodate my short leg.

Who's Speaking Here?

We're all talking. Hopefully, our voices come through . . . because even when we sit to listen, our voice is in that of the speaker: that's why, if he goes into mistake we must correct him. We are all talking here. This is one way we live together. Many other ways we don't: either because we can't, or don't want to. Who knows? But in talking we are all the same voice, and if something is said wrong we correct it. . . .

At the Desk

Culture, like meaning, occurs on multiple levels, two of which are the referential and the metaphorical. (There are others.) Most anthropology is carried out on the referential level. Not many of us are trained to deal intellectually with the metaphorical/symbolic level. Such training would involve a knowledge/mastery of POETRY — the elemental language.

Referential culture is the environmental expression or achievement of metaphorical culture. It is only when both levels are seen in relationship that either becomes reasonably understandable. Often, in the process of the environmental (material and discursive) achievement of metaphor, the risk of incomplete or inaccurate articulation is encountered. Deficiencies in the material/symbolic environment would itself inhibit full metaphorical realization. So too would imposed (external or internal) controls over the freedom to

move, think, work, etc. Maintaining metaphorical-referential congruence at the aggregate level is a monstrous problem.

Inaccurate articulation occurs when people substitute alter-
natives to the substance of metaphorical elements, for whatever
reason, on the referential plane. This substitution does not result in
elimination of original metaphorical commands; it introduces a tension between what is, and what would be. What is equals metaphor
achieved on the referential level. What would be equals metaphor
itself.

The reduction of metaphor to referential equals the reduction
of spirit to personae equals the reduction of aggregate consciousness
to individual consciousness. The anthropologist is amply prepared
to reconstruct the referential. For others, composing a full-fledged
world is more difficult.

In the Field

Leaving Home as

It is dark, going down.
A patch of wet sails
peak the dome
creating a vast ocean.
Noiselessly they await
the traveller descending
dark humid ladders
to embrace the hold
and journey
and journey
And ride
with the wet air at one's face
no hand on the tiller
And ride
the unending wave
beyond mercy or disappointment
Where lions are unknown
Rabbits their own monsters
and punishment.

Shadows in the Moonlight

Moonlight came down bright like a sun gone cool yellow, except up high the night was still a secret blue. From her doorway Olga looked out on the fields of shiny cane stalks, their arrows glistening like strange gold for as far as she could see across the way to Golconda. The moonlight was brighter than she had seen it in a long time, yet in a funny way that hid things where they should have been most plain. The black pitch road separating her lot from the fields passed no more than a rod or so from where she sat, and two or three times when she had caught movement along it out of the corner of her eye she had turned to stare, waited for the dog, manicou, or mongoose to come plain, but there had been nothing there. Once she even thought she had seen the shape of a man in the distance coming toward her house, and she waited for him to come plain too. But neither man nor animal ever came clear enough for her to be certain of what she had seen, and she had to laugh at herself for thinking she was seeing spirits.

The night wore an eleventh-hour stillness, and she heard her laugh carry for a long time over the fields. She was alone. Her house stood apart from the rest of the village by almost a quarter mile, and the houses she could see before the road took a bend were already dark. She laughed again, a little louder, more self-consciously, to see if her voice would carry as it had before in the stillness. It carried. Then Olga was quiet, and resumed waiting for her child to come home.

It was a good thing that she was mistaken about seeing a man coming down the road, because tonight she did not want to be touched. Not that she had anything against being sweet with a man on a night like this, she having had her share of that. In fact, it made her a little sad to realize the number of times she had undressed under the moon, when there was so little now to show for all that giving and taking on the damp dew grass. But that wasn't what tonight was about and Olga pushed away the sad feelings. She had to put her thoughts together before Gracie came home. She had to get them together soon, because church must have been over at least an hour ago, and the child was already late. She had to be sharp and ready in her thoughts, even though in the back of her mind a voice kept asking 'What for?', keeping high the suspicion that she herself was too late with what she planned to do. But to that suspicion she would not submit, because, even if at that very moment the child was already bedded down under the shadow of the American traveller, there would still be time enough when she came home for Olga to say what she had to say, and be free. And this time there would be no slapping, no hot-bloodedness, nothing but her telling the child truthfully what she knew about getting started. If questions came up, she would have to answer them straight. Olga had to put her thoughts together, but with the moonlight playing tricks on her nerves, it wasn't easy getting much of anything to make sense.

She never knew her mammy to be anything but a sweet woman, and although she had promised since childhood that no such thing would ever happen to her it had happened anyway, and now she wasn't sure how. She was one of the few girls of her time to stay in school until sixteen, and she was bright enough for the headmaster to recommend her to the high school in town fifteen miles away, but she never did go there. Her mammy couldn't raise the money for clothes and books.

Olga had cried for a week over seeing that chance pass by, and Bertie, the reverend's son, himself already a student at the high school, used to come to their house to comfort her. She was a lead soprano in the church choir then, and very much in love with Bertie. He loved her too, just like a reverend's son should — cleanly, truly, and with high understanding. His touch was the most painful sweetness in those days. And when on Sunday afternoons after Sunday-school he took her hand in his and led her on their long walks along the country road from the village, he usually kept her out of breath not from the walking, but from the steady leaping and settling of her heart. Like a frog with salt-water on its back.

Henry used to dog them then, alone, or with friends of his, and the many times they chased him 'Shoo black nigger' made no difference. Just the sight of him used to get her blood up, though at times she would feel sorry for him too, and if he wasn't so black she would have asked Bertie to stop chucking stones at him. But Henry or no Henry, the first hour of darkness when they had to come back to church for evening service was usually the tenderest of all, because then Bertie's arm would come around her waist and it would be as though she walked without touching the ground, until they came to the lighted church-yard where he had to let her go.

That was in 1940 when the Germans were bombing England, and the newspaper was full of photos about it everyday.

The next year Bertie went into uniform. He was just seventeen. And everybody in the village said he had to go because although his family was Barbadian his grandfather was an Englishman. That couldn't have been true because the other village boys who went into uniform were all black and their families had never seen England. She was never quite sure why Bertie went in, but he looked good in his pressed khakis the day he left with Henry and four others, riding in the back of a government truck. Henry was black and full of grins as ever, but he didn't look half as decent as Bertie.

The boys were taken to a camp in the North, past Port-of-Spain, and she did not see Bertie for a long time after that — although he did write once a week for twelve weeks, then once a month for nine months.

And all that time she was still staying in the two-room house with mammy, sleeping on the other side of a cloth blind from where mammy made some money every night. Sometimes the men used to ask her to take a drink with them, but she never paid any attention. Usually she would read until her eyes grew tired, then go to sleep. There were two men, Samuel and Marcus, who used to leave her money. Sometimes a dollar, sometimes just a shilling or two. There was another man, Berry, who used to promise her plenty of money if she would let him sleep on her side of the blind sometime, but she never even spoke a word to him. Mammy used to think that was funny.

"What kind of daughter is that you have here, mammy?" Berry used to shout, and mammy would just chuckle. "That girl sure act like a miss somebody," Berry would go on. "She walk in here, don't say a word when spoken to . . . I have a good mind to take mi belt off and give her a licking."

And mammy would really break out laughing then, "You make child to give licking?" And after laughing at Berry used to say "That girl too much of a lady for you Berry. She my great little lady . . . sometime I think she more of a lady than I know what to do with."

"She don't act like your daughter at all mammy."

"I believe sometimes she too much of a lady for me in truth. She act more like her father every day," mammy would end it.

And that would make Olga think of her father — though not in the same way she used to when she was just a little girl. Start her thinking about her father, where was he, and what was he doing, and who was he really. Because all she had ever been told about him was that he was a white man, 'bakra johnny,' mammy used to say, just barely holding back from spitting, and that would be the end of all mammy said about her father. Of course, everybody could see she was the child of a white man because mammy was black, big-lipped, had nappy hair. While she was high brown herself, and her hair came down past her shoulders in soft smooth waves. Where mammy was loose, overflowing in front and behind, she was slender and tight.

But it never did any good thinking about her father. He remained unknown, except in her imagination. At first she used to tell herself one day he would come, and although there could be no question of his living with them, at least he would bring money enough to make his daughter and mammy well off. While she still believed he would come, she used to be very excited each time the English staff changed at the sugar-factory and would spend hours matching features with the new arrivals. She wasn't sure why, but she knew her father had to be English. Not French, nor Spanish, nor Dutch, nor Portuguese, although he could have been either of these. She was certain he was English. Yet her imagination did no good because no father ever showed up. None of the English factory bosses ever came near mammy, and by 1941 she had finally come to forget about having a father except when mammy said, "She acting more like her father every day." And even then, 'Wherever he is, he might at least send something' used to be the only thought to cross her mind about him.

In the meantime, the village men on whom mammy depended were already saying things when Olga passed. Some of the others didn't speak it, but you could see it in their eyes like greedy boys watching the tree for the next sapodilla to turn ripe. But not one of them could shift her mind off Bertie. She had a lot of time to long for him too, and answer his letters. She was no longer in school. She was not about to go to work in the canefields, or in any overseer's kitchen. She wasn't thinking about going to town to look for work either. Seemed like every village girl who ever went there ended up the same way — ratting on the streets, or working in the house for some high-class family. She was going to wait. And in her waiting, her longing for Bertie, she dreamed and imagined him coming home a hero to marry her and do whatever he wanted with her after that.

In 1942 the Yankees came to Trinidad. There wasn't any war in Trinidad, but they came anyway. They were very rich, and very wild with their money. The newspaper was full of stories about the Yankee and their money. Some people were scared then that the Germans would come for sure to drop their bombs and wipe out Trinidad, but that did not prevent them from going to work for the Yankee dollar.

The Joes wanted some army base built, they wanted it in a hurry. They were paying more money a week than many Trinidadians had ever seen in a liftetime.

Men and women left their homes, trekked North to find jobs with the Yankees, and she thought of going North too, to work as an office girl, maybe, and make a lot of money, but then mammy said "Not a foot. Them Yankee ain't good for nothing but killing people."

And the paper was full of that too, how the Joes ran over people with their jeeps and army trucks, then stopped only long enough to pin hundred dollar notes to the corpses. They bought all the whores in Port-of-Spain, and it was nothing to find on a Sunday morning one or two of the mopsies or their home boyfriends beaten up or dead in the gutter. Sometimes an American would be dead there too, but that wouldn't be local people business. And although the Yankees paid good money, they made every man and woman sweat for it. Work up to twelve, fifteen, eighteen hours a day, and if you couldn't do that they kicked you off the job.

When mammy said, "Not a foot. Them Yankees ain't nothing

but murderers," Olga did not talk back too hard, because mammy didn't mind if she just sat around waiting, and that was what she really wanted to do more than anything else. She read over her last school books about Joan of Arc, and the children of the new forest, and King Arthur. She read them over more than once because her other old books were about buccaneers fighting and burying gold, and she didn't like those stories. They were for boys.

Sometimes the village men who managed to get home from the Yankee base for a day or so brought mammy picture magazines from America, and Olga liked those more than anything else she had to read. They had the best love stories. The photographs showed clean, rich, healthy, good-looking men, every one of whom could be a hero. And the beautiful girls always got in the end all that they could wish for. She used to wish it was like that for her. She was beautiful too, and she had her dream of Bertie coming home a hero to marry her. Sometimes when she pictured him in her mind it was with a different head, one not so English as Bertie's, more American. And other times when his head came the body was not so bony and narrow as his but taller, more husky and bronze. Yet it was Bertie everytime.

She dreamed about him even after she started learning how to sew at Aunt Sylvie's. She would walk down the village road to the other end, and get to Aunt Sylvie's at eight o'clock in the morning, then come back home at four in the afternoon. In both going and coming she would have young men following, riding slowly or walking their bicycle beside her. They had the same look in their eye as mammy's men, only less dangerous, and she seldom listened to a thing they said, but they helped time to pass less noticeably. Sometimes they would say things that were really funny, then she would have to laugh. But she didn't listen to a thing they said all up to the time mammy died, and even for a time after she had the two-room house to herself.

She couldn't keep them from hanging around though. They followed on the street, and came right up to the house. A few of the older men who had belonged to mammy came by the house too, but not Samuel. He died before mammy. Berry and Marcus still came, though with mammy gone Marcus turned just like Berry to offering money to let him sleep in her bed. All of them, grown men and young, would come to her house, sit in her yard and talk most of the night. It was no secret they were making bets to see which one would get into her first. That only made her long harder for Bertie to come home and take her away, but her longing didn't do a thing to the war, and Bertie remained in his camp or wherever he was training or gone to the war. After twelve months she got no more letters, but never once lost faith that Bertie would return to her. It was only the war holding them apart for the moment.

Then one night she was forgetful and didn't latch her door. Mammy had never locked their door once, but Olga had gotten the habit after mammy died. Not because she was afraid anyone would harm her. She didn't know all the prayers mammy used to say to keep out spirits, and beside, it was the savoury thing for a young woman who was temptation to do. Then one night after talking with Marcus and his nephew who was visiting from town, she forgot to latch the door, and fell asleep dreaming. She dreamed about Bertie, or someone like him, come home to marry her. She dreamed he slipped into the village after dark of night and came straight to her, so she was the only one who knew he had come home, and he had come vowing he could not live another day without her, carrying a deep passion that mingled with hers and swept them both away. She dreamed and felt him there in bed with her. She felt someone in bed with her. Gladness stirred in her as she had never known before, and even while part of her mind keep saying no, not this way, and she might even have been crying, she moved and moved until it drained away, and she passed again to peaceful sleeping.

When she awoke the next morning the soreness in her body made her want to cry. She remembered crying in the night, but in the soreness was a welcome feeling too, and her crying was as much for the way it happened as it wasn't for the happening itself. She didn't even have a name. He never said a word that she could remember, and in the dark there was no face but the imagined Bertie. Olga lay in bed and cried. Then after she heard the bread man pass got up and went to Aunt Sylvie's as usual. She did not try to run when the boys followed her on the way home that evening, but at night she locked the door, or rather latched and put a chair behind it, because there was no lock.

Then things came back to being usual for a while, until another night when she did not put the chair behind the door just to test what would happen. Someone came in. At first she thought of spirits. Then she lay quietly trying to figure which one it really was. In the darkness he came straight to the bed. She did not scream. She did not say anything. He didn't either. He wasn't long. He hardly found the right place before he was finished, and as he left she heard him placing money on the table. His body smell and the half grunt half sigh as he finished told her it was Berry. In the morning, with the money on the table, she had the same idea, and she wondered in passing why couldn't one of the younger ones think to be as bold as he'd been. But she didn't take up too much time with it. She went about her day as usual.

She wasn't afraid, but she went back to putting the chair behind the door again, until she had saved enough money from what Aunt Sylvie paid her to get away. She knew she had to go, and did not stop to wonder why, except it seemed the things she had dreamed Bertie would come back and do didn't much matter any more, and she had to find something else to do besides wait for him. She had to look after herself. And when she was ready, she got dressed one morning, packed her clothes in a bag, and while a few villagers watched boarded the bus for town.

It was noisy there, and crowded. Strange men looked her up and down everywhere she turned — but that did not start anything. That did not start her being a whore. Didn't seem like anything started her, really.

It was hard to remember.

And how would she answer the first thing Gracie was bound to ask, "What I do to make you say I getting to be a whore?" Gracie had much more fire than she had when she was young, and she could see her now, nostrils flaring, the blood pounding at her temples, demanding what right anybody had to accuse her of getting to be a whore. Perhaps it would be better to think of a different word. Only, Olga had nothing to say against whoring. Her only concern was that Gracie should know what to do for her own protection. She had nothing against whoring, the word or the deed, although in the town she had done none of it herself.

She had taken a job at a textile shop, but didn't stay there long because the work required her to be on her feet ten hours every day except Sunday, and after paying five dollars each week for her room rent, and buying food, she could hardly save any more than a two-dollars from her pay. Beside, the other salesgirls were heavy competitors, and more than once they ganged up and prevented her from making the big sales that gave good commissions. As one of them said, she was lucky she had a pretty face, or else she might never have made a wage in that store at all. And finally, although she had never forgotten mammny saying that Yankees were murderers, after three months away from the village she left town, and found herself at the American army base.

Never before in her life had she seen so many white men working just as hard as niggers. Stripped to the waist, burnt brown, sweat streaming off their backs, they were out there digging and driving piles, running tractors, hammering nails, laying bricks, just like anybody else. They didn't look the way she expected they would at all. She didn't like them. Not one of their heads fitted on Bertie's body, not one of their bodies could have taken Bertie's head. They were coarse, loud, and rough. They swore steadily so you couldn't tell when they were doing it because they were vexed, from when they were doing it because it sounded good to their ears. She didn't like them. Their eyes looked the same all the time. Not lurking like the men's in the village, nor plain hungry like the boys', but naked and flat, as though they had no secrets, and deliberately cared nothing for privacy. And she could believe what mammy said about them then, because that's exactly how they looked, like they would think nothing of killing somebody or something if it suited their feelings. They gave her a job though, marking time cards and inventory cards twelve hours a day, every day in the week, and they paid her enough.

There was nothing but cocoa forest all around the base, and St. Joseph, the nearest town where she could find a place to live was more than ten miles away. She rented a bed there, in a room with four other women, and at first she used to be so tired when she got home, she would just take off her shoes and flop down until it was time to start back to the base in the morning. But gradually her body got accustomed to sitting in the rigid straight-backed chair for twelve hours straight, and she grew so she didn't mind being confined all that time to one half of a bungalow room with three other workers, the tin roof no more than an arm's length above her head, the bare electric bulbs lower than that. Eventually she got so she could do the job without thinking how tired it made her back and neck, and although she never stopped being tired when she got to her room at night, she started feeling restless too. The women with whom she shared went out every night, but they weren't friendly. She never went out of her way to be friendly either, because that gave people a chance to take advantage of you. Suckers were a new and growing breed, the newspaper said.

One evening when she came in two of her roommates were changing their clothes, talking about some dance they were going to. A hot one, they said, and asked her if she didn't like to dance. She never particularly liked dancing, but she didn't say that. They said she should go with them. The hottest band from Port-of-Spain was playing, and it might be the last time before the police put a ban on nighttime dancing altogether. She decided to go. She didn't feel like hurrying, and they were so well near ready they went off and told her she could meet them there. The dance was at a schoolhouse less than a mile from where she roomed, and after she had rested while, she got up, put on her black satin dress trimmed with white, because mammy's year wasn't up yet, and walked over.

The school hall was crowded and hot. She couldn't find the other girls. Everyone was sweating. She saw quite a few Americans, and one or two other white boys who didn't look American at all, and for a few minutes her legs trembled with the sudden remembrance of Bertie, the expectancy of perhaps coming upon him in the crowd. There were some black boys from Port-of-Spain in zoot suits and Cab Calloway hats. Some of them looked nice. The brown-skinned boys from Tunupuna wore less flashy clothes but were better looking to her eye.

She said no to about six men who asked her to dance, half hoping all the time to see Bertie materialize in one of the half-white faces. He never did, and finally she started hearing the music and wishing one of the brown-skinned boys would ask her again. It was one of the rough, loud Yankees though who came up and said "Hi, baby! Watcha got hot?" or something like that. She didn't know what to answer because she didn't have anything hot. She was hearing the music, and smelling the rum and sweat and body powder going around in the room, and she did want to dance.

"Any poozle on the market tonight?" or something like that the Yankee asked. And she just smiled again, trying not to look too straight into his face because she had no idea what poozle was. He danced with her and tried to press his sweating body close. While she couldn't help being stiff she didn't want to hold him off too far, because everybody knew any American could make you lose your job in the morning if he felt like it.

"Blood on the moon tonight, huh?" he asked another stupid question. "Jordan flowing 'round the bend?" She wasn't even interested in catching his meaning, and so she just nodded and smiled. When the music stopped, he left her and walked away.

Then a fight started between the brown boys from St. Joseph and Tunupuna and the black boys from Port-of-Spain. The brown boys were jumping around trying to swear like Yankees, but the black boys were doing a better job at that, and beside, they had knives which they flashed across and across infront of them. There was a lot of pushing and screaming. The music played louder. Then police whistles came. As she was trying to get out of the way a brown boy rushed up, and grabbing her around the throat from behind started pushing her in front of him right through the fight. She didn't even have time to scream. Before she knew what was happening he had pushed through to the edge of the floor, whirled, and had her dragging backwards out the door. At the bottom of the steps he let go her throat but grabbed her wrist, then started running in the dark, dragging her behind him. They went for about a quarter mile down the road, then he dashed into an empty yard and flopped down under a tree. "Those bitches gon pay!" he said, out of breath. "They ain't getting out of this town alive tonight."

She was out of breath too, and she remained quiet. She was very afraid, but only because it was so dark she couldn't see what he might do before he tried. The boy sounded tired.

"You think I 'fraid, eh?" he said. "Think that's why I run, eh? You want to know something? Feel that." He put something in her hand, but she couldn't tell what it was right away. "That razor can cut your head off zap! One stroke!" He let go her wrist, but she remained sitting on the ground beside him. "Only thing," he went on, "it's my uncle's razor, and I don't want to really fight with it." Then suddenly he stopped breathing hard and said, "You're a real pretty girl," groping for her hand in the dark. She let him take back the razor, and moved away a little so he couldn't reach her too easily in the dark. "You're a real pretty girl," he said, trying to sound Yankee. Then he asked her to be his girl, and she smiled to herself because when he asked he reminded her of a yard dog ready at the same time to run or bite. She said no, she just wanted to go home. She was tired and had to work the next day. He walked her to her room then, muttering all the way about what he and his pals would do to the Port-of-Spain boys when the dance was over.

She said no the night of the dance, but she said yes some nights later, and they returned to the same spot in the dark under the tree, where he opened his pants, lifted her dress, and did what she said she would let him do. There was no reasoning behind her saying yes, either. She didn't want anything from him, he never brought her anything, and even if meeting him on the grass beneath the tree did make her body feel something, she didn't find it half so great as he claimed he did. Yet she went back time after time, until it became nothing but a regular way to spend the night. Then she stopped going.

After Lloyd it was another brown-skinned boy from La Porta who didn't take her out under the dew. He had a room in a house two doors from where she stayed. Regularly every night, sometimes as soon as she came in from the base, she would go over to stay with him. He never gave her anything either. In fact, he was bold enough to ask her to buy him some shirts, and that was when she stopped going to his room.

Who was next . . . she wasn't sure. But there were one or two others before Lou. She remembered them dimly — the way one might have sounded, the way another might have smelled — but they weren't important. They were never too important because all the time she spent with them was time spent in waiting. Not dreaming about Bertie any more, but waiting, hanging on to the promise of a husband and house of her own. A promise never made her by any one, to be sure, but a promise which though she had no reason to hold she held anyway, because that was what she wanted and she didn't see how anything else could be of much importance. Then Lou seemed like he was the one to bring that promise true.

He was one of the few Americans whom she did not find coarse. He came during her second year, when she had mastered the job well enough to do it with one eye and carry on conversations with the other girls. In fact, she was one of the senior girls at the office then, because few workers lasted long, and all the girls she met there but one were gone. She was a senior girl, and when Lou came, pink and smooth off one of the airplanes that were landing just across the field many times a day now, it fell to her to show him the routine. Lou was so openly nervous, so pink skinned and smooth, he talked so softly and with such kind words, that immediately she felt he needed her to protect him. The American staff was shifting all the time too, and when Lou was put fully in charge of the payroll and inventory department she used to stop over late whenever it was necessary to help make sure the pay sheets were done on time, because somehow she felt it had fallen to her to make this pink faced boy's life as easy as she could.

In his turn Lou promised great things. He was a Lutheran farm boy from Iowa, and when he talked she saw the little white church at the foot of his town, the town itself mostly white, except for a red school building, big rough oak trees, a blue stream passing through, and peaked roofs red or grey making the houses little spots of colour in the wide open countryside, until winter, when everything was really white for sure, everything that is except the people bundled, pink, and cheerful, clean and smiling whether they were slopping hogs or coming from church. Whenever Lou talked about his town she saw a little nest lodged between miles and miles of corn, a nest where she really could settle. She heard in Lou's voice the promise that their settling together was not only possible, but very strongly in the offing, if only he could make up his mind to it finally.

She helped him. She couldn't recall exactly how, but it was managed, and he did finally ask her to stay with him one night, though not at all in the way of the other American who had started talking about poozle — she had later found out what he was trying to say. Lou asked like a real gentleman who was lonely and shy. Yet once they were naked and hot together his tongue was set so free that all the quarter promises she had heard only at the back of his voice fell from his lips clearly. And she, a little dizzy, a little wild, was saying inside and outside a deep yes. Even as that first night was being multiplied into all the nights they could cram into six months she kept saying yes, yes, to his pleading, his tasting, his promising. So that the day he left she felt no pain.

She watched him climb aboard one of the grey airplanes headed for the east, that was true, but his orders said within eighteen months he would be home again, safe in the heart of his Iowa homeland, and he had taught her they should have faith in his orders. Beside, the promise that they should spend the rest of their lives together once the war was won had been made over and over so many times she didn't see how things could be any different. So the day of parting was no day to be sad. She had his faithful promise that once home he would send for her, and she was so full of visions of a house in the midst of the little white town, her children running home from the red school building, herself a wife to Lou, forever tantalizing him with her sweetness, that she saw the plane heading east as the first preliminary to her journey west.

She was full of visions to fill the waiting but she never saw Lou again, nor heard from him either, except once — a postcard from Spain saying he was learning how to eat bread and onions, and learning how to drink wine from a goat skin. That was when she returned home to the village — one of the times in her life when she actually thought out what to do before doing. For this reason she was always proud of her coming back, even though she had done so in disgrace — with a seven month belly. She wasn't the first village girl to come home like that, nor was she the last, and with her own house, money enough saved from the job so she had to depend on no one, she was in a better position than most who had come back carrying unborn bastards. And thank God for Grandma Thompson.

All the same, Olga hoped that Gracie would have no bastards. If the American traveller was telling the child anything about little pretty white towns Olga hoped she would know enough to put him off until he made a more sensible promise. Not that that might make much difference with this one. He was very different from Lou. With his long hair and beard, his guitar and old clothes, he seemed like the sort that had a lot of practice saying anything that was for saying at the moment. A body couldn't tell what to expect, but if she happened to pass suddenly there was no Grandma Thompson to take her place and care for Gracie.

Grandma Thompson who couldn't bear the thought of a child being born in the village without her horny hands delivering it started coming around soon after Olga came home from the base, and it was comforting to have the old lady there sitting with her blousy skirts drawn tight in her lap the way mammy some times used to sit, smelling strongly of tobacco and stale herbs, telling what to expect and what to do for the least suffering.

During the last month before Gracie came Grandma moved right in, started sleeping on the cot Olga used to sleep on as a child, and the little two-room house had a deeper feeling of comfort about it than ever before. Instead of the rumble of mammy's and some man's voices coming from the other side of the curtain it was she and Grandma talking through the blind, Grandma repeating what to do once the baby started fighting its way out, she remembering to the old lady what a sweet father Lou would have made if the war hadn't sent him away.

Then one day just before the baby was born Bertie came home. Only it wasn't home for him anymore, inasmuch as his father, the reverend, had been transferred to a church in St. Lucia and his whole family had already gone there. Olga was never sure whether Bertie came through wanting to see her. When Henry and another soldier in his camp were coming home to Palmyra on weekend leave Bertie came along too. That was all he said. He didn't stay. The few hours he spent in the village were passed mostly sitting in her chair watching her laid back in the bed under her big stomach.

"Is it hurting you much?" he asked.

"It's not hurting at all. Not yet?."

"What are you going to name it?."

"I don't know. The father's name is Lou."

"Sounds American. Is he?"

"Yes. . . . "

"Is that what you're going to call him if he's a boy?"

"I guess so. . . . "

"And if it's a girl?"

"I don't know. I will have to leave that to the godparents."

The army had made Bertie into a strong man. He was burnt browner than he had been before leaving the village, his hair was lighter and cropped short, his shoulders were wide and heavy and even his eyes had become less gleaming and steadier. He wasn't the same person that she knew before he went away, and she found herself wondering how many whores had he paid, because every one knew all the boys in the army did that. And she was ready, if he mentioned having missed her to tell him she knew what men in the army were up to, but he never got around to saying he had. Instead, "Do you feel all right?" for the second time. He never even noticed her hint at being a godparent.

"Yes. I feel all right."

"What're you going to do after the baby comes?"

"Stay here, I guess.

"You won't be going to America?"

"That's up to Lou."

"Oh . . . I see. . . . "

She didn't know what he meant by that, because he wasn't even looking at her. He was gazing off with his newly flat eyes away past her head, away out of the room it seemed.

"You're going back to the army?" she tried to call back his attention.

"Oh yes. I have another nine months. I do wish I get sent to the front before it's all over. We drill every day, you know, and keep sentry duty at night but that's not being in the real thing."

"Maybe the Germans will bomb Trinidad," she said.

"Not a chance. They're on their last legs right now. I do wish I get sent before they give in."

"Don't you want to go to St. Lucia and live with your family?"

"No. I'll probably settle in England once the war is over."

"And you won't come back to Trinidad at all?"

"Oh yes. I'll come back."

"To Palmyra?"

"Of course. Don't forget, my cord's buried here," he said. "But I won't stay. I'll visit, but I couldn't stay. Not here." He stood suddenly to lean above her, and his movement startled her. All he did was take her hand and squeeze it, and for a moment tried being sweet little Bertie again with his eyes, but the feeling didn't come close to what it was like on those old Sunday walks. Her heart did not lunge. She did not float an inch above the bed. In fact, she felt no feelings at all, and if Bertie was disappointed he did not show it. When he sat down again he seemed really quite cheerful. "What's the new reverend like?" he asked. "I hear he used to serve in West Africa."

"He's a nice man. Grandma Thompson says he visits all the sick people regularly."

"Does he ever come to see you?"

"He came to say the church would accept the child. Wanted me to give him sufficient notice for the baptism, but I haven't seen him since. He was nice, though."

"My father would have given you a lecture."

"I know. But this man's pretty good for himself too. I hear he's in with a few of the girls around here already. Besides, he has a young boy, but nobody's ever seen the boy's mother. . . . "

"That was my father's main weakness," Bertie said. "He never was nice enough to the village women. . . . "

And some other nonsense they talked, until Grandma Thompson came in saying the boy Henry was drunk, talking out of his head at the rumshop, looking for a fight, and Bertie hurried off saying soldiers had to take care of one another.

That was the last she saw of Bertie. But in the weeks that followed she saw all she wanted to of Henry, because when it came time for them to return to the camp he wouldn't go. He hid from the army jeep that came to pick up the others and remained in Palmyra. What difference did that make, really? He always used to find other places to go when he was a boy supposed to be in school, and now he was just a runaway soldier.

Like her, Henry became a mild disgrace to the village. He sold his uniform buttons to buy rum, and after they got tired of his uproarious drinking and constant fights his family put him out. Unlike with her, however, there was nothing independent about Henry. And after his family kicked him out, and he'd had enough of sleeping on the open gallery of the rumshop he came to her, begging a spot to sleep, even if it had to be on the floor.

Grandma Thompson didn't like the idea, but Olga allowed Henry to rest on her floor. He never stopped drinking, and it didn't take long for him to lose his strength for fighting and become just another tame village drunk who accepted his picong good-naturedly. He even added to it sometimes by marking time in the shop, lifting his knees high the way they did in the army, slapping his arms and shoulders meantime in something he called quarter-master drill.

When the baby came Henry was there on her floor deep in a drunken sleep, and it didn't disturb him once, her groaning, or Grandma Thompson's talking her through then bustling back and forth with hot water and towels, or the baby crying. Yet when he woke up the first thing he wanted to do was hold the child, and Grandma said no. Because he was too dirty. Henry went off and washed himself, then came back in a clean pair of pants, a shirt he had borrowed from his brother, and lifted up the child to his face. He put a dollar inside the baby's clothes and asked, "Does she have a name already?"

"No. Nobody's named her yet."

"Good. I name her Grace."

That was how Grace got her name, how she got a second father too, because Henry loved the baby so much he went off to find a job so he could help take care of her.

Henry became a fisherman on the sea from Sunday to Friday, but that couldn't be helped. The Englishmen at the sugar factory would never have hired him. On the weekends when he came in from the sea he brought the child clothes and toys, and brought things for Olga too. Gracie grew, and Henry grew more fond of her. It used to be nice, seeing him with her when he was home Saturdays. He played with her all morning before going to the rumshop, and when at night he returned, he would have two pockets full of sweets, fruits, and other little things the child might like.

Of course, by then Henry didn't sleep on the floor anymore. He was still black, true, but he was a kind man, and when one night after coming home from the sea he got into her bed, it seemed natural as anything that she should please him.

Saturdays were nice, then, and Sundays too, until one in the afternoon when Henry had to leave to go back to the sea.

Then Gracie was old enough to be away at Sunday school when it was time for Henry to leave, and he didn't like that. He missed her kissing goodbyes, he claimed. Missed her eyes telling him to bring her nice things when he came home next Friday night. Olga herself never once asked Henry for anything. She took what he brought, and let him sleep in her bed, but she never asked for anything. Henry liked to behave as though he really was a father. He liked Gracie wrapping her arms around his leg and reminding him to bring her back something next Friday. And so he missed her when she had to be away at Sunday school.

In the meantime Olga was looking her best as a woman. She was no longer thin. After the child her breasts remained high and round, her hips spread a little, and her legs took on flesh. And just as the men used to flock to her house in the days before she went to work for the Yankees, so they started coming back. One or two of the older ones had died, but there were young ones to take their places, fresh boys just starting work at the factory. These and the middling ones who used to follow her in the old days on their bicycles, they were always around, hanging about her doorstep, her yard, eager to do her errands, always bringing her gossip, bringing her yams or chickens, whatever they could lay their hands on, even though she never asked them for anything. Henry was no bother to them either. They came just the same when he was home, and sometimes he would bring a bottle to finish it with the grown men in the yard. He never quarrelled with them, and they never minded him. If he came home drunk and staggering, two or three would always be there to help him inside. Other times they just shifted their bottoms on the steps so he could get by.

After the child, and having Henry, it turned out that Olga wasn't bothered by the eyes anymore. And she couldn't tell really how it happened, but one day she had it suddenly clear in her mind that it was her special blessing to have men look at her that way. And with this in mind, she could sit in her open doorway whenever the men were around and turn every eye up under her dress, then shut her legs and turn them out again, watching all the time how the men would lose control of their thoughts, even those who tried to appear cool and indifferent. She could make them shift from thinking about rain, or sickness or the government. She would bend their minds on the sly, pretending her moves were all accidental, and after they were gone would feel a great pleasure deep inside that brought laughter, and the child sometimes asked "What you laughing at, mama?" That was mostly the only fun she had. She never went to dances, or anywhere else anymore. When it was time to buy clothes for Gracie and herself, or pay taxes, she went to town, did her business, and came straight back home. But that was only for a time.

One Sunday, with Henry gone, Gracie away at Sunday school, Olga listened to the men talking about a dance which had passed the night before, and their talk brought back memories of the dance at which she had met Lloyd in St. Joseph. She told them the story. The men made a racket about it. "You could've been killed," Reggie said, and she had to admit that that was true. "Those Yankees and those town boys, they don't play. They could've killed you, and we'd never have heard about you again." She didn't believe that was true, but she didn't stop him. The memories helped make her feel safe and cradled in the attention of the village men. She was at home, all safe, and knew she would be taken care of the rest of her life by these men for whom she was an adventuress, a mystery, all rolled into one.

Olga let them continue their racket, and while she was waiting for sundown to bring Gracie home from her Sunday walk she went on letting them catch glimpses under her dress every now and then,

smiling to see the way it made the veins at their temple tick faster.
When early darkness came, and the men started going off to supper,
Reginald did not go. He remained seated on the step beneath her
knees and when she rose to go in said, "You know, Olga, you really
could've been killed up there around those people . . . "

She stopped in the doorway but didn't say anything.

Then he got up too and said, "Let me come tonight."

And she said, "All right. After Gracie's gone to evening service."

Maybe it was recalling times with Lloyd and Lou made her
agree, she thought, as close to eight o'clock that night she lay watching Reginald put on his clothes, pondering whether Henry would
quarrel with her when he found out. It didn't seem that he should.

On Monday night after the men went away, and Gracie was
asleep behind the curtain she let Reginald come again, but on Tuesday night she would not let him, because he seemed wanting to make
a habit of it. On Wednesday night she would not let him again, and
he quarrelled. On Thursday night, just to show Reginald that he
shouldn't be stupid she let Dudley stay. He had been asking with his
eyes for a long time. On Friday Henry came home, and everything
went as usual. But on Sunday it was Reginald again, then Dudley,
and Reginald again, and Dudley, and when they quarrelled with one
another she let Winston come.

Olga couldn't remember how it first started, but somebody gave
her — left her — five dollars once, which she took and hid in the
sweat-band of a church hat she didn't wear anymore. The next one
who came brought five dollars too, which she took. Another one
brought ten which she didn't mean to take, but he left it beneath
her pillow, and she was later glad because Henry didn't come home
that weekend. Nor any other weekend. He just never came back to
the village.

And on. Three, four, five, soon all the men who came each
brought a little something which she took. As far as she knew, they
never made any agreement between themselves, but they stopped
quarrelling with one another. That made everything easy. She
simply left the door unlatched, and after it was time for Gracie to
be asleep some one would come in softly to her bed, and leave what
he could when it came near to daybreak and time for him to go. The
women of the village began wandering past her home more frequently than usual, and twice she found blue bottles of assafoetida

and scorched calabashes beneath the steps, but that didn't worry her.

Olga and her daughter never wanted for anything. The child grew up smoothly with shoes to wear to school and a new dress for confirmation. She had her own school books and a shilling every day to buy little things she wanted. As for prettiness, the child had no competition, and besides, who else in the village could boast a true Yankee American father? Gracie had days brighter than any Olga herself ever had. Olga never tied the girl down. She let her go into town Saturday mornings to see theater, or buy "Seventeen" magazines at the bookstore. The girl was singing in the choir, always had a nice dress to wear for church functions, and took her walks on Sundays with the reverend's boy who was just two or three years older than she and not from an English family but a high-class family from Jamaica. In a way this was not too different, but different enough to make a future marriage less troublesome.

In an unspoken way Olga was taken by the sweetness and beauty of her daughter, and secretly hoped the child was on her way to becoming the lady she herself might have been if the war hadn't come along to take Bertie. And she wasn't prepared when the child said no, she didn't want any high school, no more education, she just wanted to go to America . . . "I don't want to go to no high school. I old enough to go to America, and I want to go live there with my father. I hate this village."

Olga wasn't prepared, and it seemed that the child was betraying her. To grow out of the village, yes. But to say you hate it and only want to go to America? "And how about the reverend's boy?" Olga had asked. "What're you going to do about him?"

"He's just a friend." It was clear to see Gracie had no intention of spending her years with him, in a nice home with flower gardens and servants, and good-looking, clean, respectable children. And Olga didn't know how to take it, except to feel hurt for days, and outraged, because the child really had no true feelings for her father. Had never once shown an interest in the meaning of Lou's attentions for Olga. Had, in fact, been hostile to Olga's reminiscing with the village men about Lou's warmth and his weaknesses. And now, as though deserving of some special privilege in daughterhood, calling upon him as ticket or passport to some dreamed about life in America. It was while Olga was in this hurt and confused state with her child that the traveller showed up in the village.

He kept saying he was from Hollywood, but nobody was stupid enough to believe that. Any fool knew from the movies that Hollywood had the best looking, cleanest, healthiest people in the world, and this boy looked more like a long-haired stray dog than anything else. He came to the village nobody knew how, and started calling everybody "brother," but he was neither black, nor brown, nor white, and with his sickly color like a whitey cockroach nobody in the village wanted to be his brother. And, spending as much time in the rumshop as the Chinese owner himself but not drinking, the men said, he was just there playing on his guitar, singing what he called folk-songs, and buying the men drinks to get them to sing him some kind of work-songs he said belonged to the Island. Nobody was fool enough to believe he was American. Nobody that is, except Gracie.

The child was taken with this stranger right away and had more than the time of day to give him Grandma Thompson said, whenever she went to the shop, or passed him on the road. Swinging her little bottom and looking at him as though he were some sort of prize. "You ought to talk to that girl," Grandma said. "You know she think she too high-class to listen to nobody else. You better talk to her."

And Olga had said, "Not to worry Grandma. Gracie won't do nothing stupid, you know. She just trying out herself to learn what she can do."

"But it don't look good," Grandma said. "The other Sunday she carried on right in front of the reverend's boy while they taking their walk and pass this Yankee on the road. Even stop to talk with the Yankee while the poor boy stand up like a fool waiting in the grass."

"Well he better learn something quick," Olga had said. "And his father is a lady's man? He better ask his daddy what to do when his girl start making sweet-eyes at another man."

"You taking this like a joke," Grandma had said then, in a bitter and tired voice. "But you know Gracie don't listen to nobody else in this village. And mark my word . . . if you don't talk to her soon you going to be sorry. Too late, too late, shall be the cry: Jesus of Nazareth will have already pass by. . . . "

Olga promised she would talk to Gracie, but didn't. Not even after she heard that they had been seen in the town together, and when she asked Gracie the girl said no. Intuitively Olga knew Gracie was lying, but didn't feel she should cut off the child's chance to grow.

And later Grandma asked again, "You talk to Gracie yet? She not going to choir practice any more, you know."

That made Olga feel lonely. Something like that she should have been told already. Unless people had washed their hands of this case with her daughter. "She's not? . . . "

"No, she's not. You can pass down by Terrell bridge any time you like and see where she really is while she's supposed to be in choir practice." Grandma wasn't even bitter any more. Her voice just had the tiredness now. "All you young people, you're too harden. All you laughing at that boy with his nasty clothes and dirty hair, say he can't be Yankee. But he is. Watch his eyes. He no different from the madmen who passed through here in the war. Mark my word. . . . "

Which made Olga try to recall what it was like holding hands with Lou in the moonlight. Had he really been different? Had she missed something about him? If he came now to ask her to go away to Iowa, would she go? Olga searched her feelings for answers, but got nowhere. In the end she said yes to Grandma, meaning it this time. She would have a talk with Gracie. But instead, Gracie had a talk with her that day after school, saying, as though the fifteen years she had put in on the child had just dropped away, "I going to America next week."

Olga felt like she'd received a heavy blow to the stomach that knocked her breath away. But she kept herself calm and finally said, "Is so?"

"Mickey wrote to his friends and they answered they ready to accept me as one of their family and see I get to be an actress in Hollywood. All we have to do now is go to the consulate for the visa."

"Is so?"

"Mmm hmm."

"And how you know you're leaving next week? You have passage already?"

"Mickey will pay my passage. I pay him back after I start making money."

"And how about your other papers and such?"

"He's fixing all that."

"So what time next week's this grand voyage you're taking? . . . "

"Either Tuesday or Wednesday. He didn't fix that yet."

"So then, you're leaving this house? . . . "

The child won't even let her finish, but lashed out, "What you want me to do? Let myself rotten in this place? I told you to find my father, but you didn't do it. What you want me to do? . . . "

And before Olga knew what her hand was doing she had twisted Gracie's face. The child backed off with the slap still ringing in the house between them, and not another word was said until the darkness came and Gracie mumbled "I going to choir practice," and walked out the door.

The moon was getting low. It was already time for one of her men friends to be trying her door, but nobody came. At the window Olga grew tired of leaning over the sill, and stood up. Her eyes were tired from straining themselves on the road. Her whole body, in fact, felt like she had put in a long day laboring, and she stretched to ease the tiredness in her muscles. It was already late, but no matter what time the child got home Olga would be there to have that talk with her.

Gracie had never seen a real Yankee, nor heard them curse, nor heard the way they talked about poozle. Nor had she seen them wipe their feet on the mopsies of Port-of-Spain. She was too young to remember days when Yankees drove their jeeps up and down the wrong side of the road, killing whoever stood in their way, and throwing money on the bodies as though that was all a man or a woman was worth anyway. Lou, of course, was different. And if it should be that he were back in his little white town it would be nice for Gracie to go there, even if her mother couldn't, and send pictures of herself wearing sweaters with school letters printed in front and behind. They would have to go to the American consul to find out how to get in touch with Lou, and that might be a better service to the child than any advice about whoring.

Olga was a little digusted with herself for having taken so long to see, but a little relieved as well, and she went into the trunk and brought out the dresses they would wear to Port-of-Spain in the morning. She set out tea things too, so they wouldn't have to turn around too long before setting out, because they would have to catch the first bus to reach the consulate before the morning crowd. Then she returned to the doorstep and continued waiting.

The moon got low down enough to send her house shadow pointing toward the cane, still Olga sat in the doorway waiting. Once or twice it seemed laughter came back to her from across the fields, but she couldn't be sure. Everything was quiet: the night dead still.

Once she thought she saw a man and woman pass swiftly along the road, but that couldn't be, because it was too late for anybody to be heading out the lonely stretch through the fields. Besides, the man and woman she thought she saw didn't look familiar, and she didn't even hear them make footsteps against the pitch road as they glanced by. Olga closed her eyes to rest them a little while, so she would stop seeing things.

Who's Speaking Here?

Romancing America

A cadre of black American soldiers and their families were among the first people to settle villages in this part of Trinidad. They were among the first — after the maroons of Haiti and Jamaica — to establish free all-Black communities anywhere in the West Indies. These soldiers were not revolutionary fighters, though. In fact, they fought on the side of the British against the American Revolution and were rewarded with small land grants on the then fringes of the Empire for their service. For years the original settler families continued to regard themselves as 'Merikins, and asserted strong social distinctions between themselves and other Blacks who came in mainly from other West Indian islands or directly from Africa. As the villages lost their isolation, however, that xenophobic disposition went into decline. Nowadays it is hard to find, even among the old people, any who use the term "Merikin" spontaneously. But America still has a privileged place in their consciousness.

There is a romance with America. It may not be the seat of true civilization — that honor is still reserved for England — but it is a place where resourceful people can make, or re-make their lives. It is a place where one need not amount to nothing; where there is paying work, and one does not have to spend one's life waiting on the benevolence of higher-ups. America is the place where 'slave today, king tomorrow' is not an unusual experience. There is a romance with America here, carried on partly in the imagination, partly in the miming of fantasies which spin whenever the imagination is catalysed. When limers turn the talk to what they would or wouldn't do in life if only they had the chance, the geography of imagined exploits centers on "America."

In the field

Lance

Lance, who has from the first been informant and guide to me, self-appointed mentor and unrestrained critic as well, he has been to America. Although he is several years older than I am he talks and moves with a youthful energy and involvement. Men and boys usually lime in different groups. But when Lance is liming with the men, the young boys like to hang around and hear him talk. He is one of the roadside philosophers here, perhaps the dean among them. He is admired not necessarily for his elegance of language or the reliability of his thought (there are others who are individually better at these) but for his erudition in the ways of the folk, his widely angled awareness of all that's passed and is now taking place in the village, and, above all, for his having put in some years abroad in New York. He is committed to the village. He gave up America to return here, to the "lowly" life of the village gardener. In a place where so many of the young people yearn to go to New York this is strange. Why did he come back?

The young men like to gather around and get him going on his story of America. It is an occasion of sweet humour. They prompt him . . . But Lance, why yuh didn't stay in school and study like yuh family send you to do? If somebody did send me and pay for me to go to America you think? . . .

"Oh, shut your mouth!" Lance has a knack for timing. "Yuh think America is Princes Town? You think Yankees a happy go lucky people? That place is rough. That place is tough. And they don't care nothing about nobody."

The outline of his story is simple. Lance was already a young adult by the time he left for America. He had no secondary schooling, but he had a flair for learning and doing things, so the family thought they could help him — and themselves — get ahead by sending him to study engineering. One brother was a small scale contractor. With the skills Lance would bring back after completing the engineering course they could improve and expand the business. Right. First problem: Lance didn't like New York. He didn't like the brusqueness and the busy-ness of the people, and especially he didn't like the chilly weather. But he could deal with that. Next problem: he didn't like the school. The instructors dealt with him as though he were a foolish boy. None of them expected or wanted him to be intelligent. Just follow instructions. Deadlines. Assignments. Class hours. Office hours. Study this. If you need explanation of that, study the book. They wanted him to study theory, while he wanted to be doing things. He got tired of all the harrassment. He missed having friends to talk to. The school didn't have any decent trees. In fact, it didn't have any grounds for trees. No place where a man could sit down quiet in the breeze without people bumping in. Just a narrow upstairs building with dim rooms, and outside the unending noise of traffic and people up and down. Lance got tired. And after a while decided on taking a break from going to that school.

He stayed in his room and watched television. He read the books and attended classes once in a while, but in the main spent more and more time watching television. He did poorly on his engineering exams when he took them, but he was learning a lot of things with the television. As winter came on he went out less and less. He spent Christmas and New Years entirely alone in his room, and during that time came to see that getting ahead in America meant making money. So he started to think of ways in which he could do that. When the snow left and the icy winds died down he started taking long walks through the busy streets. He still didn't like all the noise and commotion, but if anything was going to happen it couldn't happen with him sitting in his room alone. He discovered the all-day cinemas and started hanging around a particular one. It was there that he met Eddie. Eddie said he was a stranger to New York too, come up lately from South Carolina, but he had relatives in the city. He also knew a way to make some quick money. ("Mafia man!" one of the young fellows who knows the story sings out . . . "Shut your mouth!" Lance straightens him.)

Lance made a number of friends hanging out with Eddie. But more importantly, he met Eddie's sister who took quite a liking to him. He made a little money too, ridiculously easy money, for just delivering messages. Until he found out that the messages he delivered were worth more money than he ever thought passed through ordinary peoples' hands. That gave him ideas how to make some true money himself. He forgot school. Engineering couldn't come near providing as much income as the little schemes he worked out. In the meantime, Eddie's sister was encouraging, so they got married. He travelled to Georgia with her to meet the rest of the family. They went by bus. It was an unforgettable ride. Through tunnels, underneath rivers, over mountaintops, across bridges that went on for miles, through countryside that went on for as far as the eye could see, they travelled for days to get to Georgia. And when he met the family, they made him feel just at home. He liked the country in Georgia, the sunny weather, some familiar trees. In many ways the people in their talk, and how they lived together there were almost like folks back in the village. But New York was where the living was, so they couldn't stay in the South.

Back in New York things went along nicely for a while, but he still never grew to like the place. His wife took good care of him and he was encouraged to apply for permanent residence. This process entailed his leaving the U.S.A. for a period. He left and came home to the village. The family was a little disappointed that he was coming home without having completed the course of study. But for him, homecoming was the sweetest thing. He felt like a fresh person. He felt like the greatest burden which he didn't even know he was carrying lifted from his shoulders. The weather was always warm; people were warmer. He could walk barefoot and garden if he wanted to. He could set his own timetable for doing whatever he wanted to do, and eat just what he wanted to eat, and besides, he was a minor hero among villagers for whom a trip to the Island's capital was a major journey. He became a real hero, to some, as his wife sent messages and money, urging him to come back to New York.

Some villagers thought she really must be a nice person, but Lance would have no part of her. Some of the older members of the family gave up on him. Some other men in the village wished they'd had his chance. But Lance was happy where he was. He refused to answer his wife's messages and made it clear he had no intentions of going back to New York. She eventually stopped writing. Now, what kind of man turns down opportunity like that? To some he was a fool. But even they saw something special in what he did and regarded him with a certain marvel.

In outline it is a simple story. But when told among the men, young and old, it is an occasion for deep drama and rollicking humour as Lance plays out the role of the fool-hero whose foolishness is much wiser than all the smart-progressive decisions others would have had him make, and say they would make for themselves. "You never been there boy," he tells them. "Wait till you have the experience. Everything that shining isn't gold." Lance could, and does quote from the Holy Bible too to justify his decision. He quotes passages about greed, and about the virtues of a simple life. He quotes from the Hindu scriptures as well. He is not Indian, but he did spend some time apprenticed to a Hindu pundit and remembers much of the Ramayana and the Mahabrata verbatim. In addition, Lance is the best gardener in the village, people agree. They get good advice from him all the time. He brings new plants and new varieties into the village from time to time, and he has been able to make things grow where it had been assumed they couldn't. So if he is a fool, he has to be a special sort of fool — one who argues with anybody that his village is a better place than any America.

The Pastor

Pastor Boysie is an elegant man. That is, while he dresses like the average village worker — except when the occasion calls for ceremonial vestment — and talks the common creole, he regards people and what they do from a measured remove which says his office is about him at all times. He does not hurry in either speech or motion, and his focus always transcends the moment. When I first met him I thought he was unmannerly.

It was during my second week in the village, and Frank recommended the pastor as a man who would have a lot of historical and cultural knowledge. His was among the original "Merikin" families, and one whose name was closely associated with the emergence and development of the local church. Unlike several others of his generation he had never lived, or worked outside of the village. From childhood he was seriously attached to the church. He had grown up in it, stayed with it through youth — the period when most young men leave to explore the outer world — and went through the graduation from member to deacon to pastor.

At our introductory meeting in the drawing room of the pastor's house Frank introduced me as an American scholar who had come to the village to do research. "What kind of research?" the pastor wanted to know, addressing his question to Frank.

I answered, "Cultural and historical research. I'm especially interested in the history of your church."

Cued by my mixed accent (I think), the pastor, still addressing the space around Frank said, "All kind of people're going about the place doing research these days." Then he turned to me, "You from America, you say?"

"This man is family to the Stewarts from Ste. Madeleine," Frank turned in. "But he living in America."

"Los Angeles," I added.

"Hmm: Oh ho. Because he don't look like no American to me." the pastor said. There was a silence. Then he asked, "How long you living in America?"

"Sixteen years."

Frank was first to stir the second silence. "The man's going to write a history about the village. That's why I brought him to you."

"I had a man come to me for some history information a while back," the pastor said. "He was a white man, and he knew what he was doing."

"Has your family always lived on this site?" I asked.

"Yes," he answered, distractedly. Then, "Americans are tall people," the pastor continued, speaking again to his fourth presence. "They have size. I remember seeing them when they come here during the war. They drive their truck right through our backfield; and when they get out they stand up tall and hale, and none of them wasn't dark like he."

I did not have a good interview on that occasion.

Randy

Randy has paid somebody through the mail a tidy sum of money to get him a job in America. It's been months since he sent off the money, but a final reply on when he would take up work in America has yet to come. Can I find out what's going on?

Clearly Randy is the victim of a scam. He had come across an advertisement in the local newspaper which said "Opportunities.

Jobs in America. Send $25 for information. Registration Guaranteed." The advertisement ended with a post office address in Baltimore.

After the first $25 they got two further payments out of Randy. Now all he had to show was an embossed receipt which said he was registered with an employment agency, and a post office box number from which no answers came to his letters of inquiry. What can I do?

I explain to him what has happened. "Why would people do something like that?" he says. Then wistfully, "I would do anything to get a job in America and make some real money."

Who's Speaking Here?

Now we will talk about old time. Olden days. Estate days.

In the Field

Mr. Landry and his family ran the sugar estate from about 1926 to 1951. Cultivation was done by hand, but there were mules for hauling the canes. Other crops were planted along with the canes — bhodi, black eye peas, in particular — which were harvested before the cane was ripe enough for harvesting itself. These food crops were sold or given to employees who merited, either by virtue of special work, or special status. The factory to this sugar estate was formerly in the nearby village of New Grant, and owned by Mr. Hawthorne, Landry's father-in-law. The New Grant factory was run by an animal tied to a shaft. Sugar was boiled in giant coppers. No chemicals added. Later pan-boiling was introduced to the factory under Landry.

Hawthorne built the Anglican church in the village.

Landry himself was a good hunter who kept well-bred dogs. He was the one who paid to have the mongoose population reduced around his estate — 10 or 12 cents a tail. When Landry's dogs hunted wild meat, the venison went to villagers who tracked or discovered the kills. Those days the estate kept animals too and butchered pork every weekend, sometimes beef. The meat was sold very cheap, or given to workers who merited, crediting those with large families.

There were other surrounding estates in cocoa and coffee, owned by The Parkers, The McCleans, the Metiziers, The Chisholms, The Rojas', and an American nicknamed "the millionaire" who's real name was Thomas. All of these estates are gone. Acquired lately by Tate & Lyle, sugar.

McLean was the first to bring a motor-car to the village, around 1917–18. A Bushe, with wooden wheels.

The roads in those days used first to be mud roads, then macadam — a mixture of metal and wood boiled together — before the authorities turned to asphalt.

All the estates kept five or six barracks each where the workers lived. The sugar estate had a hospital. There was no public cemetery: every estate had its own.

Bananas, nutmeg, tonka beans, yams — were some of the other crops also grown on cocoa estates. Rice was planted too. People mostly cooked with firewood burning in home-made fireplaces.

The average house was a wood house, with carat thatch or sometimes tin roof. More Afros than Indians lived in private houses. Indians mostly lived in the barracks. They were made of wood with tin roofs too.

Most craftsmen and tradesmen were Creoles — shoemakers, saddlers, tailors, iron-workers, carpenters, etc. But jewelling was a craft for Indian men. It was the custom then for sons to follow the trade or craft of their father. Consequently all the Ransays were blacksmiths, all the Chandlers could handle saddler work, the Jasons were woodsmen, the Robinsons, preachers, etc. Most people worked with the estates. Families also owned gardens on lands rented from the estates where they cultivated rice and vegetables.

Cloth goods were cheap — Japanese shirts sold for 60 cents. And khaki was a premium cloth. Thrifty women made skirts out of flour sacks. Bread was made at home, and in their diet Indians ate less root provision, Creoles less rice. Domesticated meat was supplemented by hunting deer, lappe, manicou, agouti, sloth, porcupine, iguana. Some estates kept chickens, geese,and turkeys too. Also pigeons/squabs.

Fresh salt-water fish was first brought to the village for sale by an Indian man who walked to Princes Town, then took the trolley to San Fernando, and bought from the fish market there. He walked back, selling all the way from two baskets tied to a pole over his shoulder, carrying his scale and his knife.

Travel above Princes Town was all by foot. From Princes Town to San Fernando there was the tramline trolley. From San Fernando to Port-of-Spain or Siparia there was the passenger train (locomotive).

There used to be a Chinese and a Portuguese shop in the village. A Catholic church nearby, two Baptist churches, and, of course the Anglican church for which the minister and his family used to live in a tree-house. Never a temple or a mosque. Indians had to go outside the village to worship, except when they held bhagwat at home. Pundits would be brought in for the ceremony. There were two Indian schools, a government school, and an Anglican school. One independent private school too.

Water for the community was kept in four ponds — two for the sugar estate, two at the McClean's estate. There used to be a lot of alligators. People used to shoot them, as they were a menace to pigs or other meat that went to the pond to drink.

A popular festival used to be hosay, the Muslim festival. Mr. Landry supported it. There never was Ramlila (Hindu) though. Carnival was also popular with the Afros.

There were no sports or recreation clubs. No dancing. No open gambling. No all-fours club. Villagers played cricket and rounders. Men and women played rounders. To gamble, men had to hide in the bush — whe whe, whappee, etc. Then they would have a bush fete, with plenty to eat and drink. The favourite drink was puncheon rum, or rum people make for themselves.

There was a friendly society.

The first movies to come to the village were in a portable tent owned by an Indian. He used to pass through doing one-night stands on a circuit from Princes Town.

A few people had bicycles in those days. A very few.

After the Rain

It was dark up the road from the rum-shop and the air was thick with flying rain. But after the bottle he had just finished at Charlie's Boodram came all the lonely way home singing old school songs and snatches of a Punjab ditty with no concern for the raindrops breaking smart against his face, no worry about the deep puddles through which he stumbled. At the head of the lane he turned down in between the barracks.

The canals on both sides gurgled with rushing water, and where pale lamplight shone above the doorways, it caught here and there the grounded shafts of the sodden carts and the rumps of animals tethered to them. From a lifetime on the estate Boodram normally knew the lane as well as he knew his hand. But with the rum sending circles around inside his head he missed his step sometimes and lost balance. It was sweet to sway in the slanted night then, right himself and say as powerfully as he could "Yoh moderass!" to everything and nothing in particular. He said it to the night, the rain, the rum he had been drinking, and yet again to none of these but a flitting sense coursing around his brain, an edge of disappointment from where he didn't know, but that threatened time after time to swamp him. "Yoh moderass!" he said defiantly, then marched on again, making deliberate angles in the lane and singing his songs in the manner of a man in good spirits.

At his gap he turned in. He wanted Rosie to be awake and made a fuss latching the door behind him, but she lay quietly on her side of the bed away from the fireplace as he took off his drenched clothes, dried himself, and stretched out beside her. He had a feeling she did not want to be touched, but he put it aside. Like sweet music the rain was drumming on the roof, the rum lust surged warm inside him, and he did not restrain himself. He pulled her clothes out of the way, and forced her legs. He held her, and although she lay a little too still, a little too loosely, he did not let go until he was satisfied and fell away to dreamless sleeping.

As he had each morning through the years, Boodram awoke with the first stroke of the bell which came faintly from across the valley on the other side of the fields. The rain still tumbled down loud and splattering on the tin roof, and the few trees around the barracks. Under the splash and rumble of the falling drops Boodram's first elation at awakening slipped away, and he lay back in bed glumly, watching Rosie getting dressed for work. She always awoke before he did, but on days when he too had to meet the overseer he would be up and dressed in a flash himself, and they would walk down to the estate yard together. But as he had for the last several mornings Boodram lay back subdued and festering. The overseer would have no use for mule-drivers today; had had no use for them a week now, and the rains still came.

Rosie gathered up the long dress and tied it at the waist. She plaited her heavy black hair and pinned it in a pad on the crown of her head. Next she wrapped the catta and fitted it on her hair then pulled the old felt hat down all around it. She wrapped the roti she would take for lunch in a clean cloth, then folded that in paper and stuffed it into the canvas sack she carried over her shoulder. She did all this without a glance his way. She did not speak. And in all her movements Boodram sensed her stiffly drawn away from him. Her eyes were somewhere between tears and anger, and beneath the general tone of weariness that subdued her face there was a sullen shade that made him recall the previous night, the way he had forced himself on her.

The rum drunk was gone now. And as Rosie wearily bent down to pull on her sabots, Boodram felt ashamed of the crude way he had handled her and had a sudden compulsion to say something kind. He called softly, "Rosie."

She did not answer. He had to call three times before she said, "What?"

"I didn't mean to wake you up last night," he said.

"What?"

"I didn't intend to wake you. I must've been drunk."

"You always drunk these days, so what?"

"Well, I didn't mean to do nothing you didn't like."

"Everytime you always say that," she replied, getting her hat. "This not the first time." Her voice said his crudeness was a habit and Boodram didn't like that.

"What the hell you expect then?" he snapped, sitting up. "And you's mi wife. So what you expect?"

"Just behave a little decent sometimes is all." Rosie kept her eyes lowered and wouldn't face him.

"Decent!" he exploded. "What decent? So I ent decent? I minding you all this time and ent never take no other woman and I ent decent? I could get woman you know. I ent bound to come home here at all, you know."

"Well get then," Rosie said, pinning her hat in place and reaching for the cutlass behind the door.

"Ah go show you," Boodram shouted, getting out of the bed. But before he could get his feet properly on the floor she was out of the door and gone.

It was still dark, and some rain blew in before the door slammed shut behind her. Boodram got back into bed. There was no sleeping anymore. He lay there and listened. The morning was filled with falling water. No birds, no jingling harness, no voices on the road outside. He had to listen hard for the grumble of the big sugar factory just little more than a mile away. Only number one was running, the second mill being idle, waiting for the canes that could not reach the yard because the heavy rain kept falling. Rosie and the other women could work clearing up the fields and making them ready for the new rattooning. They had already cut most of the last canes and carried them to large heaps along the traces where the mule carts ran. But in the rain, no mules were running. No carts were bringing canes out of the fields to the big derricks where they were weighed and loaded onto the locomotive trucks for hauling to the factory.

When the rain first began the Company did not stop the mules immediately. But after three days of steady raining the fields became thick and deep with heavy mud. The mules started falling with their loads. And when two were so badly crippled the driver had to send for the overseer with his gun, the Assistant Manager sent every driver home saying, "Don't bother coming in again until this rain is over."

Boodram lay in bed. He wondered when the rain would finish, and thought how pleasurable it would feel to be braced on the shafts of his cart again, racing load after load through the rutted traces. He loved racing against the other drivers through the long slow turn that opened into the derrick clearing. They all lashed their mules at this spot screaming Hi! Hi! Hi! to come close up in the line as possible, and get weighed, then dash off to the field again. He wondered if Carter felt the same. But rain kept everything to the cutters only. Rosie and the other women put in regular days while everybody who was cart-man could only wait for the clouds to pass away.

The rain was spoiling everything. Not a day's pay for the week, and for the first time in twelve years he was behind in the tally for the season's mule champion bonus. Just when he and his mule should have been out there pulling up on Carter, here he was lying in bed, listening to the drum and patter of falling water. And the rain made him drink too much, even though that was the only ease he had while waiting. At Charlie's, as a rule, there were always other cart-men with whom he could play draughts, tell stories, sing, and sometimes wrestle. But that was spoiling too. Longer the rain lasted, less the money they had to spend, and Charlie liked to give them talk whenever he had to trust them rum and cigarettes, cheese and biscuits, and other little things it took to help make the time pass. From time to time talk brought talk, brought hard words, and those who fought had to stay away, while others who didn't fight but were offended stayed away too, until those who came would sometimes say little to each other, just sit there mostly staring at the rain, and cursing sometimes the way he did at everything and nothing in particular. Last night he and Charlie had the shop to themselves. Boodram had tried to keep it cheerful, but the Chinaman couldn't sing, he couldn't make jokes for himself, and he took draughts far too seriously. Boodram had to spend the last two shillings in his pocket on puncheon to make the night lively, then he had come home through the rain to Rosie.

She never liked him going too much to Charlie's. "Why you go dey for to spend yuh money on rum? An' we have a child to mind?" she seemed constantly to remind him. Soogrim was no child. And Boodram never had thoughts not to mind him. But when you're

twenty-one, twenty-two years old already, you're no more somebody's child. When Boodram was twenty-one Soogrim was already
two years old and only God one prevent them from having more
children. Soogrim was his pride, though. The boy had brains. And
Boodram knew he would never stop doing what he could to keep him
comfortable in his studies over in Canada. But at times a man had
to do for himself too. Everything in its own time. And Soogrim
wasn't doing bad in Canada.

He didn't look bad at all in the last photograph which came
from Toronto. In fact, standing in front of the tall university
buildings with books under his arm Soogrim looked like somebody
eating well, dressing well, and having something left to make the
spirit well too. So what Rosie had to tell him about going to Charlie's
for, and about minding Soogrim? In fact, she wasn't looking so good
lately. With time to study her these mornings as she dressed and
went out leaving him behind, Boodram discovered new lines around
her mouth, and a stoop in her shoulders. As though she was carrying
a load even when she wasn't in the field. The thought of her growing
old made a little sadness for him. She seldom looked him in the face
anymore, and her style gave Boodram feelings she was going through
a grief in life that maybe she would never tell him and yet want him
to understand and know. She was a good woman though. She could
read, she never shunned work no matter how she felt, and even
though she quarrelled sometimes she never went so far as to make
his days unbearable. Why did he have to tell her about finding
another woman? He never had and knew he never would, as long as
Rosie stayed in the house beside him, and she knew it too.

Boodram's feelings rose and fell with the rain, when sometimes
it went down to a low murmur then came rumbling back again
against the barrack paling. Two drips which came in where the roof
leaked were steady. Boodram got up and emptied the pan which
caught that water. Then he was drawn to the table drawer where he
got out the photograph that was taken when he won the last mule-
driver's championship. He looked good in the picture: not skinny,
not beefy as the overseer who was handing him the bonus money, in
good health and spirits like a champion driver ought to be. He liked
the way some hair fell over his forehead, the way his thick eyebrows
and big moustache made him look a little fierce. The overseer had
no hair on his face, and beside Boodram's dark complexion his pale

skin made him look weak and underhanded. Boodram wished that
he had a picture for all the other championships he had won over the
years, but the Company had photo-taking only for the first time last
year. Before that, it was just the bonus money and rights to choosing
the first mule when crop season came in January.

Boodram went back to bed. He thought about some of the
drivers who had challenged him in past years. A few had come close
to winning, but none had ever challenged so hard as Carter. Like
Boodram, the fellow seemed to be somewhere around forty, but he
drove as though he was in charge of a mule for the first time in his
life. He had come especially to take the championship, some people
said, for as soon as crop season began and the mules were in their
traces, he had broken away more reckless than Boodram had ever
been, more brutal with his animal and loaders than anyone else in
the fields. Nobody knew where Carter came from. Some rumoured
that he was a Moruga man, others that he came from Tobago. He
had an end room in the barracks, but he had neither wife nor child,
and he made no friends. His black face was a constant frown as
though he was caught in a battle with some serious unfinished
business all the time. His gruffness even with the time of day said
he had one purpose on his mind. The other drivers left him alone.
But everyone was watching because cropover was less than a month
and a half away, and he was still ahead of Boodram in the tally.

It was near ten o'clock when Boodram finally put thoughts
about the championship aside and started a fire. He hung his limp
khaki pants and shirt above the fireplace to dry, and made himself
some tea. Then getting out the playing cards he sat at the table to
play a game of solitary. Soon tired of that, he left the table, pulled
on the stiff warm khaki clothes, and throwing an old oil-skin around
his shoulders went out to see his mule. He changed the tether, gave
the animal some feed, molasses and water, then came back in and
stood for a while over the half-door studying the sky. It was grey and
heavy, just as it was the day before. No sign of blue, no birds, and
broad rain-flecked puddles filled the road between the barrack
buildings.

A few hungry chickens pecked the road, and somewhere from
behind the second barrack somebody had a tassa going and singing.
But even as the voices came through the rain they sounded hollow
and Boodram said to them and no one in particular "Why all yuh

ent stop that blasted singing?" He was restless. He should close the window, remain in his house and wait. But instead, he went to the box beneath the bed and got out the jar in which they saved their money. Several fives, twos, and one dollar notes folded tight were right on top of the silver, but he put them aside to take out two shillings. When he replaced the jar he smoothed back Rosie's skirt and ohrni on top of it to make them appear undisturbed, then after emptying the leak pans once more he set out for Charlie's.

It was pay Friday at the estate, and a few people who had provisions and fruit to sell were under the eaves of the shop with their trays and baskets. Inside, Charlie had many glasses washed and turned down behind the counter, and the Indian boy who usually helped on paydays was there, but otherwise the shop was empty. Boodram called for a nip of puncheon, and while he waited for the rum, sat on a stool to gaze out at the rain. Through the shop's door he could see down the road between the schoolhouse and the church, across to the pond that served as a reservoir for the factory. The water was the same color as the sky. On the other side of the pond was the factory, angular and grimy, coughing small billows of steam and a stream of great black smoke into the air. Beyond the factory the grey-brown fields rolled on one after the other, out to where the women moved like slow ghosts in the misty light. They had things all to themselves out there in the rain.

"How the mule doin, Mr. Boodram?" It was the Indian boy.

"Good, good, . . . " Boodram answered.

"That's the best mule the Company ever brought here in a long time," the boy said. "I bet he's just waiting for the rain to stop."

Boodram smiled, and he offered the boy a drink from his nip.

"Not when I'm working," the boy said.

"Go on, take one," Boodram pushed the bottle toward him. "Tell Charlie I say you're taking a drink with me."

The boy took a little of the rum in a glass and said, "You know, Mr. Boodram, everybody saying how this Carter beating you this season. But I don't believe so, you know. I watch you a lot of times racing across the fields, 'Hieeh! Hieeh!'" the boy bent over imitating a cart-man with the reins in his hands. "I don't believe nobody beating you. When I get mi own cart miself I'll know a lot of things to do just from watching you."

"That's good, . . . " Boodram said.

"I watch Carter too," the boy went on, "and I bet if the Company let drivers work in the rain you'd show him who is the best man . . . "

The boy's confidence in him made Boodram feel good, and he smiled again. Then Charlie called, and the boy had to go.

Boodram waited for an hour, but none of the other cart-men came. One or two of the shift-workers came in, but he didn't have much to say to them. When he got tired of sitting alone he bought another nip for his pocket, and walked back through the rain.

In the barrack room Boodram hung the oil-skin on its nail and put the shilling he had not spent back in the jar. He got out the cards, and again played solitary. He measured the rum by drops into his glass before he sipped. He talked to himself for cheating, then answered back as though he were two people.

He played against himself this way until the rum ran out, then bored and ever so slightly drunk Boodram folded his arms on the table and waited.

It was after four o'clock when Rosie came back home. An early dark had already begun gathering in the corners, and Boodram said "They keep you late today, eh?"

"We waiting all this time for pay," she said with weariness and irritation in her voice. "Since one o'clock we waiting and what that paymaster doing? He and the time-keeper there they counting, counting, and still when people get to the window for what they put in your hand they still making mistake left and right."

"All yuh ent cuss they tail?"

"How yuh gon cuss? Is the white man paying, and one o' we keeping time."

"Them does get pay in office though. Them don't have to stand up in the rain."

"Well I done fuss miself up enough already," she said, setting down her things.

"They should have a office for we too, then nobody having to stand up in no rain."

"Won't make no difference. We in the rain whole day anyhow."

"And they should get a new paymaster," Boodram let his voice rise with defiance. "That jackass they have always making mistake and saying is the time-keeper fault."

Rosie wiped the cutlass and put it away. She took off the old felt hat, then she went to the fireplace and started a fire.

"I hear somebody saying today the field so muddy you sinking in up to your knee," Boodram said.

Rosie didn't turn around to look at him, she made no answer. When the fire got going well she straightened up, and taking two envelopes from her bosom threw them onto the table. She poured some water in the basin and took off her clothes.

"I don't know why they keep the cutters working," Boodram said. "It's no good for the canes."

Rosie answered nothing to this either. She hung her wet clothes on a line above the fire, then started to wash the mud from her arms and legs. Boodram's eyes followed everything she did, but not once did she turn around to meet his gaze. He looked at the envelopes — one was her pay, he knew from the size and brown color, and the other must be a letter from Soogrim.

When she was drying off herself he asked, "We get letter from the boy?"

"He write," she said.

"When you reading it?"

"I have to cook first. You eat today?"

Boodram picked up the letter and toyed with it. "Soogrim a good boy," he said. "Whoever thought I could have a son to go through schooling and studying for lawyer?"

Rosie was busy drying, and she said nothing. She was younger than Boodram, but already her breasts were long and slack. Her back was shaped into a solid curve from years of cane loads balanced on her head, and where once her cheeks used to dimple with shine when she smiled the hollows were lined pockets of permanent shadow. She was very pretty when they were first married, Boodram remembered. Her back was straight and firm, her shoulders soft. There used to be lights in her eyes when they sat in the dim evenings, and her laughter then was enough to make him go on inventing tales of the kind men tell only to women who take pleasure in everything that they say. But over the years of marriage they had found less and less to say to each other, and as Boodram watched Rosie cleaning herself he felt a deep wish to wipe away that silence, bring a real laugh back to her face again and have her look at him with wanting.

"I wish I could read," he said, fingering Soogrim's letter again. "When the boy come home he's going to be a big lawyer, eh? . . . When he coming home, Rosie?"

"Two more years," she said.

"He's a good boy. When he come home we'll give a fete for the whole village, eh? . . . Dhalpurie, goat and rum for everybody. . . . "

"That all you thinking 'bout?" she turned on him. "We don't even have a decent house for when he come, why you don't study that? All you want is rum and fete. . . . "

Boodram didn't want to argue, but he said, "How we building house and pay his studying too? Is money we making to do all that? And ent nothing wrong with thinking 'bout a little fete when the boy come. Everybody in the village like him. And don't forget, we're not the only ones helping pay his education."

"If you didn't have so much rum fete yourself maybe we could do more than build house." Boodram said nothing to that, and Rosie added, "If you stay out the Chinese rum-shop you know how much shilling we save?"

"You shouldn't say a thing like that Rosie. I don't spend money every time I go by Charlie."

"Well, you're there every night, and you're always treating somebody. As for this week, you're going day and night, through all the rain. But when you get ready to march off tonight, don't forget you didn't get no pay this week, eh."

"You don't have to be so hasty," Boodram said. "How 'bout all the other paydays? And the bonus? For the last ten years every June 1 bringing home bonus. What happen to that? You not the only one in this house working."

"Well, don't forget you didn't work this week."

"I'm not the only one, none the cart-men work. Rawan couldn't get a mule through that mud in the fields. It's not my fault the rain wouldn't stop."

"The rain, the rain," she said mockingly. "You didn't work this week, and if you don't watch out you won't win no bonus this year either. I hear this Carter well in front of you."

"Who say I don't win this year?"

"Just remember that — you not working, you not winning the bonus, and we have a son in Canada to give everything we can send him."

"Who say I don't win the bonus? You think anybody could beat me on this estate? For ten years I cart more cane than any other driver, and I gon do it again this year."

"Everybody know that Carter far out in front of you. That man got will. You don't see him hanging 'round the Chinese shop. One look at him you could see he got will. That's why he in front of you already."

"We'll see what happen. If all this blasted rain didn't falling I would've done pass his ass already."

"Curse the rain," she said. "Curse it. Everything's the rain, but if it wasn't for me, we wouldn't a have no money to send Soogrim studying in the first place."

"What wrong with you? The boy win money for heself. He have brains."

"He have brains, but is who buy his shoes and clothes? Who pay San Fernando taxi all the years, then money for books? . . . "

That wasn't fair. Boodram had done his share, and the estate council too. The council it was who paid for the boy's high school in the first place. "You talk crazy if you like," he said, "but everybody having a fete when the boy come back home."

"Just remember when you talk about fete that you ent working."

"Well everybody see the raining. And if the boss say no work, no work. But I'm still champion driver, and when this rain dry off, I showing you, that Carter, and everybody, what champion is."

"Just remember when you get ready to go spending money on rum you're not working, you're not winning no bonus, and we have a son in Canada to send for. That's all I'm saying."

The rain still played drumming noises on the roof, and all the while they talked Rosie had been attending to her pots. Burnt pepper and bigan choka gave a good smell to the room, and Boodram forced back the anger swelling in his chest. Her cooking pleased him. It would be nice to say something so. But from the way her face was set, from the way she kept her eyes down on what she was doing, he thought it better to say nothing. Eventually she put food on the table, and when they were finished eating Rosie got up to take his dish away.

"You not going to read the letter?" Boodram asked. "I want to hear what the boy saying."

Rosie didn't answer. She finished taking away the dishes and wiped off the table before she sat down and opened the letter. It was a full page long. It said that Soogrim was well and hoped that they were well; that the weather in Toronto was cold, and that the boy was getting along well in his studies; that he missed them very much, and finally, that he needed five hundred dollars to pay on a motor-car because he was taking a little work to make some money driving, and he had to get around and keep up with all he had to do in town and his studying. Boodram was at first pleased, especially with all the big words the boy had used in the letter, then shocked. "A motor-car! What he want motor-car for, he think he is big shot?"

"You hear what the boy say? . . . He want a car so he could do a little work. And Canada a big place, you know."

"So how he getting 'round all this time? Look at me! I don't even have a cart of mi own. That mule and cart out there belong to the estate, you know. We send him to get education, not for no work and getting around." But as soon as he said that Boodram's irritation again gave way, and he felt a little ashamed. Rosie was looking at him, and it was she who had really encouraged the boy with his studies, she who had from the time he was a child started saving money so Soogrim could go away to the university. It was she who made him carry the boy's name to the council and show them how he would do good. "And beside, what happen to any motor-car when he come home now?"

"I don't know," she said. "Sell it, bring it home — I don't know. The boy want a car, he must have good reason. Is the thought of not having money to spend on rum that's hurting you. You're always boasting in the shop about your child, but when time to do something for him, you quick to turn your back."

Boodram argued half-heartedly, then finally gave in.

"You have to win that bonus now," Rosie said, and Boodram agreed. He didn't really think the boy should buy any motor-car for so much money, but Rosie had a sweet serious look on her face, like when she was saying prayers, and he didn't want to go on arguing with her. He knew she would work hard. She was re-reading Soogrim's letter, saying the words to herself, and the pride she felt showed all over her face. Boodram felt pride in his son, too, yet watching Rosie's lips mutter the boy's words to herself he felt like shouting 'But he can't drive no mule though! I is the best mule-driver in this whole estate! This whole country!' But he didn't. What did mule-driving and being lawyer have to do with one another?

Boodram left the table and went outside to check the mule. He tested the rope around the animal's neck. He drove the stake to which it was hitched deeper in the ground. Then he went to see the cart. It was just as he had left it earlier, the thick rubber wheels blocked by two large stones, the shafts sunk lightly into the mud with the tail pointing up to the sky. He fussed over the stones for a while, then went back to see the mule. The animal stood with its tail to the light wind, silent, unmoving, and as Boodram stood patting its unresponsive rump he could not stop the rush of nasty thoughts about the rain coming down, forcing another wet tomorrow. Rosie was inside reading her letter. For him, another night, and the days of waiting. The only place with life was the rum-shop, but at the thought of another night alone with Charlie he mastered himself, and went back inside.

Rosie spent more than an hour with the letter while Boodram's restlessnes grew. He played with the cards for a little but soon got tired of that. He couldn't talk with Rosie while she was reading, and finally he just sat and listened to the rain. When he could no longer sit still Boodram said, "Think I'll walk down by the shop and see who's there. Rosie, you got a shilling?"

"Where your money?" she said.

"You know I don't have."

"You want to buy puncheon, find yuh own money," she said without looking up from the letter.

"But look," he pleaded, "I'll bring you a little something too. You know puncheon's good for the cold weather."

"What cold weather? If you want to talk about cold weather you should be up in Canada. That is cold. You hear what Soogrim say. . . . Every morning the place is full of snow, and I have to walk up to my knees in snow to get to class. . . . That is cold. Snow up to your knees."

"Well, I don't mind if it ent so cold, but a little puncheon's good for the wet. Beside, I don't like going to the shop without no money in mi pocket. How would it look for a man who is champion not to have a shilling if somebody ask for a drink?"

"Boodram, sometimes you talk like a child. How would you like it if Soogrim come back home and find you a drunkard? Would you like that? People saying . . . the boy is a gentleman, but look at the father, he a damned drunkard. . . . "

"I no drunkard. All I want is to go down to the shop and pass the time. . . . "

" . . . Have a drink and talk nonsense with your drunken friends. What good that do for you? Stay home and rest yuh body nuh. Make plans, so when the rain over you could break out the mule and win the bonus." There was something in her reasoning, Boodram admitted to himself. All the same, when the rain stopped then would be time enough to make up a mind for winning the bonus. Without saying any more he gathered the oil-skin over his shoulders. Rosie, back to her letter, did not look up as he closed the door behind him.

Invisible rain-drops pattered steadily on his head and shoulders but Boodram did not hurry. He walked as though it were a dry night with stars out, and neighbors loitering about the road after their evening meal. But his feelings were far from merry. At the shop the vendors had all gone home. The yellow light from the open door limped a short way into the dark, and when Boodram entered, Carter was the only customer sitting at the counter. Charlie was nowhere in sight. Boodram had never seen his challenger in the shop before, and as there was no friendship between them he did not speak. He leaned against the counter and waited.

The shop was as cheerless as the dreary night — no laughter, no singing, just a feeble hiss from the Coleman lamp and the patter of rain. Except for a few moths fluttering around the light there was no stirring, and Boodram did not like this. He wanted laughter and jokes, the living voices of men around him. The emptiness made him very conscious of being there penniless, with Carter at the other end of the counter drinking.

"If you want Charlie you better knock," the black man's voice came. "He gone in the back to eat." Boodram turned around, glanced at Carter, banged his fist on the counter and continued waiting. Carter had no right to speak to him, no matter how lonely he was, for he felt bound to speak in return and there was nothing he wished to say to Carter.

Charlie did not come right away, and for the long while Boodram waited, the flat hiss of the lamp, the pattering rain filled the distance between himself and his challenger. By the time Charlie did shuffle in from the kitchen, the silence between the two drivers was so charged, Boodram was wishing he had been more open and said something to Carter.

When Charlie asked Boodram what did he want, Boodram furtively signalled him to come close, and in a voice that he hoped Carter could not hear told Charlie he wanted a puncheon that had to go in the book. Charlie fetched the rum and Boodram downed the drink in a hurry to feel the warm glow it spread inside him.

"You want another one?" Charlie asked. "One drink, two drink, all the same. You good customer. You pay me payday."

Boodram hesitated, glancing up to see if Carter was listening, and his challenger said, "What's the matter Boodram, you don't have money? Came take a drink out of my nip."

Boodram frowned, first at Charlie, then at Carter. The Chinaman stood passively, scratching his ribs through the sleeveless merino, his squinted eyes blinking quickly. "I don't want your rum," Boodram said. "What you think I is, a drunkard?"

Carter laughed. "Boodram you's a funny man. I ask you to take a drink out of mi bottle, and you say I calling you a drunkard. You a funny man." Carter laughed again, and picking up his bottle and glass moved closer. "You got worries Boodram, or else you wouldn't be so sour. Take a drink man," he offered the bottle. "Take a drink and relax. Look how dark and wet it is outside, you want to stand there unfriendly in all this rain?"

Boodram hesitated. He had expected Carter to curse back at him, and did not quite know how to take this offer of friendship. He stood hulking with one palm on the counter, and Charlie who had waited quietly the meanwhile started to laugh. "Look at him, look at him," he said, pointing at Boodram. "He want the drink, yes?" Charlie laughed like a little boy.

Confused and uneasy Boodram thought of Rosie sitting at home with her letter. He couldn't go back right away. He wished there were more people in the shop — men he had known for years, men who knew and respected him as the best mule-driver, a better man than themselves. "What you want with me?" he said to Carter.

"I don't want nothing with you," Carter sounded sincere in his voice. "Listen to the rain, man. You come through the wet and dark because you want something with somebody?"

"I left mi house to come here and be with my friends. I come to pass the time with friends. . . . "

"Is the same thing I trying to tell you. So you don't want me for a friend? . . . "

"I don't know you Carter. You come from wherever you come

from and I don't know you. I left mi wife and come through the rain because I want to be with people I know. Friendly people."

"So how you going to find out if I'm friendly when you keep to yourself and I keep to myself?"

Charlie withdrew to his high stool behind the counter, and Boodram thought about what Rosie would say if she saw him drinking from the same bottle as Carter . . . 'Man don't have no mind,' she always say that. 'They just like dogs . . . vomit up something one minute, then turn around and lap it up the next. . . . ' But she didn't understand that sometimes a man had to do things he didn't quite like, especially when the hours passed slowly and there was so little chance to feel the rub, join with the voices of other men. No man Boodram knew would have been satisfied to sit alone at night with a letter, regardless where it came from. And while Boodram was thinking, Carter poured a long shot into the champion's glass then one for himself. He raised his drink waiting, and Boodram, setting his thoughts of Rosie's criticisms aside took the rum.

Carter refilled the glasses and they drank again. "You a lucky man Boodram," he said. "You have a hard working wife, and a son in Canada studying. I don't have no wife, and I always hear fellows who married never hard up. How come your wife let you leave the house without even a shilling to buy grog?"

Boodram's pride went up. "If I want a shilling to buy grog I don't have to ask mi wife. What kind of man you think I is?"

"I don't know. If I had a hard working wife like you I don't think I'd leave home tonight . . . a night like this."

"Man want to be with other men too sometimes," Boodram said. "And with all the rain I'm tired staying in the house."

"Me too. I wish the damn thing would come down heavy and stop once and for all. Then we could get back in the fields. There's nothing I like more than having that mule in mi hands . . . feel him jump up and get when I tell him, make him stop where I want him to. . . . "

"That a good mule you have. He old, but he know the fields backwards. He know every gully, every jump, and when I used to drive him sometimes I could close mi eyes and just let him take the road."

They had another drink. Boodram was thoroughly warm inside now, and the shop became less of a dreary place. He owed Charlie twelve cents, but that wasn't much. Even Rosie wouldn't mind that.

The evening passed while they talked about the breeding, training, and handling of mules. Carter turned out to know a good deal more about mules than Boodram had expected, and it was not long before he felt a mild admiration for his challenger. The bottle jumped lower and lower, and when Carter wanted to change the conversation and talk about women Boodram wouldn't let him. "Think you goin' to win the bonus this year?" he asked.

"I don't give a damn 'bout no bonus," Carter replied. "I love to drive, and one of these days I'm getting mi own horse. And when I get through training him, I want to see who stand up next to me. . . . " Carter went on to talk about his future animal, with his eyes seemingly fixed on some time to come when he and his animal would rule, unchallengeable champions of the fields.

Eight o'clock came and Charlie half-closed his doors, but Carter talked on, the faraway gleam growing stronger in his eyes. He wanted a black mule next time if he had to drive a mule. He would bathe and brush it at night, and when they took to the fields in the day he and his mule would flash over the ground like swift shadows, swift and unbeatable. It was only when Boodram said he thought it was time to let Charlie close up that Carter put a halt to his vision saying, "I shouldn't be talking like that to you, you're a mule man yourself. Maybe you've already had the kind of thing I'm looking for. . . . "

"Never owned a mule in mi life," Boodram said. "I drive them, don't care 'bout having none mi own."

"Why not?" asked Carter.

"Why should I? The estate bring fresh animals every year and I can always get a new one when I want."

"No," Carter said, shaking his head, "no man. There's nothing like having your own mule. If you're going to be champion you ought to have your own mule."

"I don't want one," Boodram repeated. He was a little tired, and felt he had to say something final to Carter. "I buying motor-car," he said.

"A motor-car!" Carter whistled, then grinned. "So that's why you don't have money to buy grog, eh? . . . A son in Canada, and you're getting a motor-car! That good! Boodram, I always thought you were a smart-man." Carter poured the last from the bottle and continued. "If I didn't want to be champion I'd let you win the bonus yourself this season. I could just see you now, Saturday mornings driving about making people jealous. . . . " They both laughed.

"I'll give ride to everybody," Boodram said. "Children, everybody. I won't be like them people who put their nose up in the air and pass straight. I won't be like that at all."

Carter slapped him on the back. "If you want to make some quick money for your car, I know just how you could do it. You ever bet the races?"

"No."

"Well, I have a godfather have two horses running tomorrow, and they sure to win. They always win. You could never go wrong putting your money on them. All you have to do is bet one, you make all the money you want."

He had never been a betting man, but the idea of some quick and easy money appealed to Boodram. In a flash he saw all the things he could do if he won a few hundred dollars, but he hesitated, uncertain if he should trust Carter's word.

"When you go home tonight, tell your wife," Carter urged. "All you have to do is bet, and you get plenty money for your car."

Boodram thought about that. It would be nice to make five hundred dollars or so, then he could go to Rosie and say, 'Here . . . take this and send it to the boy . . . two hundred.' No, he wouldn't say it like that. He would wait, and when she started wailing if he didn't win the bonus he would take the money from its hiding place and hand it to her without a word.

"If you want, I'll lend you money to bet," Carter was saying. "You're a good man, Boodram. Under all the bragging you do, you're a good man."

"What time is the races?"

"We have to leave here ten o'clock to make the first one. You going to go?"

"Well, if you say it easy to make some money . . . "

"Yes, man. I telling you. You could bet my money if you want. You think you will go?"

"Well, why not? No work for we on the estate nohow." They both laughed.

"And I'll have plenty of money," Boodram said.

They parted in the rain, Carter setting off to his barrack room, and Boodram to his. When Boodram got home the fire was out, the lamp turned low, and Rosie was curled up on the narrow bed asleep. He hung up his wet oilskin, then turned up the wick and picked up Soogrim's letter which was lying beneath the lamp. He stared at the blue-ink words which he could not read and felt proud that his wife knew what every one meant. Then suddenly the thought crossed his mind — suppose after all, Rosie was reading what she liked, and not telling him what really was in Soogrim's writing?

He held the letter closer, and stared hard at the writing, but that didn't make him understand. He looked at Rosie, but even in her sleep she seemed so haggard he could find room for nothing false about her. Boodram felt ashamed for having thought she would trick him, then he thought about how happy she would be if he just put five hundred dollars in her hand all at once. She would be surprised, and her face would light up, maybe, the way it used to before Soogrim went away. One bet on the horses could bring all this money — money for Soogrim, and happiness for Rosie. Boodram put the letter aside, and stealthily tiptoeing to the trunk got out the money jar. He was not quiet enough, however, and Rosie awoke. "Boodram, what you doing?"

"Nothing," he answered, trying not to let her see the jar in his hand.

"Put it back," she said, her eyes fixed on him. "That we child money."

"I just want to count it," he said, emptying the money onto the table. She watched him from the bed like a silent cat while Boodram spread out all the dollar notes, pretending he was counting them, and when it seemed her eyes weren't so strong on him he quickly crumpled one of the tens in his palm.

Rosie jumped out of bed in a flash. "Put it back," she cried. Boodram stood up. "Put it back," she kept saying, trying to get at his hand. He pushed her away, and she fell sitting to the floor. Suddenly, as if a great weariness came down on her at once, Rosie folded over and began to cry.

Boodram began to feel foolish, and all he could say was, "Stop your crying. . . ."

That only made her wail a little louder. "Oh God," she moaned, "mi son goin' starve in that cold country. Twenty years I work hard, hard, hard, and now this man taking the money to drink rum . . ."

"Who going to drink rum?" Boodram said. His foolish feeling fell away and he roared, "So I didn't work too?" He couldn't help himself. He wanted to drown her out. "Didn't I work too? What nonsense you talking? Get off the floor. . . . "

But Rosie had both hands clasped around her knees, rocking back and forth as though a death had taken place. In this state she would hear nothing he said, and it really was useless talking. He sat down in the chair. "Stop that damn nonsense," he said, trying to make his voice stern and kind at the same time.

She didn't hear him. "Oh God, he going to kill me and mi one child. . . . "

"He's my child too," but she didn't hear a word. Boodram cursed, more in frustration than in anger now, but his stream never penetrated Rosie's keening. He cursed her liberally for taking him to be a jackass without sense or father feelings. Then he added a few moderasses for the neighbors whom he knew were listening. At last, with a curve of his arm he swept the money into one heap again. Then stuffed it back into the jar. All except the ten dollar bill that was in his pocket. He replaced the jar in the trunk. Rosie, her head bent to the floor just kept on with her crying, and there was nothing else for Boodram to do but slump back into the chair.

The bed remained cold for a good part of the night. Rosie fell asleep on the floor, and Boodram sat fingering the money in his pocket, thinking, until he too fell asleep at the table. Near daybreak when he awoke, Rosie still lay snoring on the floor. The lamp had burnt out, and in the dark Boodram hid the ten dollar bill carefully in the roll of his pant leg. Then he went to the bed and stretched out. Not until he was fully relaxed and about to fall asleep again did he realize that it had stopped raining.

When Boodram came awake again Rosie was already gone to the fields. First he checked to see if the ten dollar bill was still in his pants, and it was. Then he opened the window and looked out. It was about nine o'clock, and although the sky was still cloudy a weak sun had come up. That was good, but Boodram felt a little uneasy about his misunderstanding with Rosie. For a moment he was tempted to put the money back into the jar, but then what was there really to worry about?

It was Saturday, and the cutters would work half a day. But by the time Rosie got back home he would be at the racetrack. Then

later on in the evening when she was wondering if he was still drinking rum he would show up and hand her enough money to send to
Soogrim. He might even be able to do more than that. Remembering how he had talked about getting his own car with Carter the
night before, Boodram thought he might even be able to surprise
Rosie with that too. He had never dreamed of owning a car before,
but after talking about it with Carter the possibility seemed very
near, and it was easy to imagine himself sitting behind a steering
wheel with Rosie at his side very happy and proud of him.

Then he had a bright idea. Instead of betting only ten dollars
on the horses he would bet forty or fifty, and make real big money.
Carter seemed sure that his godfather's horses would win. Boodram
went to the trunk and searched for the jar, but it was gone. He felt
a little angry, and a little disapppointed too. He started looking in
places where he thought Rosie might have hidden the money, but
gave up when he discovered the jar, empty, upside down among
the dishes.

Boodram dressed then. He rubbed oil through his hair and
over his feet, he tried a few steps in his leather shoes but they hurt
too much and he took them off. He rolled his pants cuff carefully,
and after making another half-hearted search for the money he left
the house.

The children were out in the road, and some of them hailed,
"Boodram, man. . . . " He greeted them with the usual "Righto . . . "
but his mind was far away. Today he was not Boodram the champion
mule-driver, he had his eyes on other things. Today he was going to
make a lot of money, enough for his son's car, and maybe his own,
but in any case enough to make his wife proud of him. Let Carter
keep the mules, it was much better for a man to have a car. It would
be a good surprise for Rosie. And on Saturday mornings he could
drive around with children running behind the bumper and hanging
to the running-board. Even Carter would have to say, 'Yes . . .
Boodram, you's one helluva fella.'

Boodram reached the shop. Carter was there, and so were
several of the other cart-men in clean khakis and some wearing
shoes. He didn't spend much time talking with them. He shouldered
through until he was beside Carter who sat at the counter. The black
man was sullen again, and he took his time saying 'Hello' to
Boodram. They had two drinks in silence, but Boodram didn't mind

the other's attitude. He was busy with his own vision this morning
— a shiny black car, a surprised and happy face for Rosie. Even if
he didn't have a lot of money to start, he'd heard of people making
fortunes starting with less than he. And today was his day. He could
feel it. When Carter was ready they started the three to four mile
walk to the racetrack near Gasparillo. The sun was still not very
strong, but most of the clouds were gone and a dry breeze gusted
from across the fields.

"You have money?" Carter asked.

"Ten dollars," Boodram replied, pulling the money from his
pocket.

"That's all you got? You can't win nothing if you don't take a
chance, you know."

"How much do you think one bet would win?" Boodoo asked.

"Can't tell. Maybe a hundred dollars, maybe more than that,
according to how much people bet. But don't worry, mih godfather
horse bound to win. They win all the time."

"Well listen, if I bet one horse and he win, then I could put more
money on the next horse when he's running, right?"

"Yes, sure. If you want to do that."

"Well you have to tell me. I never bet no racehorse before. You
sure your godfather two horse going to win?"

"Surety. They win all the time."

The business of betting was not too clear to Boodram, but he
had a good feeling as they struck the main road from the estate, then
followed a back trace through Tarouba to the Gasparillo junction.

"I too glad this rain done," Carter said as they walked between
two fields of uncut cane. "By Monday it dry enough to work the
fields again."

Boodram was glad that the rain had stopped, but he wasn't
thinking about the fields anymore. "If you could make so much
money betting horse race, how come you want to work so bad in the
fields?"

"Every man have his weakness," Carter said with a serious face.

"Then what happen to all the money you making betting?
You're not a fete-man."

"Going to buy mi own mule, I tell you. And when I make some
more after that, I buying a racehorse too."

Boodram wasn't sure that Carter was smart for wanting to do

this. If he had money to buy racehorse he wouldn't want a mule. But that was Carter's business. He was going to buy a motor-car.

By the time they got to the track the sun was bright enough to cast strong shadows on the ground. There was a good crowd packed into the stands and all around the rails, people from several villages and many from as far away as Port-of-Spain and Arima too. A race was on. The excited voices rising from the crowd caught Boodram. Suddenly he was afraid that they had delayed too long in getting there and had missed the race. He started wildly for the crowded rails, with no regard for the muddy water that splashed up on his pants, no ear for Carter's insistent "Slow down man, slow down. That ain't we race. . . . " Mud splashed up onto his shirt and face, but Boodram did not stop until he was squeezed in tight against the rail.

They were in time to see the finish of the first race, and when the loudspeaker announced the winner Boodram asked, "Your god-father horse in this race?"

"No man," Carter answered. "I telling you all the time not this race. We betting number five and seven."

Then Carter led him to the betting booths. It was all very complicated for Boodram. He didn't understand about the numbers too well, and with people pushing and shouting, he felt a little at sea in the confusion. When Carter tried telling him the name of the horse on which they were betting, Boodram couldn't get it right in the noise. He therefore handed his money over to Carter to bet for him. There was nothing of the sullenness about Carter as he took the money. He grinned and disappeared in the crowd. Boodram struggled to remain where he was, content that Carter would return and everything would be alright. But it was difficult to hold the same spot in the steady drifting and pushing crowd, and Boodram found himself inched further and further away from near the betting window. He kept watching, but Carter was a long time coming back where he could see him, and gradually Boodram's original distrust of the man returned.

The roar of cheering voices went up loudly once again as the second race ended, and Boodram felt that he may have been a fool for not handling his money himself. The loudspeaker announced which horses had won, placed, and showed, how much money each paid, and Boodram was a little surprised that the announcer called some amounts in small numbers. He thought a little about that but wasn't quite sure what to make of it. After the third race was announced and Carter still had not returned from the ticket window Boodram started to let himself feel exactly what he did not want to believe — that Carter had run off with his money. He started stumbling through the crowd not quite sure which way to turn, getting angrier at all the people and faces he didn't know pressing around him.

As the crowd surged to the rails for the close of the third race he allowed himself to be carried along. Boodram ended up almost where he had stood during the first race, and just as completely as he had disappeared Carter erupted beside him. Boodram's relief overwhelmed his suspicion and rage as Carter shouted, "You had mi looking all over the place man. Why you didn't stop where I left you?"

"I was looking for you," Boodram shouted back.

"I circled all about then thought maybe you come back here. Come, come, let we see how they finish."

Working in tandem they shouldered their way to a position where they could see the horses coming around. The noise grew louder. The horses came around then rushed past in a clatter of mud and color, and little men bouncing high up on the out-stretched animals. Boodram had never seen anything like it. There was a sweep and power, an intensity beyond any he had ever dreamed racing his mule across the canefields, yet it was familiar to him. He knew it deeply enough to join pace with them, shouting, screaming for the gallop, straining them on to the last moment, then it was over.

"You see that! You see that!" Carter shouted. "That jockey sweet too bad."

"Who he?" Boodram asked.

"That the man they call Holder. You see him?"

"He riding in we race?"

"Bound to. What you think make it so sure we winning?"

"He does ride your godfather horse?"

"Every time."

"And you make the bets already," Boodram asked.

"Long time." Carter winked, and then he smiled.

For the moment Boodram stood enchanted. The excitement of the race brought a taste to his mouth and if he had money he would have bought a drink. He was going to get money so he could buy a drink, and he said to Carter, "You have money to buy one? I pay you after the race."

"You ent have to pay nothing," Carter said, raising a nip out of his pocket.

They drank, and Boodram felt cheered. He smiled. They grinned at each other. They drank again and waited, and when it was time for their race to start they were already there at the rail, and didn't have to do any pushing.

When the horses went off the voices went up, and Boodram's was among them yelling on his ten dollars. Then suddenly he remembered he did not know which horse he was cheering. "Which horse? Which horse?" he turned to Carter.

"Number three. . . . "

Boodram returned to yelling, and an old mule hand, now he could imagine himself handling "Number Three." As the horses rumbled around letting loose a shower of mud behind them, Boodram felt himself a jockey clamped onto the heavy back of the big horse with the air burning his face, and in his hands the reins that held back in the turn and loosed his animal in the straight away. The horses came down to a final thunder of hooves and voices, "Number Three" crossing the line half a length ahead of all the others. The shouting tapered off, but not with Boodram. He hugged Carter and stamped his feet in the muddy ground. And after the winner was announced over the loudspeaker, Carter led him off to collect their winnings.

Carter was still gleeful as they left the cashier's cage but Boodram looked at the money in his hand with a terrible disappointment. "How much money you win altogether?" he asked.

"Same as you," Carter answered, still bubbling. "You see that horse? See what I tell you? Man, you can bet on him every time. He bound to win."

"Carter, I want to know how much money they pay you altogether," Boodram repeated, and this time Carter straightened up and looked at him with a serious face.

"You think I cheat you?" Carter asked. "Well talk up man, you think I cheat you?"

"No, I don't say that, but how come I only get back thirty dollars and forty cents?"

"Well what you expect? That's what the horse pay. You ent hear them say so on the loudspeaker?"

"Oh ho," Boodram relaxed. "So is this we put on the next race now, right?"

"If you want to do it. You don't have to do nothing I say, you know."

"Is alright," Boodram said. "Let we buy a nip and then put the rest on the race."

"Alright," Carter's face broke again into smile. "You a real man Boodram. You glad you come to the races?"

"Let we get the rum," Boodram said.

They bought the rum then placed their bets at the window. They drank and pushed themselves back to the rail and waited.

When the seventh race started it was just as before, except in this one the number five was their number. The horses swept around the curve smooth as water. Everybody shouted. Boodram screamed them to the straightaway and there became silent. Number five was boxed in and struggling. Boodram thought the reins into his hands and strained the horse forward. His teeth clenched, he crouched. He sawed the rein for attention, then gave it all away. But none of that helped. Number five crossed the line in the pack and Boodram felt the starch which held his stomach and shoulders together slip away and leave him.

He was greatly disappointed and couldn't stem the anger welling up inside him. Anger against Carter who had led him to believe in winning, anger against the jockey who let the horse get boxed in, anger at the horse, the other people pushing and jostling in the mud. Yet he could not show his anger. For it was important too to let Carter see what an independent man he was.

"Well, it's a risk we're taking, not so?" Boodram said, reasoning for himself as much as for Carter.

"But Holder don't lose race like that!" Carter seemed deeply at a loss. "I never see him lose race like that."

"All race is a chance, you know." The words came even as Boodram was making up his mind to say them. "We have any more horse we could bet on?"

"You have money to bet?"

"Four dollar. . . . "

"Ent that your last?"

"Leh we bet if we're betting, man. We come here to bet. You know any other horses?"

Not only did Carter not know any other horses, he didn't want to bet his last ten dollars either. Seemingly overcome by an unfair trick of fate he returned to echoing, "I don't see how Holder could lose that race . . ."

"Bet 'Teardrops' in the last race, . . ." a voice came from behind them. When Boodram turned around there was a short black man wearing ragged pants and a mashed felt hat, looking him directly in the eyes. The stranger had a face wide and pointed like a new puppy's, but he had a look of age and distance about him too. He smelled sour. "I know what I'm saying," he went on, looking at them steadily. "Teardrops in the last race . . . not to place, not to show. To win." And with that he turned to wander off through the crowd as though he had other business to attend to.

"You hear that?" Boodram said. "Come on. Leh we make that bet."

"You stupid or what?" Carter wanted to know. He didn't share Boodram's movement. "Some jackass you don't know talk, and you're going to put your money on what he say?"

Carter had a point. But something about the old man's intruding way made him seem like luck to Boodram and he said, "Is chance we're taking."

"Not me."

"Then make the bet for me. . . ."

Carter took Boodram's money and went back to the cashier's window. When he returned Boodram asked, "You didn't bet at all?"

"I bet, yes. But not on no Teardrops. Whoever hear a horse name that?"

"Who you bet then?"

"Tiger Prince carrying number seven."

"You know him?"

"You know Teardrops? . . ." Carter was back to his sullen self again and Boodram left off.

They watched the race. As before, people crowded to the rails and the horses went by in a loud clatter deep in the smell of horse sweat and leather. But Boodram was less excited now. He didn't have to get involved in riding Teardrops home. He didn't have to work himself up and scream for the winner. If Teardrops didn't win, then all the money was lost and there would have to be a way to make Rosie understand man must take a chance and if luck's against him, hold strain. The sour old man with his puppy face was a giver. Not everybody who walked the roads was like that, but Boodram had faith in this feeling.

Tiger Prince was struggling as the horses made the last turn. He ran second to last around the curve, and when the horses streaked down the straight for home he was still there. Teardrops won the race.

Out of the forty dollars that he won Boodram offered Carter five, but Carter wouldn't take it. He said he had to talk to his godfather about why Holder lost the race, and went off by himself through the crowd. Boodram pushed his way out of the noisy park, but with all the people and cars and bicycles squeezing out one narrow gate it was almost six o'clock dark by the time he crested Tarouba hill with the racetrack behind him. Thre were others walking along the narrow stretch between the canes before coming to the main road, but he walked alone. He didn't want their company. He felt a little stupid for thinking earlier that morning that he could win enough money at the races to put some in Rosie's hand for Soogrim's motor-car.

And buy himself one too! How could he have been so stupid? Just the same, he wasn't going home empty-handed, and even though the rain had stopped and drivers would be back in the fields on Monday he didn't feel any surge of excitement at the thought. Let Carter win the mule competition. Underneath, a new feeling that was somewhere on a leash, not well opened up yet, was taking hold. It was all right for him to come home in the dark; rain never again would upset him; and he could tell Rosie that wasn't really him taking advantage the night before last.

Some children were at play in the road, and a few women stood in the clean sand talking when Boodram approached the barracks. He didn't call, but some of the children did and turned to follow him. When he came to his room they went on, and Rosie was there at the half-door window leaning on the sill looking out. She opened the bottom half to let him in but she didn't turn around after he brushed past her.

"Look, I have something for you," he said, putting the forty dollars on the table. She turned and looked, but didn't say anything.

"Is only forty, but I get that with ten." She faced him with her elbows propped on the sill, her hair combed loose, and a deep quietness about her eyes which hid whether she was surprised, or glad, or anything about the money. "See, if you did let me take more. . . . "

"So you eat?" she asked.

"I coming straight home. Where I gon eat?"

Rosie moved then, to make a plate from the rice and bhagee which was still warm on the fireplace. She placed the plate on the table, then when he sat down to eat she went back to leaning against the half-door with her back to the outside.

"They're having race again next week," Boodram said through mouthfuls of food.

"You going?" she asked, after a silence.

"As man, I'm bound to go. You coming too, because you have more luck than me and together we bound to win plenty money." He didn't mean to say all that, but he felt good once he'd said it.

She laughed then, a teasing girl's laugh which said he was talking foolish but she was pleased and maybe happy to hear it.

Boodram finished the food and asked for a cup of water. Rosie brought it, then took his empty plate from the table. When Boodram finished drinking he went to the door with the last of the water to rinse his mouth. Then handing back the cup, "You check the mule yet?" he asked.

"What kind of thing you asking me . . . You know I does feed mule?"

"Well, leh me go feed him. . . . "

Boodram went outside to feed the mule. He brought a bundle of canetops and dropped it before the tethered animal. Then he took the bucket which hung from the cart axle and brought water from their barrel to the cooper's trough which the animal could reach. When he came back inside the money was still on the table. Boodram fidgeted for a little. He stood with his hands in his pocket staring at the money while Rosie finished washing the pots and dousing the last coals in the fireplace. Then she sat at the table with her eyes somewhere between Boodram and the money, and started idly braiding her hair. Boodram fidgeted for a little longer, then making up his mind he reached boldly for five dollars of the money and thrust it into his pocket saying, "You don't mind? . . . "

"What I gon mind for?" she said.

"Well, I'm just taking a little walk," he said, and started for the door.

"Boodram," she called, in an almost careless voice, "you're going to stay long?"

He turned around. "What happen, you 'fraid somebody come to trouble you?"

"No," she said. "Nobody going to trouble me."

Then still on the verge of going, but looking at her closely he asked, "You want I should bring back a nip gi you when I come?"

"If you like. . . . "

Outside, up above the clear sky was clustered with stars. Boodram didn't know them by name, but he could read the sign for rain. It was not there. In the dry road some women were still chatting with small children playing in and out between their skirts. Come Monday morning the fields would come alive again with voices, the hurried trot of loaders carrying cane bundles on their heads, and the rattling of carts making new ruts back and forth to the scales. He would be ready. But tonight it was time to taste a different empire.

Down at Charlie's shop the gas lamp sent its regular slash of yellow light through the open doors. Boodram could hear the voices of his friends there, some already raised in the singing which Saturday nights were made for. News travels fast in the village. It had more feet and mouths to carry it than a man could cipher, and they would know. It would be the first thing when he got there for one of them to come up and say 'I hear you win big, boy!' And Boodram felt a satisfaction deep beneath his heart when he thought how he would do. Just as the words were coming, and all eyes were turning his way, he would shoulder up to the counter, pull out his money and pound it down on the counter. He would let them slap his shoulders if they liked, look Charlie in the eye and say 'Puncheon for everybody!' After all, what is five dollars to spend when a man could win forty . . ?

In the Field

Joseph

Call me Solomon. Solo traveller, sometime word-maker, whose summary is in the science of Anthropology — although no one believes that. When I walk the village path they see me as one of them, a mild liar, who has travelled perhaps far, and returned. They travel too. And they have stories too. And they like to match stories with me. Joseph has a powerful story everytime. I have never managed to best him. Stories about freeway escapades in Los Angeles, New York ladies, or the world's tallest roller-coaster just don't take him. He knocks me new everytime, and carries me away. And gets carried away too, although he's the one doing the telling. It takes him with the first utterance. His lips curl in a pleasant sneer, his eyes pick on mine. The story is a powerful possession, and he has to shake and dance as he tells it. His voice takes on fresh octaves.

First he warms up with a story of how a huge mappipre snake attacked his head-lamp while he was hunting. Knocked out the light, and coiled again to strike at him. But he had the right prayers. And all the snake could do after that first strike was take itself off into the bush and find some other ignorant animal to bite. Then he tells about the times when he used to hunt tiger-cat in the forest. That was in the days when there was a real forest: before the oilfield people and the marijuana growers turned the place into a zug-up jungle. Gun traps everywhere now. You can't walk the woods in peace. Monkeys too. He used to shoot them because he and some of his friends used to like monkey meat. But monkeys are very sensible.

When you're about to shoot them, they show you their young ones. They hold them up for you to see.

Then there were his days as a "bad-john." He used to terrorize people. But there was another "bad-john" badder than he, an Indian fellow. Once this other "bad-john" was paid by an Indian man to kill his wife. The assassin stalked the woman. But when he drew his bead on her, he found she was pregnant. The assassin didn't shoot. He returned to the husband and said, "You pay me to kill one, but when I look, is two. You didn't come nice. . . . " Then he shot the husband. To hide the body he buried it in a river bed, deep, then buried a pig ontop in the same grave. When the police dug to find the dead man, all they found was the body of the pig.

Joseph knows where to end his stories too.

Bhola and Mr. Jay

Bhola encouraged Mr. Jay's friendship by offering to be godfather of one of his children. Later, on the basis of this friendship Bhola manipulated Mr. Jay into allowing his house to be broken down and moved further away from the junction so Bhola could expand his shop. "Yuh house already old and falling down, let me break it down altogether and move it for you, nuh? . . . " Bhola then encouraged Mr. Jay into a truck-owning partnership, _and_ used Mr. Jay's capital to finance his own separate trucking and other operations. Mr. Jay, lacking in business sense, didn't understand what was happening.

Mr. Jay put up half of the initial down payment on the truck, then what income derived from the trucking operation was used to repay the full price in monthly installments. Naturally, this left no income for Mr. Jay. When it was time for the truck to undergo official inspection, Mr. Jay's share went toward buying new tires. He was then convinced that it was "smart" to save these new tires, not use them for heavy-duty work, but have them taken off the truck and saved. The tires were later sold without Mr. Jay's knowledge to another of Bhola's partners. The jointly owned truck was used to haul goods at a rate which paid $16.00 per job for both driver and loader. Bhola's independently owned truck earned 30 cents/100 lb., capacity 2,600 lbs. When the joint operation was bled to the level of an irretrievable disaster Mr. Jay was advised to sell the truck at a loss. He had sunk his life's savings plus borrowed funds into the truck, and he refused. He chose instead to become sole owner of the truck. Mr. Jay now owns the shell of a truck that is rotting away on blocks, and he is broken for life. Bhola's own truck still plies the road, and his shop is prospering.

Kay's story

There was a woman who came into $90,000, but she could get it only on a certain day when the bank closed early. A number of people were in line ahead of her when she got to the bank. In order to beat the clock she offered $5,000 to the person immediately in front of her and the person accepted. She repeated this eight times, and made it to the cashier's window a moment before closing time. The people who accepted her grants got no money because the window closed after her. She got $45,000. Moral: You must spend some to get some. And people can be used through appeal to their greediness.

At the Desk

In the village, when situations of need occur people respond without racial bias — most of the time. Here, the general situation of chronic need seems to stimulate the potential for transcending racial antipathy. It could be otherwise. Is it reasonable to expect that as the community becomes "prosperous" the potential for race conflict will increase?

Indians are more adept at exploiting situations of need for personal gain. Example, water crisis. Indians who own delivery trucks usually get contracts for water delivery from Indians working in the county office. [It is rumoured that some trucks dump the water before it gets to the needy so as to make more trips, more money.] Indians will more readily cultivate individual relationships with a special purpose — or "hidden agenda" — in mind. Mr. Jay and Bhola.

Afro-creoles, on the other hand, hold absolute independence as an ideal. As a rule they wish to be in debt to no one, and abhor the personal relationship which has as its prime goal some sort of economic advantage. Afro-creoles want no liens against their time, their energy, or their person. At times they will even refuse to pay legitimate debts when the situation demands from them an obliga- tion, rather than offers an opportunity for self-expression.

Indians accept that liens come in variety and are inescapable. They exploit them.

Indians say, and many accept that, 'you must stoop to conquer.' Afro-creoles say so too; but they don't really believe it. They don't like to postpone potential conquest. What they really prefer most of all is the assertion of power.

There is a profound cultural difference based on whether "the metaphorical" or "the referential" takes priority, and the direction of flow between them. For Indians, enriched reference can stimu- late metaphor. For Afro-creoles, to start from the referential is to start empty.

In the Field

Young and Old Limers

The young men as a group do not lime inside the rum-shop — where the heaviest lime takes place. They lime beneath the eaves, or beside the road outside the shop — any convenient shelter that keeps the shop within view, within easy reach. From time to time one or two pass into the older group that limes inside the shop. The selection is based on mutual recognition that the young fellow is ready to imbibe both drink and "wisdom," and contribute an experience or two of his own in the illustration of some general observation — such as the nature of the road, the integrity of women, the best way to pro- tect a wicket, or how to grow the best garden plants. He must also be willing to accept the leadership of his elders.

This passing-in happens without formal ritual, without formal announcement even. The young man's progress from his group to the fringes of the adult group takes place as a slow unconscious pro- cess, so that no big thing is made of his readiness, except at times when his youth may be subjected to mock challenge. It is important how he deals with such challenge. He may mock his challenger in return, may defend himself by calling in an outside source to verify his manliness — either an age companion or older man — but he must not ridicule or disrespect the older challengers as he might those of his own age. The highest compliment the young fellow will likely receive from his elders occurs in his absence, when there is agreement — "He's a nice young feller. He nice too bad . . ."

The older men sometimes lime in the young domain, and participate in their conversation. But they are not leaders there. They are on the fringes. And a satisfying lime will require that before it is over, they spend some time with their own older group lime. Young limers end the lime with their own group too, whether they are being inducted into the older group or not.

Strangers buy drinks, hang, and listen in the lime.

Talkers, whether they are strangers or not, or whether they buy drinks or not, are the center of the lime.

Liming is an unchallenged male activity.

Overheard

Young fellers too lazy. They waiting for the seriousness in life to jump up and catch them but they'll fail. They're too lazy; and they don't believe in anything. They have no belief. And without belief a man is nothing.

Calypso

From Guayaguayare to Moruga to Point Fortin, along the backroads between oilfields, she was known year by year as "the guabin," "the bird," "the fox" — whatever the annual name for a woman of pleasure. She was known in all the dance halls, and by all the musicians. Among feting women she was dean: having had more fights than many, known more men, in more different places, but also because wherever she went, no matter the circumstances, whether at a grave-side or the dance hall, she attracted men like a natural magnet. Even after she was not young anymore, had lost too many teeth, and grown round in the middle, it was still the same. She couldn't dance as long and as hard and was not so quick to throw the first punch anymore, but the men still were drawn to her. Young boys, middle-aged duffers, even a grandpa or two, all paid obeisance to her presence. And she could boast still that she taught more men in village after village what they should do, and didn't give a damn about the respectable women who disliked her because every time they got on their backs for a man they went deeper into her debt. She cussed sweeter too.

Bad Blood

We had the habit of taking lunch together those days when court was held in Princes Town. Rick Mohan, medical officer for the district, DeLeon the warden for the county, and Randolph, sergeant in charge of the police station usually had to be around to give evidence in one case or the other. Wilkinson, ex-county councillor and lawyer without license, Sampson who used to be a sanitary inspector and myself, we made up the six that day. It was a sweltering Wednesday in September with off and on showers during the morning. By the time court was over, just before noon — the magistrate didn't like to miss lunch with his girlfriend in San Fernando — the pavements were steaming, and the short walk from the court-house, which was really a large room in the police station, across the square to Lim Chow's restaurant had us all drenched in perspiration. It was a relief to get upstairs and find our corner on the shaded verandah where Lim Chow usually set up a table for us.

From there with our backs to the square we could see clear across town out over the cane fields rolling on past Fourth Company village, on to the Central Range blue in the distance. Or we could turn and look down on the square surrounded by shops and cafes, the two bank branches, doctors' offices, with the market-gardeners squatting over their produce spread out on the sidewalks. The road from San Fernando to the east runs right through this square. It is busy. And at noon the thoroughfare was a delight for those who liked to sit back and watch people. You had taxi drivers busy hustling fares, every man with his own style of motion and language. Vendors who knew the sun would spoil their things calling out for buyers.

Children out of school in their little uniforms buying things to eat, or chatting, walking arm in arm checking out the goings on themselves. All of this, and you have the country people too, shy and jumpy the way they cross the streets, or standing around in families holding together as if they needed protection. And they did. Especially the females. The town idlers leaning in the cafe doorways or loitering on the pavement made a gauntlet for women to pass through. Of course, some women liked that. You could pick them out by the colors they're wearing, and their movement. Some of them, their bodies keeping time with the music in parts as they pass where the shops had loudspeakers. This was Princes Town, mid-day. By night, an empty, over-sized village, except for scavenging dogs and late travellers, but on court day this was the seat of County Victoria, gateway and commercial center to scores of little villages lodged in the eastern hinterlands all the way to the coast.

We liked Princes Town. Though each of us came from different parts of the island we had all grown up in villages ourselves, and took a common pleasure in the mixed bag where we had shops and services, but plenty of space, tall fruit trees, and gardens too, plus an easy mingling of people no matter what their colour or position. That is a good thing to notice when you have it, because people in this nation use colour and position as a rule to set themselves off from one another. We liked court days too. They brought out everybody, and after a morning session in the stuffy court-room it was nice to have a different kind of talk over some drinks and some kai-si-mein soup, followed by fried rice and curried beef or pork. Chinese really know how to cook pork.

It was almost two o'clock, and another heavy afternoon cloud was covering the sun by the time we got through eating. Sampson called for another half of scotch with ice and soda, and we went on talking. But our talk about women took a strange turn that day. Instead of the juicy stories it was our habit to share, we got on the topic of older women we had known who had somehow made themselves unforgettable in our youth. Wilkinson had a good one about Tante Bella catching him with her daughter. When they thought she was going to thrash the girl and make life hard for him by going to his father, she sat them down instead and gave them advice. He ended up marrying the girl. "Tante Bella's dead and gone now, but I'll never forget her. That was the best talking-to I ever get in mi life," Wilkinson ended.

Ruby, our middle-aged waitress had a nice lazy rearend walking away, never mind her missing front teeth, and it was a pleasure to watch her move around our table. When she brought the next set of drinks and leaned over to get our empty plates and bottles you could see the firmness in her arm reaching up and across her breasts. Wilkinson tried to catch her eye, but she wouldn't give him her attention. And I was about to make a remark on that when Sampson said, "I remember a time with that old lady from Lacotan Trace they used to call Gran-Gran. . . . "

In his day Sampson was a cutting figure on his Norton motorbike, decked in his khaki suit with scarf flying. People used to call him "Spy-Smasher," the dashing sanitary inspector who never allowed enforcing health codes or anything else to stand between himself and a pretty woman — married or not — in his territory.

"When I first came to work in this part of Trinidad," he continued, "she was one of the first villagers who tried to make me feel at home."

"An old lady like that!" Randolph raised his voice in mock surprise.

We all laughed.

But Sampson let that pass. He was clearly moved by the story we had just heard. And while it can't be said that he was jealous of Wilkinson, the time had come for him to share something he apparently carried deep within himself, so he continued. "The fact is, I didn't want to come here in the first place. I liked living in Port-of-Spain."

"But you come from a village before that, not so?" challenged Wilkinson. He had no respect or empathy for the country-born who turned their backs on their birthplace and gave themselves to the city. "What's so great about Port-of-Spain to make you want to stay there? It's one of the dirtiest places I've ever seen in my life."

"That's certain parts you're talking about," Sampson came back. "Charlotte Street, Henry Street, and. . . . "

"Not only where you have market," Wilkinson cut him short. "How about the la basse? You can't get anywhere in Port-of-Spain without passing through the smell, and that smoke! They're forever burning trash there — what little the corbeaux don't have scattered in the streets. . . . "

"You're exaggerating," DeLeon said. He had family living in Port-of-Spain and visited there frequently. "It's only some times of the day when you have the burning. And we have other ways of getting into town besides that main road."

"But that is the main road," Wilkinson was primed to argue again. "And . . . "

"Why all yuh don't keep quiet and let's hear what Sampson's going to say!" Randolph exploded. He glared as though we were supposed to be afraid of him, and Mohan who wanted to hear Sampson's story was already saying "Shhh! Shhh!" too. The argument cooled down.

"Anyhow," Sampson picked up, "much as I liked living in town the big man in the health service those days said I had to go, and so they posted me to this place here."

"How come something like that happen? You must've voted DLP or something?" Mohan said with a laugh.

"Me? Never!" Sampson was emphatic. "I don't have anything against Indians, but I'm a staunch PNM voter. I even canvassed for the minister that year and all. No, my voting didn't have anything to do with it. His daughter did."

"Ah hah! So you went in the man's flower garden, eh. . . . " Randolph led our exclamation and laughter. "So what you expect if they catch you picking, eh? What you expect?"

"Well wait, wait. Let me tell you," Sampson raised his voice over our merriment. "I'm going to tell you how that happened."

We subsided to listen.

"I didn't know who she was. But carnival Monday night that year I went to Despers' yard — that's one thing I still miss about Port-of Spain. You can't beat that place for steelband. Anyhow, it was there I ran into this young thing. And to make a long story short, we had a good time that night. We jumped up Tuesday and Tuesday night too, and things went nice. All this time I didn't even know who she really was."

"You mean you didn't even get her name?" Mohan asked. "You're jumping up with somebody all that time and don't even know their name?"

"Name, what?" Randolph said. "You think they're telling you, even if you ask?"

"Those Port-of-Spain women say and do anything carnival time," Wilkinson put in. "They only have one thing in mind."

"Well she did give me a name," Sampson went on. "Said she was Sylvia Macarno, so to me she was Sylvia Macarno. And the thing real nice, so I decided to keep following it up. It was Friday after carnival, when I decided to drop past the high school she said she was going to that I found out who she really was. I timed it to drop by just casual like when I know they're just coming out of school. But when I see her come out, she walked past me like she didn't even see me. So I give a quiet psst, and started to follow. . . . "

"She didn't look back, right?" Wilkinson couldn't restrain himself.

" . . . Right . . . "

"She made a mistake telling you the school," Randolph said.

" . . . Right. And she walked straight to this big limousine, and a chauffeur standing there holding the door open. Then it hit me. So I asked one of the other girls, 'Who is she?' That's how I found out who she really was."

"So what did you do then?" Randolph's voice was hard, and the official police look gathered in his eye. "You give it up?"

"No. Why I must do that? In fact, I thought to myself, Super! Because the fellow who was chief clerk then had a thing with her mother that some of us in the office knew about. I thought, Nice! All I have to do is play with discretion . . . Nice!"

"And that didn't work?" Mohan didn't want Randolph to come in with one of his lectures. We all knew the temptation with high school girls, and especially how bold they were.

"No, it didn't. They found out she was giving it to me anyway, and right after that this chief clerk came and told me I was being transferred. 'Well boy, the boss says he's giving you a chance to move,' he said. 'What boss?' He was the only one I knew to make such decisions. But not this time. 'The big man,' he tells me. 'The minister. He put you down for promotion in the country.' At first the chief pretended not to know what was happening, but when I press him it come out. 'She not for you,' he said. 'You're a jackass if you don't know that thing is foreign exchange. . . . '"

"What did he mean, foreign exchange?" Wilkinson questioned with his air of the self-made economic expert. But we all knew what Sampson meant. Foreign businessmen and trade officials receive royal treatment in Trinidad. The best of everything is put at their disposal, including female companions. They are the new royalty, with access to a whole preserve where average local Trinidadians like us can't set foot. We knew what Sampson meant, and we ignored Wilkinson.

"But what about the girl?" Mohan pressed. "If she really wanted to be with you, nobody could stop that."

We knew that too, and we waited.

"That girl . . . that girl, . . . " Sampson was shaking his head. "If you think she really cared about me, or anyone else, you don't really understand our women."

"Self-centered, . . . " DeLeon said. "No sense of tragedy in them."

"So who want tragedy?" Randolph bellowed. For him tragedy meant wreckage and blood and broken bodies. But that was not DeLeon's meaning.

"Randolph . . . Randolph, . . . " DeLeon said, and I shouted to cut that off because I didn't want Shakespeare at our table that day. I wanted to hear what Sampson had to say.

Mohan didn't even sense the difference. "And suppose she was the one you wanted so bad you could die for her? What then? Suppose you really wanted her for life?" he persisted.

"You mean like Romeo and Juliet?" and we could hear the snicker in Sampson's voice.

"Like that . . . yes. . . . "

"I ent promising anybody that one," Sampson said. "That is a style Indians have, but it's not my style. You miss one, catch another — that's my philosophy. Enjoy life."

"But it would've made you damned happy to be with her all the same, not so?" Mohan sliced back.

"True, true. And when I came to this part of the country I still raw from the way I got cut off from her. I had hard times in me for everybody — the clerks in the office, the junior officers, shop owners, people on the street, the lady who cooked and washed for me, everybody."

"Especially the women," DeLeon put in with his smile. "Sampson, you're a good one."

"Well, I didn't have much to do with them at first. . . . "

"I remember that. But then time came for open season. Anything wearing a skirt pass in front of you getting chopped down."

"Well. . . . "

"People used to call him ram goat," DeLeon said, raising his hand, explaining again to all of us. "And some villages he couldn't dare pass there after dark because the fellows were waylaying for him. Not so?"

We all knew the story about Sampson and his lust for women. It was legendary and we had heard it many times before.

"So how Gran-Gran Mande come in the picture?" Mohan asked. "You went after her too?"

"No, no, no. She did have a nice looking grand-daughter, but that was a tough family, boy. I wasn't tangling with that one."

"So what happened?"

"Wel, one day, making my rounds coming back from Moruga, the rain caught me. It was crop season, and the rain made mud everywhere in the road. Besides, the tires on my motor-cycle then weren't the best, so I decided to pull up at the junction with Lacotan Trace. The only place for me and the motor-cycle to shelter was under Gran-Gran's house, so I rode in and stopped the bike."

"How come you didn't park at the shop? You could've sheltered there," Wilkinson's voice was skeptical.

Sampson passed his hand before his face in a sign of disgust. "That fellow, Singh, who have that shop, he was always trying to give me something. He kept a nasty place too, damned nasty. Flies everywhere. And when they got into the salt meat and made worms he sold it just the same. Drains around that shop stayed green in the rainy season, but you couldn't get him to do anything about that. I cited him too. More than once. He was one of the first people I cited when I worked that village as sanitary inspector, but it didn't cost him a thing. The magistrate charged him a few dollars is all. He paid. That was that. He went back to his nasty ways just like nothing had happened. And everytime I saw him on my rounds he offered me something. When rice was hard to get, he offered me. Flour, rum, onions, whiskey, he was always offering me. So I never liked to stop in there except on business. . . . "

"If was me, I'm taking everything he offered, then make him put up more," Randolph said. "That's the only way to deal with people like that."

"Let Sampson talk!" DeLeon was impatient. "I want to hear this Gran-Gran business."

"Well, anyway," Sampson went on, "I'm downstairs under the house sitting on my cycle, and then I hear her calling me. When I look up she said, 'Come upstairs, nuh. Come in the gallery.' So I went up. She called me upstairs, and we sat down in two rocking chairs side by side on the gallery."

"I sat there with her, looking at the rain. I didn't have much to say, because it's hard sometimes not to give people an opening for questions you don't want to hear. But she was a lively old lady. Her eyes look yellow and watery like a lion. . . ."

"Where you ever see lion?" Wilkinson challenged.

"Never mind that," Sampson set him aside without loss of a beat. "You know what I mean. Somebody who looks at you and they size up everything in a hard way. She didn't have much in the way of wrinkles for an old lady — I later found out she was in her eighties — no trembling in her voice, no feebleness in her movements. She asked the grand-daughter who was living with her then to bring out tea and sweetbread, and we sat there looking at the rain, making small talk about weather, and crop-season, and the bad roads.

Across the junction from the gallery the shop door was open, and you could see a bunch of fellows in there loud-talking, and laughing, and carrying-on. You could hear them through the rain. And then I must've slipped into a trance, or something, because suddenly I'm hearing Gran-Gran saying, 'You see them? Listen to them!'

'Who?' I said.

'You hear how they carrying on? Big hard-back man and they can't find nothing better to do.'

It wasn't so much what she was saying. It was her caustic voice that bit me. She was looking steadily at the shop now. Leaning forward, her hair wrapped tight in a blue headcloth, she looked like a mongoose ready to attack. 'Look at them.'

When I looked more closely at the fellows in the shop I notice one or two of them were older men, dressed in the raggedy clothes village people usually wear except on Sundays, pot-bellied, but I couldn't see much more from the distance.

'Especially that one in the red shirt . . . there, . . . ' Gran-Gran went on.

I could see the red shirt, but I couldn't tell much about the one wearing it except he was tall, and seemed to be one of the ring-leaders. 'But you have good eyes to tell who that is from a distance,' I tell her.

'I know all of them.' she didn't take on my compliment. 'I watch them come in the world and I see them growing up. I could tell them in the dark if I have to. And that one — he has respect for neither man nor God. He's spoiling all the young boys and them.'

I had heard some talk about a fellow in the village who was a coming "bad-john." Not a warrior like those true hooligans we used to have during the war, you know, but he was a stickman who had cut some other fellow over a girl, and he was banking whe whe for a merchant in town beside doing other things the police didn't like."

"Hmmm!" Randolph interjected. "I know the fellow you mean. I can't call his name right, but he used to be a pest around here till we get him put away. His father was a fellow named Boysie, from St. Mary's village. . . . "

"That's right," Sampson quickly took back the talk, "that's right. She told me that. But anyway, we're there, and Gran-Gran has this look on her face, and I'm listening. I watch her, and right under my eyes the old lady change. She goes from mongoose to monkey, look-ing sharp but sad, with a far-away glaze coming over her eyes. 'No respect at all,' she said. 'None.'

'Well you know how it is when you're young,' I said.

She settled back with that look. 'That's how it has to be,' she said. 'With he, his line, and all who come under him, that's how it has to be.'

'Why so, Gran-Gran?"

She didn't answer me. She set out talking again, but she wasn't answering me. I could tell she was on some sort of journey going back into the past, and I listened. . . . "

'After the big fire here in the village we had a streak of bad blood pass through,' she started rocking in the chair.

'Is so?'

'For a time it get into everybody.'

'How such a thing happen?'

Gran Gran's voice had a quality just like the rain now — drony but up and down as she's talking. 'We had it bad here,' she tells me. 'Neighbors cursing neighbors, man chopping man . . . '

I sat there and I listened. She wasn't talking to me, but she was saying something for me to hear.

'Somebody get vex with shopkeeper Singh,' she went on. 'and they burn down his shop. At least, so we know it. Some say is he who burn down his shop himself so he could get money from the insurance people.'

'You can't tell these days.'

'It's true too he build back a new shop in style — with an upstairs for himself and his family. When bad blood come again, I want to see if that will burn down too. Bad blood is a terrible thing you know. It does take you and rotten your mind so you forget everything that's good to live for. I know. I pass there myself when we had that sickness. And when it take me so, I feel shame. I feel drenched in weakness and shame, because I's a christian woman who believe what the Bible say.

I look in the mirror and had to say — That is you Mande? Anybody could see bad-mind shining in mi eyes. Mi mouth crooked. I look just like that old lady they used to call Madam Souccouyant around here. She was a souccouyant, it's true. She could fly. I can't fly. I never was able to fly. I never had any business with the devil over nothing. But you could see dread and ugliness shining from mi face. When that bad blood raise in me I didn't stop going to church, yet I forget all the Christian teaching I grow up with through life. And I know one of these days I will have to pay. Recompense — I will have to pay. . . . '

I listened. . . .

'The night Singh's shop burn down I stand up in mi gallery here and watched the fire. They rush to the pipe to get water, but the pipe dry. Only wind coming out. That's when they used to lock off the water nine o'clock at night to six in the morning, then nine o'clock in the morning to six at night. Nothing coming out the pipe. Some of the neighbors come and ask could they take water from my barrel. I tell them, Take. But the little water we neighbors had in our barrels couldn't manage that fire. Red and blue, that fire burned. The rum and the pitch-oil Singh had in there blew up and shoot big flying sparkles clear up in the sky. And those of us with house nearby we start worrying about where the sparkles landing, and who else house going to burn. We had to give up and let the shop burn down, and turn to wetting down our own houses.

Mr. Lawrie was helping put out the fire with my bucket, but then he start taking away my water to wet down his own house. Mind you, he has water at his place, but he's taking my water in my bucket to wet down his house. And when my son went to get bucket from his hands Mr. Lawrie wouldn't give it. Vinroy had to fight him to get it. I stand right here in mi gallery then and I tell Lawrie — I tell all of them — Not another soul cross my yard to take water. But some of them still coming. Eh heh? I take up mi cutlass and I go down by the barrel. I stand up there and I have mi poonyah ready. And so help me, I was ready to chop them.

When they see me, some of them curse and they call out, Who you think you could chop? You old woman, who you think you could chop? Come in and find out, I tell them. Come in if you want to see blood here tonight. They call, and they carry on, but they stop taking mi water. Vinroy and mi last daughter who was still home at the time, they wet down the house and save it.

Those were terrible days around here. A person had to be fierce. If you didn't stand up for yourself, bat bite you.'

I watched Gran-Gran. I listened and I watched this old lady, trying to picture her with a cutlass in her hand, ready to chop somebody, and I couldn't. Maybe she could be hard, but I couldn't see her bringing blood from nobody.

'With the shop burned down,' she went on, 'it wasn't any trouble at all for me to see straight in Ram Beharry's whole yard. Not that I make it a habit to mind people's business, but when things happen before your eyes to see, then you see. It was Beharry, they say, who Singh paid to set fire to the shop. He was an Indian just like Singh, fresh out of Corosan, and we used to know him as a fellow selling coals before he moved into the village. In those days it was no pitch oil stove — pitch oil was for lamps — no gas, nothing like that. People cooked with coals. And who couldn't afford to buy coals chopped wood.

Beharry was a quiet man. He used to come in the village sitting on his donkey cart piled high with bags of coal, and you could always tell it was he coming when you hear the harness, but you wouldn't hear his voice. All the other coal-men calling out, but not Beharry.

He was clear out of Corosan, bony and black as the coal he's selling, but for around his eyes and mouth that always red. And these Corosan people, they to this day have a reputation. They happen to be very wild people. They don't read. They don't know a thing about church, and they will kill in a minute. Life don't mean very much to them at all. So when Singh rent Beharry a lot next door to his shop, many of us didn't like it. We didn't feel we could trust him. But there wasn't nothing we could do. Singh was from Corosan too, and Beharry was his family. So he rented him the land, and Beharry moved down here with his wife, and they build a little house next door to the shop.

Beharry still sold his coals. He would leave and go up in the forest for a whole week at a time and leave his wife here by herself. She was a young girl. Singh had her working in the shop. And although they were family, people used to say Singh took her for himself.

But that didn't prevent the village boys from asking.

They would hang around the shop, and every chance they get they'd have talks for her. She was a young girl. And it didn't take long. Soon one, and then the other, the young boys started getting in Beharry's yard, and my boy, Vinroy, he was head chief in the movement.

I used to ask him, say, What happen to you? Why're you so hungry for this man's wife?

I didn't bring him up, I didn't teach him that way. But all the talk I talk, was like he couldn't help himself. He wouldn't listen. He tie himself up with this man's wife, and not to say he wasn't young and handsome too. Wasn't a girl in this village he couldn't get if he wanted, but no. He stick up with this Indian girl — and not only he. All of them. But he, my son Vinroy, and one we had around here used to call Pappa Boysie, they were the chief ones.

Naturally, where you have two he-rat going after the same cheese you're bound to have bad blood, and that's what they had between them.

I talk to Vinroy, I lecture him, I pray for him — no use. While her husband off in the woods making coal, Soonia-girl would leave the shop come dark saying she's going down back to do her business, and one or the other of those two, sometimes both of them would be waiting for her down there. So they're going.

I talk to Vinroy. I tell him go, get away from the village and go by mi sister in Point Fortin where he could get a job in the oilfields. He won't go. His brothers come and talk to him, his older sisters — he won't listen. He's around here working now and then in the garden, but not thinking to make nothing of himself. Not trying. Just hanging about with the idlers by day, and joisting over the Indian girl by night. Bam, it come, he and Boysie stop talking to one another. That was an attraction!

Singh put in a section in his shop where they could stand up and that shop was the most popular place in the village. All hours of the day, in the night, you could find the idlers — and some decent men too — in there, drinking and talking that loud talk they do, some of them eyeing Soonia, and all of them eyeing the explosion between Vinroy and Boysie.

I often wonder why men like to swarm like that. If you want to bring them out all you have to do is put a willing woman in a given place, and here they come. And once they start swarming trouble bound to follow.

After the shop burned down they take to sitting out in the open with their drink. They had the habit so bad they sit down right there between the burnt up galvanize. They cleared a place out of the ashes and continued their drinking right there. They even gave it a name and all, calling the place Katanga. I don't know where they get a name like that. But if you hear them — See you at Katanga, boy . . . You stopping by Katanga tonight? . . . Katanga! Katanga! Go by Madam Tee and tell she Katanga send you . . . they used to stop the children and send them, getting their dew from Madam Tee.

And I have to tell you, that lady could make some dew! She had the best hand in this whole part of Trinidad. When you drink from Madam Tee, you're drinking the best, bar none. No doubt about that. And the little boys and them used to like making message for Katanga because they get to keep any change. They get something for their pocket. So they'd hang around waiting for the bottles to empty so they could run for more at Madam Tee. Day and night. Those were the golden days for mountain dew around here. With the shop burn down, not only Madam Tee but one or two others well get in the business. Some of them didn't even know what they're doing, but they're getting their molasses and going off in the bush, and com-

ing back with what they call rum. And selling it. Anybody who had
rum to sell could sell. Not even the police could stop them.

One time they send a squad-car full of police to shut down
Madam Tee, because she was the biggest, and an Indian fellow who
was jealous sent for them. Long before they get there she already had
the news. She just hide herself away, and they went in there and take
her coil and mash it up and put out warrant for her arrest. But the
police wasn't stupid. They knew where she was hiding, but they're
not arresting her. And Madam Tee was smart. She save her best coil
and leave the spare one there for them to mash up. The minute they
get in their squad-car and drive off she's back boiling again. Nobody
didn't 'fraid no police here. Police had to look the other way when
they pass Katanga.

Hard-back men, young boys, all the rough and tumble in the
village and some decent ones too, Katanga was their hang out. Rum.
Drink. Curse. Gamble. Fighting. And when the rain start, they're
scattering under people's house and you can't tell them don't shelter
there. They're cursing you and daring you to come down and put
them out. But I didn't use to take them on.

Soon's the sun started going down you could see them there in
Katanga. And as soon as it turned dark their noses turn like dog
pointing at Beharry's yard. That made some of the young women in
the village here vex. Quite vex, with their men friends, and with the
Indian girl too. Until Thelma, Reverend Solo's younger grand-niece
who was living with Boysie at the time took matters in her own hands
and came down to call her out.

Boysie was Thelma's mister but he wouldn't stay at home.
Sometimes at night when Beharry was off in the forest and he catch
Soonia ahead of Vinroy he wouldn't go home at all. He and Vinroy,
they're head and head trafficking in Beharry's yard. But Vinroy
didn't have no woman and child to mind. Thelma had just give birth
to that same one you see there in the red shirt when she come down
here one moonlight night from their house near Mootoo hill on the
Barrackpore road. She come down just as the moon start coming
from behind Manoe's chanet tree, and the army was there in their
Katanga as usual, drinking, and Boysie's there too.

Thelma was a tall woman. She come down the road all in white,
her head tie. When she reach infront of Katanga she take up a stand
and raised her voice for everybody to hear. She started cursing. She

call out Boysie. She tell all who had ears to hear what he had in certain places, and what he couldn't do with it. She call out Soonia too, and tell her to stop sending her lice home. Soonia no sooner hear Thelma's voice than she duck inside and shut her door and window and blow out her light. Thelma carried on. She raised her dress to show people where she got the lice, and show them what Boysie had at home that he was leaving to line up behind Tom, Dick, and Harry to get to the skinny Indian girl.

Naturally, the army start laughing. People coming out of their house gathered around, and everybody laughing. She talked, she called at the top of her voice what she wouldn't do.

After a while Boysie couldn't stand it no more. He run out in the road and he slapped her. But Thelma was good for herself. She took hold of his collar and she butt him so fast he sprawl on the ground. When she put the coconut on him so, somebody say, Oh God! She break he nose! But Boysie get up. And when she went for him again, so they start to wrestle. They wrestled. They rolled on the ground like two alligators. And when he finally managed to get on top of her he start to beat her. Licks everywhere. Cuff, and choke. And when she tore off his shirt he jumped up looking for his cutlass to chop her. Vinroy dashed out to take him on then, and told him he couldn't do that.

. . . Stop beating the woman! Vinroy tell him. If you want to fight, fight me.

Oh ho! Is that drive Boysie mad and he come for Vinroy. You want this one too? . . . he's saying. You think you're man enough to take this one too? . . . And they grapple.

People try to hold them back and cool them off, but too late. All the heat they had sitting inside them for one another boil up and it coming out. I never knew Vinroy could fight so. They grapple toe to toe, man for man, until Vinroy, when he bend back Boysie so, he bend him to the ground and went down on top of him. Then licks start. He knock Boysie senseless, and they had to run for water to revive him.

All this time the moon already up and over the chanet tree, everything bright, and they bring Thelma in mi yard here to help her wash the blood from her mouth and face. Some of the women tried to console her. But Thelma didn't want that. As soon as she catch her breath she back in the road again calling Boysie . . . So you beat mi? You beat mi? You beat mi good. But this is the last time you're raising your hand against anybody. You hear that!

Boysie didn't hear her. He couldn't hear a thing. He was still sitting on the ground waiting for his senses. But she repeat, and she repeat, and then she went off. She wouldn't let nobody walk with her either, she went off by herself.

That night Soonia wouldn't open her door at all.

From mi bedroom late at night I could hear Vinroy and others knocking and begging her to open. But she won't open the door at all. Then they start pelting. I don't know who it was, but one of them pick up a stone and pelt it, then all of them start pelting. They rain stone on that galvanize so, nobody nearby couldn't sleep. As for Soonia, I don't know how the child made out in there by herself that night, but morning time bring a different story.

It was half-past five when they wake me up. I hear Manoe's voice. . . . People! Oh people! . . . and from the way he's sounding agitated I could feel already something bad happen. I open mi window and look out. I could easy make out Manoe in the road, standing infront Katanga, and hear him . . . O God oh! People! People! . . . but I couldn't see what it was put such fright in his voice. I get in mi clothes. Neighbors, everybody run out.

When we get there, it's Vinnie. I see mi last boy-child flat on his back in the canal. His eyes wide open, but they ent seeing a thing. He lie down like everything in him mash up, and now it's my turn to bawl. I couldn't help miself. To realize Vinnie dead! . . . Mi last one . . . Mi sweet-child . . . I fall down. They had to carry me back inside, bring me upstairs and put me to lie down. I lay down, and I try to rest, but if I say mi body didn't cry for vengeance I lie.

How that happen? Who kill mi son?

We bury him. But police never find out.

They come and they talk to everybody. They take down evidence from everybody about Boysie and Beharry. They even carry those two to the station for questioning because they were two who could have something against Vinnie. But they didn't hold them.

I couldn't take it. I couldn't take that. Mi son dead, and the police not holding nobody because they can't find evidence to please them. I went down on mi knees. If people couldn't see who kill Vinnie, the one up above could. And he could do somethng about it. I went down on mi knees. I prayed, and I asked — strike down the wicked murderer. I called on The Spirit to see the one who kill mi son suffer. I prayed for them, all who helped cause it to murder one another and suffer down into the ashen grave. Spare none. Fix a sign of The Beast on the murderer, his offspring, and their off-spring, down to the last one.

Son', Gran-Gran turned to look me in the eye, 'hope never to have old people pray on you, for the Spirit will answer.

The Spirit answered.

Less than two months after we bury Vinnie, the day for his forty days, in fact, they find Boysie in the woods near Corosan. They find him dead in a little pond of water where woodsmen used to bathe. Snake bite him, and he dead right there. At least, they say snake bite him. But it was Beharry who found the body, and it was Singh's truck they used to load the body and carry it to the Princes Town police station. Doctor there say Yes, snake bite him. Matter close. The body swell, and they wouldn't let Thelma bring him home. From the police station to the undertaker to the burying ground. Fast. Right away. Matter close. Thelma bawl — Even though the man was no good I know how she feel in her belly.

As for the Indian girl, what happened was like water running off duck's back. She was just a young girl, and Beharry send her back to Corosan, out of the way for things to cool down. Some people say she had child up there that was dohgla and they threw it away. I don't know. She didn't come back until after Singh built back his new shop, and then she was carrying twins some people say Singh give her and not her husband Beharry.

But look how things work, eh . . . Since Singh's madam died, Soonia is full mistress in the shop. Beharry not selling coal nor going to the woods again, he's driving truck for the shop. And the young boys and them, they don't remember a thing about Katanga. But they can't help themselves liming in that shop, carrying on just like their fathers used to do, or even worse, because it's not only no work nowadays, more of them are making money selling tampi. All they do is make a trip to the woods, meet their partners from Port-of-Spain, and they have money for beer and whiskey in the shop. They don't want dew, this generation. It's beer and whiskey. When that money done, it's another trip for more tampi and that boy there, Thelma's son, he is the ring-leader of the lot. . . .

'Police know about this Gran-Gran?' I asked her.

'Yes, they know. But what they could do about it? Is so it has to be — what they could do about it?'

There was nothing I could say when she finished . . . what they could do about it?"

Sampson was misty about the eyes as he repeated the words of Gran-Gran's lament, and some of us felt sad with him, but Randolph was not taken in. "That old woman fool you, boy," he said to Sampson. "She didn't tell you Thelma was her husband, outside child, right?"

"Mnnh mnnh!" Sampson couldn't help showing surprise. "No. She never mentioned nothing like that. Is true?"

"All these years you are here in this county and you didn't know that?" Wilkinson sneered. "Her husband was no saint you know. I used to hear my father and his friends talk about that man. . . . "

"Sounds like you're getting ready to say Boysie was his outside child too. . . . " Mohan was sarcastic.

"You hear that too?" Wilkinson shot back. "Is possible," he said, assuming the air of considered thoughtfulness that was his professional trademark, "is possible."

But that would have been taking it too far.

We went through the routine emptying the scotch before us. DeLeon shook the last drops into Sampson's glass and said, "Yuh good man. Yuh real good. I never knew you could tell story like that."

"He didn't tell no story," Randolph flurried. "What he say about that case really happened."

"That's not what I mean," DeLeon said patiently. "I know about the Vinroy Callender murder case too — and how you fellows couldn't solve it. I mean Sampson tell the story nice, man . . . talking like the old lady and everything. We have to drink to that. We can't let this pass so . . . Ruby!" he called, holding up the empty bottle.

When Ruby came, all the talk already had me stirred up, and as she came with the empty tray in her hand, her eyes looking right through me, I felt an urge for her I never had before. In all my years of knowing Ruby and enjoying seeing her walk away I never had such an urge to be next to her. When she got to the table and stretched her arm out for the bottle I said, "What're you doing when you get off from work?" It came out just like that.

Ruby bunched her ripe lips against her open front teeth and gave me such a big schupse, everybody broke up laughing. I laughed too. But I know I wasn't trying to be funny.

At the Desk

Why do they leave the community center to crumble and rot down? They all claim to live for peace and unity, with concern for each others' well-being — "All ah we is one!"

The village council never meets. Why do they neglect these emblems of a new national consciousness? That are designed to transcend race and class — two problems inherited with the history of colonialism?

I don't quite understand why they have such little or no concern for keeping up the council or saving the center. They tell several stories to account for why the council does not meet: People do not like the autocratic style of the president, but he has government connections and cannot easily be replaced; there has been some mis-use of funds, and the treasurer is not to be trusted either; the officers wouldn't undertake repairs when the rot first began at the center, and now it needs too much work, too much raw materials; the government officer in charge of community development in the county — an Indian fellow — would like to see Indians take over the council and community center, and wouldn't bring help as long as creoles are in charge. On his part the government officer, with whom I spent quite a bit of time, claims he has been trying to meet with representatives of the village council for months without success. The government expects some initiative to come from the people. Government doesn't have money sitting down to throw at people when their own laziness cause them to lose what they had in the first place.

Some people blame the government: others blame the Indian development officer for not carrying out government instructions which he gets from Port-of-Spain. They blame each other. Nobody volunteers for blame. Nobody claims authorship for this mistake. What people say is lacking is leadership: and they look at me.

b.

Whenever I talk with old women in the village, they love to reminisce about the past. Especially when there is more than one together. But they are not the only nostalgic ones. Whenever I get together with adults, men or women, a favourite topic is "the wonderful past." Sometimes the nostalgia is so intense, I feel myself the desire to rush out and work for the restoration of this wonderful era they remember so vividly.

c.

I obeyed the tug. After a session when the talk was about gayap — informal cooperative association — when people did not need money to get things done when generosity and good will were automatic aspects of everyday life; I obeyed the tug. I tried to arrange for the organization of a co-op.

We have had two meetings: one at the house I am renting, the other at the Baptist church. Several men came. But we couldn't seem to get past why the village would never have a successful co-op in our talk. Why the village would never have a successful venture of any kind which required trust and cooperation. It was confidentially hinted over and over, that only one or two people were trustworthy, but the trustworthy ones had no organizing or leadership skills. Those with skills were not to be trusted.

I wonder if all this talk, the nostalgia and confidential revelations of distrust, is a way of helping them transcend some harder anxieties? Things are changing here. The estate is now operated by a manager with a skeleton crew on their various tractors. Indians have moved with confidence from the class of field laborers into the skilled trades and entrepreneurship, and they are clearly on a faster pace than the Afro-creoles in the business of "progress." Gayap is dead. Without cash now, nothing gets done. A village that was relatively self-contained and independent is now part of an outreach which does not stop at the government offices, but flows across the neighbor's fence and invades the space between relatives. It is money. It is work. It is travel. It is goods, and building materials, and new things like television, and the yearning to own motor-cars. It is the growing indifference for one another. There is an aggression here against what one can't see, but feels powerfully nevertheless.

My presence and interests exacerbates the situation, I think. I have a motor-car. I do work which I alone make up. My apparent comfort and ease puts them in mind, I suspect, of how it was, or might have been, when they were at ease too. The verbal presentations I get are something different from much of what actually happens. They invoke the "old-time" for me, and show me the old ways of growing, harvesting, and preparing food. But they also frequently ask me to ride them to the supermarket in town where they buy packaged food from Minnesota, South Carolina, Canada, Australia — processed foods that have very firm niches in their lexicon of taste and habits.

Perhaps if I were not here "old-time" would rest where it is, in the old mahogany bureaus, and the receding corners of their minds — to be invoked on ritual occasions. Of course! Aren't rituals central to the transcendence of discrepancies? My presence, in a sense, is ritual occasion. It is certainly not their everyday. And their talk is not really just for me, but for themselves too — a mechanism which invokes a wholeness they need to feel, the courage they need to face collapsing into a different future.

The Second Desk

During the last few weeks of fieldwork in 1976 I encouraged villagers in reviving an old custom of performing the kalinda — complete with stickfight — to celebrate the New Year. Some of us had been drinking and talking about "old times." The idea for a revival did not originate with me, but I encouraged it, principally so that I could make a film recording, and ended up being deeply involved in its

organization. On the day of the event, while it was in full swing —
one could not call it much of a success as far as celebrations go, but
the drums did play and several stickmen danced, even if there were
few truly intense encounters — a young lady from the village whom
I did not know, who knew me only from a distance, came up spontaneously and kissed me on the cheek.

She did it with a certain show of defiance — initiating a kiss
with a stranger in public is not the sort of thing a young lady would
normally do — and gratitude. At the time, I wasn't sure why I
deserved this. And perhaps I still don't fully grasp her true intention.
But after months, years, later, I have come to rest with an understanding of her action as her way of saying 'thanks' for being stirred
somewhere in her cultural personality, some center that otherwise
lay suppressed beneath more artificial exigencies.

The Community Center

We in this village don't pay much attention to the Prime Minister's Better Village Competition anymore. Not these days. In the beginning, yes. Because in those days, you know, we all loved Prime Minister Williams. He was a man who captured all our feelings, and we loved him. I remember when he first started lecturing to the people, before they elected him, we used to go by bus all the way to Port-of-Spain to hear him talk. That was lovely. We would leave here all hours of the day, sometimes not knowing how we getting back, but to reach there at the square in Port-of-Spain to hear him talk. And that man could talk. He was a little man, but when his voice rumbled so, and called out knowledge from the ages he used to make you feel weak one minute. And in the next, when he brought up the way to deliverance out of the ground you could hear and feel God talking through that man, and you had to love him.

Those were good days, yes. And we would leave here by bus, sometimes not getting back home until two or three in the morning because the last bus from town wouldn't get to San Fernando until after midnight, and then the Princes Town bus, if there was any, wouldn't come on this road but drop us at Mathilda Junction where we would have to start walking. Sometimes we would hire a car to take us, wait, and bring us back again. But we didn't always have money to do that. Those were good days. And even if the rain caught us on the road coming home we didn't mind. The little wetting we could take, because inside, the promise had already gone from lees to strong liquor and we could feel the world turning to bring us up off the ground into an upright position again. Our people were very upright in Africa, you know, before they brought us to this part of the world.

And when he was elected and became the voice of government we all said, yes. A new leaf, a new day opened for the people of this island and nobody could stop us now. All those years when you had to bite your tongue for the Englishman, when you had to hide in the bush to hear drum because otherwise the police would arrest you, all of that over. This we country now. And whatever happen it's because we make and the whole world was going to see how we could make.

Like everybody else we in this village formed our village council. Church members, those who didn't go to church, some of the Indians who still lived separate in the old estate grounds, even some of the rag-tag who didn't do nothing but hang around the shop drinking rum whole day, everybody came out. We formed together and made our council. We elected a president and officers. My oldest daughter and my second son took office and before we built the community center meetings used to take place right downstairs here under my house. It used to make my heart feel glad to see everybody talking and working together. I was born and lived my whole life here in this village, and families I know who never talked to one another were sitting side by side under my house at these meetings. Indians who I didn't even know could talk English good were there making speeches.

I gave my son some money to buy galvanize paling to bar up that side of the downstairs where rain lash in so meetings didn't have to stop when rain fall. I gave them my Coleman gaslight to use, and while they were down there making speeches, or planning what to do, or if somebody was showing the rest how to make baskets, I upstairs in the kitchen readying ginger beer, or mauby, or tea, or coffee for everybody. Those were good days. Because not only here in our village, everywhere in the country people were doing as we were. Getting together, and working to make our community better. That man, Prime Minister Williams, brought out in us the very thing we were lacking — pride, self-respect, love for the likes of ourselves — and these were the very things we needed to make village life complete.

We've never wanted for food here in the village, nor for things like medicine and clothes either. Many of us among the older heads know how to use the plants growing in our gardens, and we could buy a piece of cloth and make any kind of dress or suit we want to out of it. When it comes to sickness of the soul, we're first rate at dealing with that. Nobody nowhere could handle church better than we. But it was a different matter with pride and self-respect. The belief that we were the backward part of the country was strong in our midst, and we had to overcome that. So when Prime Minister Williams could stand up and show the people Trinidad was the measure of any country in the world, when he could prove and convince that Trinidadians writing the names of those others who called themselves lords and kings in the book, then what we have to be ashamed for? Times changed. We could walk the road with pride and see the future changing. We could see the promise in that change and we built a community center.

Mr. Bynoe give the land, Wendell the carpenter give free labor, and so did Mr. Bailey who know how to do mason work. Raggoo gave his cart to haul lumber from the saw mill. Shopkeeper Singh hesitated at first, but then he too let his truck men bring the cement from San Fernando without charge, and gave the workers nails and things like that when they needed. And old as I am I went down there and help pass up the boards while they're building. The other ladies and myself, we cooked. Everybody pitched in and we had a great gayap. Mr. Manny and his sons went hunting the night before and they brought back manicou and quenk. People brought cassava, dasheen, and fig from their gardens. Some bring water nuts. One or two brought rum made right there in their backyards. Whenever you have gayap you have to have that because it's the grease to make work flow. Those who didn't have things from their yard to bring went to the store and bought oil. Some brought flour and salt to make dumpling, and sweet drinks for the women who don't take strong. Pastor Richards blessed everything and we built that community center in two two's. We brushed the yard. We had a good time.

The following Saturday we went back again, this time with galvanize the council paid for, and paint. We had gayap and got the painting done and the roof put on. We built it from the ground up and finished everything. That place was the center of pride for all of us.

But look at it now.

I turn my head whenever I have cause to pass that way because it makes me feel bad to see what become of our center. Wild bush and the ants and scorpions have it now. I hear there's a strange Indian man sleeping in there at nights, but if so, he must have a special blessing to protect him from the snakes and centipedes who're the new owners now. It's there, our shame, our disgrace, our defeat. And I don't like to see it. Anybody coming to our village for the first time seeing that, if they really see it, they get a good understanding right away of our state of affairs these days, and it's not nice.

We have street lights and people have TV in their drawing rooms now. Water pipes not only in the yards, but inside the house, people have these days. You could hear radios blasting from one end of the village to the next. And some of the young boys working for oil money build houses big enough to have school in. No more wood smoke in the kitchen, it's gas stove if you please. No mud oven. Who bothering to bake bread, when you could buy that thing the shop sells wrapped in fancy wax paper just like they do in Port-of-Spain? There are more motor-cars in this village than used to be in the whole of Trinidad before the war. We have plenty noise, and light, and busy-ness. But the heart's gone. And if you want to see where it went, pass by the community center.

So as I was saying, we don't pay much attention to the better village competition anymore, because that is what started it. Whatever you call it, the sickness that mash us up, it started with that competition. We entered in the first year and we were good. We did the dancing, we had woodwork and handicraft, we entered in the stickfighting. We had garden produce and bouquets. That year we should have won, but they gave us second.

The next year we prepared for them.

That Chinese boy who the government have selling choreograph or whatever they call it, for village dance these days, he wasn't even born yet. But you have to watch these Chinese, you know. They're a wily people. Plenty things they don't know, but they're masters at pushing themselves to the front. And they don't give a damn about black people. They don't like us at all. I see with my own eyes a Chinese boy here in Princes Town, a creole-Chinese, the boy curse his own mother calling her dirty nigger, and saying he wished every nigger would drop dead. That is their way. But the government have this one, paying him to tell people about village dance. You think the likes of he could've been anywhere in the same circle with Tan Rosa? Bele, bongo, Shango, Castillian, pasillo, she was the queen of all. From San Francique to St. Mary's, Mayaro to Sangre Grande, people knew Tan Rosa.

They used to come for her in motor-cars when they had wake anywhere, and all she's walking with is her qua qua. Same thing every Saturday night, especially around Easter time and Christmas season. Everybody want Tan Rosa to come to their dance because when she's there, and she step out, everything liven up. When you see Rosa pick up her skirt and decide to flare those petticoats, nobody could touch her you know. And if you're watching you're bound to catch the fever yourself. She was queen. Rosa never wanted for anything. She never had to walk with a cent in her pocket because people glad to give Rosa whatever she wanted. She was queen, and there'll never be another one like her — Lord bless her soul.

But Rosa it was who took over the dancing in full that second year. She trained everybody. Gentlemen from Rio Claro, Arouca, Hardbargain, Fyzabad came in their motor-car to take Rosa, she wouldn't go. She stayed right here working, making everybody practice night after night, and everybody support her. Every night we're at the community center, and while Rosa's practicing the dancers Mr. Thompson's sitting in one corner with his tools carving. Madam Benoit in another corner with the handicraft makers, and outside in the yard the stickmen holding their talk and making up new lavwhe. Me, I'm too old for all the twist-up and shimmying they have to do in the dance, but they make me treasurer. Everybody trust me. I'm just the old lady who born, raise, marry, and settle here. They trust me. And I have mi little book taking down contributions and dues. I don't really need the book because nothing's wrong with my memory, but it look nice and business-like. That year we prepared for them good, and when time come for competition shopkeeper Singh gave us his lorry and driver and we're gone to Port-of-Spain.

All the way driving to town the stick-men and them singing, and Ma Solomon's son, the one they call Gingerbread, leading on the keg. We pass through all the villages. We pass through Claxton Bay, Couva, and Chaguanas. By the time we get on the Princess Margaret Highway it's already dark and we could begin to see the lights of St. Benedict's up in the hills. Lal Beharry is a good driver and that night he's giving us a smooth ride all the way. Some of the stick men and them have their heads band in red, some in white. They stooped down with their sticks pounding the floor of the lorry in time with their singing. The dancers not all dressed yet, but the ladies carrying their starched petticoats and their flounces, some with their hair half-ready, and the headties resting in their hands.

When we get to San Juan they open the rum. We didn't have Fernandez or nothing like that, we drinking what we make by our own hands. It's the best. You can't stop that. All who taking take, and when the bottle finish somebody else passing another one. Only Lal Beharry we wouldn't let him have any because he's a terror behind the wheel when he take in one or two. We tell Lal he could drink all he wanted for the rest of the year, free, but not that night while he's driving. Everybody else sweet, those who take and those who're not taking. Sing, clap, we're joyful. We know we're prepared, and everybody ready to give up their best in the competition. When we reached the beginning of Port-of-Spain, all going past the railway station there, we bounce up on another lorry just like ours carrying people belonging to some other village from the east. They're singing and beating their drums too. Before long, we meet another one from Arima, I think it was, and everytime Lal Beharry pass them they pick up speed and begin following.

By the time we take the road going to the concert hall we're in a long line of cars and lorries, some of them quiet, but most of them singing like we were, and the town boys who don't have anything to do but idle beside the road calling out as we pass, 'Aie country! Country booky!' They want to know what part of The Main we're from. If we could talk language. And so on. They're full of taunting, down to whether our girls wearing bloomers and all. But we ent mind them. Some of our stickmen want to get out right there and settle it, but we cool them down because we didn't want any police interfering with us before the competition, since Port-of-Spain police are naturally biased against country people. When we get to the hall, Lal Beharry park the truck and everybody finish their last-minute dressing. They give me the handbags and purses and other valuable things to hold, and we go inside.

It pleased my heart to see the way it was inside that great hall. There is the big stage facing everybody, and to the front there is the Prime Minister with his company, and all the other ministers and them with their company. It pleased me to see all of them there, brown and black like me, intelligent, and brilliance shining from their faces. When I was a girl, you think that could happen? All through my years as a young lady, and later as a mother of eight, anytime any congregation of dignity came together in this country it was usually one or two white people at the fore. Some brown ones used to think they were better than we, but still there were very few seats for them in the row of honour. If you were brown, you had to stand down, just as we black they expect us to stay back. But when we take over things change. No white in front, brown in the middle, black at the back. You sit down where your rank place you, no matter what your colour. And the only reason white people weren't there is because they can't stand that. They can't stand the truth when it means that black people outrank them. And some of them even go around saying how it's hate we hate them. We don't hate them. What we must hate white people for?

I stood on the side of the road myself in this village back in 1952 when the English governor and his lady pass through on their way to see where it was Columbus first landed. I ran after their car myself, and handed a bouquet to the first lady when she made them stop the car and get out with a graceful curtsy. And the governor, tall in his white uniform and cork hat, gold medals shining all over his chest, what a splendid fellow! He didn't disdain when I offered my hand, he shook it. And I went down in my own curtsy then because they were aristocracy. You could feel it. We don't hate white people, we prefer to give honor where it is deserving. We are not an ordinary people, and when we see jackass standing up to pretend he's man it don't make no difference what colour the skin. Jackass is jackass, and we say so. And we know, besides, we know that hate is a thing that consumes the hater. It takes and makes him rotten inside. Hate has a lot more in store for the hater than it does harm for the hated. So why we must hate them?

When we went on stage that night, when the lights come on and they finished introducing us to everybody, Rosa didn't wait for the people to stop clapping. I'm standing to one side with the chorus, since all we do is answer in the singing, but I'm watching everything. Rosa give the signal right away, and the drummers start. The chantrelle call out her song, and when we answered the whole hall could hear we. The ladies picked up their skirts, and when the men opened their arms the ladies mince their steps like butterflies and you hear the petticoats make a breeze. It is dance from then on. The ladies taking their turns dipping and turning out, the men around and behind them. Then all together. Everybody spinning in unison, the men going down to one knee and up again. Then Rosa comes like a mama butterfly, her scarves and petticoats flaring, lighting here, touching there, spin, fly, close the wings, then sail again, and the drummers with her. The people couldn't wait. They couldn't wait for Rosa and the others to finish before they launched into clapping. They stood up, and that whole house roared when Rosa finish and take her bow.

The Prime Minister was on his feet and everybody around him. People calling and laughing and clapping all at the same time. And we, we're happy. The drummers ent paying no mind to their sweat, and all of us standing without words, speechless in the dread of that deep down happiness what come when you know people have been touched to let loose the full spirit in their souls. After that, we didn't even hear what the other villages did. We hear, we couldn't listen.

The stickmen went outside to take their rum and get themselves in readiness. We ladies leave the stage. The kegs, they bring them up, and some drummers from Williamsville came on to play. I know them, because my third sister used to live in Williamsville until her husband died, and I used to spend time there with her in the garden. When her oldest daughter got married I was head cook for the celebration, and those same drummers were there, only they weren't playing kalinda that time. It was calypso. But when they sit down on those kegs, one of them rolled the buller and the cutter picked up the beat. You could feel heart-break and sorrow creep out everywhere in that hall, because you're hearing the drums call for blood. And when that goatskin cry thirst, man have to listen and somebody answer. I looked for the Prime Minister and he's on his feet like he himself ready to take off his jacket and fly up on the stage. Some of those around him, especially the older ones, they're tapping and shaking their heads in time with the music, and one or two even answering in the lavwe. Because by now the chantwell calling, and the chorus answering not only on stage but here and there in the hall as well. The stickfighting start.

Stickfight is a bloody business, you know. I mean it is a dealing in blood. But the first fighters and them didn't draw none. That was Williamsville and Mayo. And I guess since they're from the same part of the country the fellows were friendly and draw an agreement between them. At least, that's what the people said, and they gave out Mayo was winner in that one. When our turn came we sent up our own drummers on the stage. Old Mr. Lavalle was on the cutter, and that man knew where to find the warrior in everybody. He brought the hall to attention, and when the fighting start, except for the drums, the lavwe and the dancing, everything quiet, everybody waiting, because you know before long something is going to happen.

The first match between one of ours and one of theirs brought blood. When Mr. Bobby who live in the last house before the church going down the hill from me carayed with the fellow from Tarouba, when Mr. Bobby stomp his front foot and stretched, you could tell that the fellow was no match for him. In two two's it's whap! whap! and the fellow cut. Blood running down the side of his face, and people lose their mind. They throw money on the stage for Mr. Bobby, and so it went. When the men pick up the money they bring it to me for safe keeping, and I'm watching from the side. Mr. Prime Minister out of his jacket now explaining to the ladies around him how Mr. Bobby did it. And when the drums pick up again he sit down, but everybody's still hot. The coolest one there is Mr. Lavalle. He's leaning forward on the little keg, just beating between his heels, and my heart's coming up to mi mouth. I want the fight but don't want to see it, because to tell the truth, something hot and painful wrench inside mi belly everytime I see a man's blood or even think of it. But I'm watching. And so it happened. Man after man, they go up on the stage and get cut. Three for us, and three for them.

Then Tarouba send up a fellow they called Mussolini. He's big and he's tough-looking. His head's shaved clean and it's shining in the light, and he had muscles standing from the back of his neck on down. Mussolini jumped in to caray with Springer, and when I watch them, mi body turned cold, so I'm frightened. Springer look nothing but a little slip to Mussolini. Springer is a slight man. He hardly reach up to my height and when he carayed in front of the fellow Mussolini he looked like David before the giant Goliath. But Springer could play stick, you know. He come from a line, all of them are natural born stickfighters. They're thin, but they're quick like tiger-cat and they're slippery.

When Mussolini charged on Springer, he went for the head. He fired. And same time he fired Springer side-stepped and put his stick in Mussolini ribs. They caray again. And Mussolini hot to come back, he fire for Springer's head again. This time Springer step inside, and put a short stick right across Mussolini's neck. Eh heh! Mark up one for Ethiopia. Because Mussolini ent fighting again. He sprawled on the stage with his two heels beating, and the whole hall in uproar. Quick as a flash the St. John's ambulance brigade people rush up and take charge on stage. They tend to Mussolini until he could sit up. Meanwhile people're on their feet, they're calling they're shouting, and quite a few of the women have their hands over their faces. Some of them crying. Some of the men arguing whether Springer hit a legitimate blow or not. The Prime Minister sat looking steadfast at Mussolini, and you could see from his face he's feeling sick. I don't think he was ready for that kind of thing, and that was what helped bring about an end to stickfighting in his village competition.

We won in the stickfighting that night. Springer gave us the victory, and everybody could see that. But when it came to the handcraft and the carving, they thief we. Madam Benoit had baskets for all occasions. She had the one for flowers, and the one for keeping bread. Those were out of straw and coconut branches. She had the basket out of coconut husk we used to use for hanging plants. She had clothes basket, and the old-time shopping basket that they make now with wood in the bottom. She didn't have any wood in hers. She used bamboo, straw made from the banana trunk, weaving grass, coconut branches — things that grow all around here in everybody's garden. And not only baskets — Madam Benoit and her helpers had handbags, purses, hats, bracelets, little boxes for people who have jewels. They had slippers and fans, and even down to the old-time tray we used to have for fanning rice, and the flat one we used in making farine.

Madam Benoit and the other ladies had many things to show how we country people could do, and have been doing for years. In my day we grew up knowing how to do things for ourselves. The men cut mortar and pestle out of poui. And when we harvested rice we didn't carry it to no mill. We pounded it ourselves, and the husk that leave back with whatever grains we used to feed to the animals. Nowadays you take your rice to the mill, and the Indian man's giving you back half of what you take, and charging you! So we showed them all that.

Not only Madam Benoit and the ladies, but Mr. Thompson with his wood craft. Of course he had mortar and pestle. And if you see his work! Everything smooth finish. Not an edge to be felt anywhere. He had trays made out of cedar, and a whole chair which he made from one piece of mahogany trunk. He had a box mill some of us older heads still like to use in grinding our morning coffee. He had toys that children could play with, bowls, little wall hangings shaped like maps of Trinidad and Tobago. He had little saints, and a big crapaud that could frighten you until you realized it wasn't real. Who say we shouldn't come away with first prize that night?

Well, the judges say. They had this half-mix woman from I don't know where they find she, a man they say from India, another one from America they say is professor on village people. They had a local woman, the wife of some doctor from Port-of-Spain, and a young fellow with a beard striving his best to look wise but coming off like my fourth son used to be when he first left home to live among town people. His pose couldn't hide the discomfort he's bearing with his blood going one way, and his thoughts going the other. Those five they had to judge us.

You could see the Prime Minister wasn't pleased. When they announced the winner they gave everything to Tarouba, except the dance. It would have been too brazen to take that from Rosa, so we won in that. But for the stickfight, they say Springer hit an unlawful blow and that disqualified him, so we lost that. And for the handcraft, they didn't like our baskets because, they say, they were too rough. We had hand-made roses with leaf stems decorating ours, but that wasn't good enough. The other village had plastic. They had plastic in red, white, and blue and that they cut up in stripes to weave their baskets. It look nice, but where you ever hear about plastic growing in any village here in Trinidad? Some people in the crowd gave out boos, and you could see the Prime Minister wasn't too pleased.

In the wood-carving, they say Mr. Thompson's chair was too stiff and didn't have the right varnish. The furniture that won look like anything you could buy from some store in Port-of-Spain, and none of that ent make in this country. Japan, Korea, America, the Italians, that's where that shining furniture coming from. And it always fragile when you match it with our own that we make here.

You can't use it hard. It not make for people like we. We thought they
wanted to see what people here could do with their own hands. With
their wit and their talent. But they didn't want that. They say Mr.
Thompson's chair too hard. They say his coffee mill wasn't shining
enough. They didn't even try it to see how he made the screw and
handle and everything to work. They say our baskets and handbags
too coarse. They say Springer's stick too dangerous. And so they gave
the grand prize to Tarouba. They didn't even give us second. They
gave that to Williamsville because they had plastic baskets too. They
marked us third.

The Prime Minister didn't like it. He didn't like it at all, but
what could he do? When they made the announcement you see him
give a slight applause. He gave one or two claps but there wasn't any
joy in his clapping. They rushed police men up on the stage then,
and others came to guard the Prime Minister and the judges' box.
They behaved as though we were going to fight them. And some of
our stickmen were hot, but we ladies knew better than to let them
get themselves in trouble.

On the way home we were an unhappy people. I gave everybody
back their belongings, and we finish the rum. While we're drinking,
everyone talking over and over again, how such a thing could happen. They thief we. Some of us tried to console Madam Benoit, Mr.
Thompson, and the others who'd worked so hard. "What you gon
do?" I said.

"Never me again," Mr. Thompson said. "They could have village
competition with money and love for prize, never me again."

"You shouldn't say that," I answered, "because it is still our
country."

"Who country?" It would've been better if Madam Benoit was
hot. She was cold and bitter. "You see what they give prize for? This
is country for people who have money to buy whatever they're selling
in town. They don't want we."

"I done with that," Mr. Thompson said.

Rosa was the only one who didn't feel empty. "Time is changing," she said. "A new breed taking over."

"Well what kind of take over they're taking over, if they don't
know what they're taking over?" And Madam Benoit was right.

If you don't know what you have, how can you tell what to
want? And if you don't honour what you have, you can't build

anything on it. You're left naked for all the vultures who pick and feed on the covetous.

I can't lie. I tried to keep our spirits up that night, but inside, my heart hurt me. It still does, whenever I remember.

We came all the way home, and it was almost two o'clock in the morning when we got here. Lal Beharry, bless his soul, drove like an angel. He didn't look for a single drink the whole time.

When the rum finish, Uncle Red who could sing a lavwe better than anyone made the heart-break worse. He start up —

> The length o' mi bois
> Is the length of yo coffin
> Oi, oi, oi . . .

We joined in the chorus, but I really didn't want to sing that. We didn't really have anybody dead, we didn't kill anybody, and I felt it would've been better for us to sing something from church. But we didn't. We sang that song about killing, and maybe it was good for getting rid of the murder some us had at heart.

When we got to San Juan, the police stopped us. They say no singing on the road that time of night, and they followed us for a while to see if we'd start up again.

But God's grace was with us and we controlled ourselves, and Lal Beharry drove like an angel, and we got back here safe to find people waiting to receive us. Bright lights were on in the community center, and when the lorry stopped the people inside started singing —

> Welcome, welcome back my friends
> Bring your victory home . . .

They came out the door singing. The old people were there, and some young ones too, even some children among them, and it made us feel good to see them there, so glad to see us, even though they already had the news that our village lost in the competition. We didn't have television in those days, everything was battery radio. But the competition was broadcast from right there in the hall, so they knew. They consoled us. They had hugs and kisses for Rosa. I told them how much money we made — forty-two dollars and eighteen cents — and we had refreshments while everything was unloaded off the lorry.

For weeks after that, people around here attacked the judging. The school-master wrote a letter to the newspaper, and my son went to see the local councillor. But after that, nothing happened. We didn't expect anything to happen anyway.

People continued coming to the center with their bodies but many hearts began dropping out of it. The things we had taken to Port-of-Spain for the competition lay jumbled up in a corner for a while, as we talked about having an exhibition that would bring people to see our work in the village.

The talk dragged on, and we never could come to an agreement on how to make the exhibition. Somebody said we should call in a government officer to help us organize, and we did. They sent an Indian fellow, and he turned everything ole mass. He started off nice, but after a while ended up holding separate meetings with the Indians on our village council. We didn't mind that at first. But when some Indians started claiming that if any exhibition took place in the village it had to be in their end — not the village center, mind you, but in their end — we could see what was happening.

At the next meeting we take a vote — everybody could carry home whatever it was they made or helped make for the competition. People did just that. They called on me for how much money in the books, and they want to distribute that as compensation between the same people who made things and went to town for the competition, but we couldn't do that. What about the stickmen? I asked. They risk life and limb. That put an end to that question, but people carried away every piece of the wood-carving, while we're still planning on holding the exhibition, and everybody agreeing to bring their pieces back for the time we decide.

Then a new mark buss. The government officer told his friends in private the reason we lost in the best village competition was because the party — not the Prime Minister, but his party — had interest in currying favour with Tarouba. With us, our village, they had no problem. We were known for our full support of the party, the Prime Minister, everything. Tarouba was different. Tarouba was hostile ground for the party. And so to sweeten a different change somewhat they turned us aside in the competition and gave the grand prize to Tarouba.

Up to today I don't know if that's really a true story. It made sense, but it could've been no more than rumour, the kind that make people hate one another wrongly. Yet it made sense, and people seized onto it.

In time, however, we agree on a date for the exhibition, and put the news in the papers. We get them to announce it on the government radio, and we pay for handbills that we sent out to other villages and stick up wherever we could in Princes Town and San Fernando. The decision was that while the music, eating, and drinking would take place at the community center, tables with the handcrafts would go up alongside the road in the Indian quarter. That way, visitors would be encouraged to see the whole village, and mingle with all the people.

On the morning of the exhibition it rained. Rain started coming down around six o'clock in the morning, and more the day went on, blacker the sky became, and it was rain and more rain until after one o'clock in the afternoon.

A few of us took the wetting during the morning hours to get to the center, but most people didn't put a foot outside. The one or two of us there made with what we brought. Miss Margaret and myself, we started a pelau, and Jaikaran's wife with his daughter started their fire to make roti. Not a man came to help us.

We did the cooking and we had a few sweet drinks, but the drummers never quite got to the center. They stopped under the shop to shelter from the rain, and naturally had to take a drink or two to warm the body. That way, one thing led to another, and next thing we hear is drumming full blast coming from the shop, and all the merriment that should've been at the center going on over there.

The drinkers called on shopkeeper Singh to sell, and, naturally, he had to oblige his customers. When the neighbours see this, then they brought out their little sugar-cakes, and pone, and souse and other eatables to sell too.

By the time the clouds cleared, everything is happening near the shop. A few ladies ambled down to the center, but they didn't bring anything to make for visitors to see. And, in truth, we had no visitors. The local councillor came around twelve o'clock. He ran into the center through the rain for five minutes, then left for where the noise was to do his little drinking and talking. About five other outside cars came, but nobody reached up to the Indian quarter.

And there would've been no point in that anyway, because, with the rain, none of the tables went up, and there wasn't anything for any visitor to see there.

At the junction around the shop more people gathered in the late afternoon. That's where the music was. The drumming and the singing. In the end, we carried the food down there. To make back what we could, we carried the pelau and the roti down there hoping to sell, but ended up sharing it out anyway because by then people already spent most of their money on rum and beer and nearby eatables. They like the food, and they ate, promising to pay. But it would have been foolish for us to expect anything out of their promises.

And it wasn't long after we carried our trays down there that the police sergeant came. He and a constable. They wanted to know, did the men have a permit to beat drum on the road. To tell the truth, nobody even thought about that until the police came. We're an independent country. We ent thinking about permit to play we own music — that was for old-time days when white people couldn't stand to hear our drums and singing. They still can't. But they're gone now, so why we should have to get permit?

But the police and them only looking for a little grease-hand. Some of the men talked with them, and soon one or two ladies brought eggs and put in their car. They get dasheen, yam and green fig. Mr. Manny promise next time he went hunting he'd bring a manicou and pass by the station. The police get in their car and drive off. But what spirit it was that they interrupted, the whole thing break.

People start arguing whose fault it was the police had to come in the first place. Some vex because more visitors didn't come to the village, and they start accusing.

"What're they coming to see?" Mr. Benoit shout out. "What're they coming here for? You have something to show visitors? And even if you have something you think they're interested in that? All yuh village people too damn stupid."

"And who is you? Who is you?" Madam Zell shout back. "Where your mother get you? You think you ent country people too? You don't have no right opening your mouth to call people stupid. I come out mi house to have a good time — not for nobody to be calling me stupid."

"You're stupid, yes! Damn stupid!" Mr. Benoit disrespected himself. "Serious business happening here — you think this ent serious? This showing you the whole business about government and what kind of people ruling Trinidad, and all you want is a good time."

"Aie! That mi wife yo bawling at!" But Mr. Benoit didn't even hear Bajan Prince call out.

Prince and Madam Zell, they don't have no children. But you never see them one without the other. In their garden, going to church, going to town to do market, always it's two of them together. She belongs to here, but Prince was a newcomer to the village then. Her family never took part in the council, nor anything like that. They work hard, but they were a people onto themselves. Nobody knows how Bajan Prince got in with them. He's a little man who likes to stay pretty much to himself too. But he's hot-blooded.

"Aie!" Prince called out, "Aie, that's mi wife!"

But Mr. Benoit didn't hear him. " . . . Good time belong in your bed, or go down under the tamarind tree . . . " Mr. Benoit went on. "This is serious business. All yuh can't see? Village people dead in this country. They don't give a damn about we . . . " Mr. Benoit letting go everything he has penned up inside him, but with the little drink she had in her Madam Zell didn't care.

"You vex 'cause I never went under no tamarind tree with you," she called back, and everybody laughed. Everybody jamming around these two now. It's drama. "You never get," she throws, "and you don't have none to get," Madam Zell, as she turn and show her backside in Mr. Benoit's face.

"That rotten thing you have?" he called back. "Dog don't want that!"

I always say woman shouldn't curse with man because men have too many hurtful things they can say against us. And Mr. Benoit knew most of them. He shamed himself saying things about Madam Zell, but not for long.

Right when he's giving it to her, and the crowd laughing, Prince couldn't take any more and he rushed forward with one cuff in Mr. Benoit's mouth. That's what the crowd wanted.

Fighting break out right and left, with everybody scuffling. Prince and Madam Zell trying to put Mr. Benoit on the ground, one or two trying to part them, and others looking at neighbours they don't like or have a grudge against and cuffing them or butting.

Some of the older heads, with Jaikaran and Mr. Joseph from the council wrestling to part people and bring them to their senses. Then Mr. Manny told the drummers to play. "Play!" he said, "play!" And he tried to raise a kaiso. Nobody much paid any attention to his singing, but the drumming cooled things down after a while and those who had to go home left, while others still there arguing, and nobody with money, so we gave away the rest of the food. When people're eating, they don't have time for fighting.

That was a day! Neighbours dredging up long-time hatreds, and cursing one another face to face. It looked so bad, I felt shamed to the bottom of my heart.

As for the village council, people dropped off one by one, after that day, so that in a little while the government officer didn't have nobody to talk to.

All weekly meetings stopped.

The young boys took over the center then, and started carrying on their idleness there — with the one or two young girls who couldn't calm their weakness, with their tampi, and their slack talk. When it came time to brush the yard, they wouldn't do it. They didn't build no center, they say, so why they must brush yard. Or do anything else to take care of the building?

Meanwhile, the ladies carried home all the things they had brought in for doing hand-craft and different kinds of baking class. We had a pitch-oil stove. One night it disappeared. We had a sewing machine — same thing. The drums that Mr. Lavalle had made special for the center, they walked. Then somebody came and took off a window. Well, you see what we have left. The galvanize is gone. The cement floor and the few bricks we had to the front are still standing. They're holding up the vines, and giving shelter to the crapauds and scorpions. I hear an Indian man sleeping there at night, but I don't pass there night or day if I could help it.

I still have money keeping for the council. I have eighteen dollars and fifty-seven cents that belong to the council. But nobody can't claim it because there is no council.

As for the Prime Minister better village competition, I sit here in my home and watch what they're doing on television sometimes. They don't have the crafts and stickfighting anymore. And what dancing there is is watered down with everybody doing the same thing again and again. They have what they call drama. But what that is is people dress in old-time backyard rags showing how stupid they could behave. But all of that's to be expected, I believe, since it's not village people doing things for themselves, but the government paying young people like that Chinese boy to go around and show villagers how they must do on stage.

Now and then when Madam Benoit or Tan Rosa pass in we remember those past times. We look at the young people today, how they walk so aimless, and we have a promise — when one of us dies, whoever's left behind will see to it a proper bongo takes place. I want good dancing, with qua qua and drum, and whatever else people want to play. I want strong singing. Village life may be going, but it ent dead yet.

From the Field

Baptist, Circle, and Shango share much in common. Some Baptists don't like Shango, others are Shango-baptists. A few villagers are Shango devotees completely, others follow Circle exclusively. The Astral Spirits who are the powers in Circle are very busy. They keep constant tabs on their time. The Prince of Zenda with his mark, the skull and crossbones, is a leading Astral spirit. All Astrals dress in evening clothes, and when they come together for some Circle business they conduct their meeting in a businessslike fashion. They don't stand stupidness. The Astral meeting is a banquet. The Astrals travel back and forth through the universe. They are busy and usually manifest for a short time only. Astrals are like saints: they must do good work in order to reach the top — just as with Catholics. Therefore they give many benefits — in medicines, with financial problems, and general help.

Melville Herskovits was an anthropologist who early recognized patterns of cultural retention ["Africanisms," he named the details of retention] and syncretism among Blacks in the Americas as a positive trait. His analysis of Afro-American culture emphasized this "creative" aspect which the slaves brought forward, he argued, from their West African background. It is remarkable that after the weeks of fieldwork on which their text *Trinidad Village* is based, Herskovits and his wife co-worker found that "retentions of African custom in immediately recognizable form are relatively few" [287]. Their explanatory proposition was that protestantism had a devastating effect on African custom, driving it, where it survived, into subtle forms of "reinterpretations" [304]. Many anthropologists have been uneasy with the concept "reinterpretation." It is not widely called upon.

However the psychological process might best be specified, it seems clear that West African religion devolved into folklore more rapidly and completely in Trinidad, and other British colonial areas in the Caribbean, than in places like Haiti, Cuba and Brazil. These last two continued to receive unacculturated Africans in numbers late into the nineteenth century. Haiti had a successful revolt which brought former slaves to power. Trinidad, on the other hand, never had a successful anti-colonial revolt, and the African slave trade to their island territories was outlawed by the British in the first decade of the nineteenth century. No fresh Africans. The loss of contact must have been a factor contributing to the decline of African culture in the territories.

Further, for some decades before the British seized control, Trinidad had emerged as a land of opportunity for plantation developers and other entrepreneurs. The process of "development" led to an influx. Culture-bearers from various countries in Europe, Africa and The Americas, as well as from China and India, were brought into everyday contact with each other. In this complex situation cultural competition became a fundamental characteristic of the society, as did the mediating process of creolization — a pattern in which new combinations in culture, language, and personality emerge. Syncretism — the reconciliation of differing belief systems — is an historical aspect of the creolization process.

The Orisha are African powers. Shango is Orisha. Ogun is Orisha. Amanja is Orisha. Oshun is Orisha. Africans can understand African powers much better than Trinidadians. Nevertheless the Orisha are still beneficial. They will give help with medicines, and financial advice too. They are the older spirits. They don't have the businesslike manner of the Astrals. They are more eccentric. Their meeting is the feast. And whoever worships them does so through the central practice of ritual sacrifice. Orisha and Astrals can communicate in their own peculiar language.

While among devotees some Yoruba deities or orishas have come to be identified with Catholic saints — as in Cuba, Haiti, Brazil — among others they are recognized as demonic entities. Many Trinidadians today still know nothing of the legendary life of the Yoruba king Shango, or the myths based on the legends. They think of Shango as a set of superstitious practices that are really nothing more than devil worship. Maybe dangerous devil worship. Groups of devotees are small, family centered mostly, and scattered in the Black folk communities of the city and in some rural areas. Recently, some members of the Black intelligentsia have joined the folk in working for a revitalization of the religion. They emphasize the historical role of Shango in the development of Trinidadian culture, and both the cosmological and international worlds which may be accessed through this form of worship. But the pentecostal sects are growing much faster in Trinidad, and among them, the African "powers" stand for nothing but unmitigated evil.

One of the interesting devil figures of old village lore is the diablesse, the female enchantress who walks at night, and who is recognized by the uneven meter in her step because one of her feet is a cloven hoof. She is the figure in seductive petticoats, wearing a lush perfume, and a hat which shields the greater part of her face. She works the dark road, emanating warmth, and the promise of easy adventure. But she's the female devil, who leads men astray, and often to their demise.

In the legends of the orishas one finds the story of Oya — Shango's favourite among his three wives. It is told that Oya lured Shango, king of Oyo, to the *iroko* tree in the forest where, disguised as an antelope, she evoked her excellence as tempestuous woman and power, and in so doing succeeded in winning the primary place in his affection. But Oya was not all seductress: she was the wife par excellence. She could manipulate Shango, and withhold secrets from him, but she was the confidential companion and staunchest aide when his rule was threatened. She was the one who stood beside him when in consternation he looked upon the ruins of his palace, accidentally destroyed by his own hands, as in an intemperate moment he sought to prove he still had control over violent power. Oshun and Oba the other two wives had already fled home. Oya it was who accompanied Shango on his last journey, when in deep remorse he left the kingdom and walked to a distant place where he hung himself. She accompanied him in death too. For when she got the news that he had hung himself, she, too, hung herself.

Oya — orisha of the River Niger. Oya — orisha of the wild winds . . . orisha of light and fire.

Would Shango have travelled to The Americas without her?

Would she have let him? It seems quite reasonable to conjecture that she came along, to suffer with the other orisha their exile, their rejection, the loss of their children. To be brought low, from queen to female devil, in a region where memories of the shrine survive haphazardly, as half-remembered dreams.

Yes . . . it is interesting how the orishas came to be dealt with as devils in these parts. How their worship was forced underground. Even among some bold ones who claim to be devotees of Shango, Ogun, Obatala, Shokpona, care is taken to include the rosary, and a Catholic prayer or two during ceremonies. Perhaps this is a strength — the art of syncretism. Perhaps it is a confusion — the romantic memorializing of a great loss. Then again, who is to say we don't have here the seedling of regeneration?

When Oya Dances

On mornings after Oya dances in my dream the sun sucks in his face to crawl pale and lonesome across our sky. Such are not pleasant days. For at the heart of what pleasure we take in respite from the burning rays is an awakening. We see with inward eye the passing, our own transcience, and for a spell lose touch with the formalities that protect us.

I leave early on my walk as usual into town. The three miles float the same as time in its deliberate passing, indifferent to whether I hurry or take pleasure in my stride. I perspire for the cool wind and hear silence going away, rolling with it the sound of birds and trees, the occasional motor-bike, cars, the villagers themselves being stirred by their early morning bowels. We are ever immersed in satisfying some need. Some search. Some hunt. If not for land, then water. Money, warmth, food — of which we seem never to have enough — or even the other. Today, the sun pays no attention.

Aloof and pale, it takes the high path, and the women selling yams on the sidewalk become faces of the unconquerable hunger that holds us. Faces of the tunnel that known well how to warp its sides, change shapes, and in a thousand ways deceive us. Suck us on, my friend. To plant the fields, catch fish, sit up with the dead, shake mangoes from the trees, skin goats, mix concrete, feed babies, train our heads, and present ourselves to others. It is there on the faces going by me along the road. Fresh morning faces. Rested. Peace curls almost within reach, they say. And for the moment let's not think of mirages. Let's forget the jeering, slashing refrain — Almost caught again, that time: come forward.

And me, the wanderer, ex-pastor of the flock who walks this town and all the country roads around? They say, I know, That one there has lost his senses. Touched. Mad. From over-working the brain. From too many days bare head under the sun. Or, somebody put him so. My passing moves them to recall among themselves that Claude, the youngest of three brothers who inherited the pastorate from his father had been called. He was chosen. He was named, identified the main voice in the family home, the pulpit voice which carved a path for life in the village.

Among themselves my passing moves them to recall that when Ma Holder died her son living Sangre Grande side brought his out-side woman to occupy the house. Nobody in the village had ever seen her before they showed up — he in a garbadine suit and silk shirt, she wearing a red dress that made its own music standing in the dry goods section apart from the village women, while he fired one or two with his old friends in the rumshop. He never introduced her. But when he left to go back home to his wife and family she remained behind, and everyone understood.

They will tell you if you remain to listen that he took to coming every other week-end to the village. That between time Emelda was her own woman — a hot-blooded pyol, it was plain to see, who fooled them at first and started going to church. The young men were after her, but she had no time for them. She attended church regularly. And then, at last, it became clear what her object was. Pastor Claude in his prime of manhood . . . who could when he preached move the sky to open its doors and reveal all the wonders of heavenly existence. Who could make the trials and travail of earth seem like blessings when compared with the contorting agony of everlasting death in hell. They saw how his voice made her tremble. They saw how she helplessly opened what she had to catch his eye-beam. She was his trial.

They welcomed this at first. Their young pastor whom they loved, whose ordained mission it was to lead them through the arduous pitfalls of this life and bring them to the stars, in her he faced his trial. They gloried in anticipation of his triumph. They waited for the day when this evil woman — what else could she be, this hot-blooded pyol, living her secret sin so openly for a man with wife and family? — when she would be broken to confess the demon in her flesh. And in their silence goaded her on. Behind her back they noted how her gyrations came more intensively and with unmasked intentions. They watched the champion pastor gird himself, and revelled in his warriorhood. They will tell all those who wish to hear that they even knew when he took to praying alone in the church every fo'day morning — his lonesome Gethsemane. They will describe him on his knees before the cross, and they didn't have to hear his words to know what he was asking.

They knew when the pyol diablesse took to shadowing him in the dawn, how she came out in her shawl for early morning walks timed so her rumbling heat smote him in the face first thing, as he emerged from his audience with the Saviour. They knew when he weakened too. At first they were shocked that he might break. Then visions of his coming back from the brink triumphant, in glory, drove them to anticipate a deeper ecstasy, and they waited.

Then one day he fell. His prayer had gone well, and yet when he came out the door of the church and saw her taking herself by in that first light he followed her. Single-mindedly followed her. As if to say, 'Yes demon. Today I will meet you in your cave. I will smash you. I will bend you and smash you into a thousand pieces. I will discard you to the wind. I will finish you forever.' But things didn't turn out that way. The pyol woman gave and gave. When he thought 'Ah, hah! I have finally broken the bottom' she did not cry submission, beg forgiveness. She gave some more. Claude dangled on the brink a while, but before long she became his major ministration.

At dawn, or dusk, in broad day and the deep of the night she was his tutoring obsession. The thunder in his voice ceased to roll. The beam-flash from his eye curved down, and spent what little force it had mocking what he used to be. He lost his message. Like an obedient slave he threw himself again and again to her bottomless fire. When Ma Holder's son came on his week-end visits and the pyol woman had to do her duty, Claude went insane kept away as he was from doing his. When he took to shaming himself outside the shop on such occasions they had no choice — they stopped going to church. They stopped asking Claude to visit the sick, and took their babies elsewhere to be offered up.

They were disappointed. They believed just the same that there was a divine teaching in Claude's fall, and they tested their interpretations on one another. As he dried up to a shrivel in his own agony they grew cold. Then they became enraged when the diablesse who wasn't even baptized moved herself off the back bench and took a seat in the front pew. As though she had control over the pulpit. They asked Claude to leave. They voted him down.

At first he refused to leave, claiming the union between blood and privilege. His brothers put an end to that. One day Claude came to the woman's house with a grip and a bundle in his hands. He had dried blood on his shirt. His brothers had driven him out, he said, and he needed a place to stay.

You can't stay here, she told him. This is Malcolm's house. I can't bring no man to stay here. . . .

When he wanted to leave his things for a while, again she said no. And they saw him come down from her gallery, take the road out of the village with his things in his hands.

That night he came back again and asked her to let him in. She wouldn't. They watched him. Nobody offered to take him in, no one asked how he'd make out. Nobody wondered whether he'd walked to Princes Town or Point. They never asked whether he'd take the road to Moruga.

They watched him come again and again to Malcolm's house, and nobody told him when the woman left. Nobody told him when the brothers visited her too, and that soon after they did she hired a taxi to take her and the clothes and wares she had out of the village.

He talked for a while to the empty house, thinking she was in there, thinking that with a few more words she might be moved to let him in. The villagers watched and laughed. Soon the children followed him, and gave him names.

He walked then. He walked first east, then to the west. It was the soothing thing to do. He walked, and if his feet took him to the village he passed the church without a glance, but looked at Malcolm's house wistfully, consoling himself that one day she would be there. . . . That's what they will tell you.

But not one will stand witness for the founding deities. Not many could say that they have witnessed the powers present themselves, or that they have come to know the pain, the agony the divines are undergoing. The pyol one they say is demon. I know her as the thought through which I am to be invaded, through which the echo comes that swallows me, that shuts out my heartbeat and rolls me from time through memory to the vision of our divines caught in agony, driven to delirium over their children in exile. It fell upon me secretly. Perhaps without intention, or knowledge on her part. But I've come to be the witness of our exile, our sojourn here without the dance, that ecstasy or flight which is our bridge to ease and calm submission. No hymns of redemption here. And when she up on her delicate hoof goes into dance, when she, orisha of the tempest rings me in her whirling arms what could I do? When the whirlwind conjures her posture toppling the bone in us, what am I to do? Clamp my jaws, yes, and battle for sterility? Or give way and be ladled on the path which flows from exile through submission?

I chose the dream. They had other names for it, but then, how could they know? Oya, the wind that sweeps all before her, is never careless with the dance. She is the messenger of fire: devotion is her major key. I chose. And those who see me clearly catch much more than an old man clothed in rags. They see the light to which I've been re-born. The young ex-pastor drummed out of his village had a great deal to learn. There was much early pain in leaving behind the geography to which he was first born, and in the beginning his only thought was to make distance. Guayaguayare, Toco, Chaguaramas, Cedros, he walked the corners of the land, his sack carrying nothing but a few books, the papers, fruit, some bread. He slept beside the road, then walked, and read, and talked where he could with others who like himself were sucked into that geography of motion in exile. He walked, he talked, he ranged with others who'd been dislodged into the ranks of the undefeated, until at last he came to give himself to light. Now he returns, and in his passing faces west by day, east during the night, his face always before the sun. They see me passing, make way for me to pass, not in reverence, but in that dilate state of fear concealed as humour. They laugh. They grin. The black, brown faces open, the teeth clatter about. The eyes squeeze tight with laughter. What a world!

In the heart of town the haberdashery with its pleading high-pitched song amidst a clash of prints, pots, pillows, hangs as the over-burdened image of those unending needs we address with trifles. It leaves an empty feeling, compounded by the Indian on his stool hunched over the horoscopes spread open on the counter hunting his correct aspect . . . *Jupiter in Virgo says — a time for expanding business goals and interests: you must spend to make; control impulses; be practical in financial matters and the goal is yours; do not be arrested by friends or manners along the way; keep track of expenses. . . .* Shop-girls, clerks, drivers, laborers, gamblers, drunks, big-bottomed women hung in cloth and half-filled shopping bags, police, councillor, priest and judges too, we are all chaff on the celestial wind that comes from where it is not given us to know, on its way to where we'll never find out.

I walk, and on such a day it is the yearning comes. I wonder why I have no home. Why prosperity never anchored me. Nor land, nor blood of any kind. It is the wind. I feel the tug of geography. Up and down. Around. The hills and fields. The trees, and sandy stretches curved around blue water going far away, going far away, and up and overhead, to where I'll never know, but go I must as it takes me. It is on such a day I walk in battle with that need for pride and permanence.

I go to the back window where they pass out old-age pension. I take my place in the morning line and shuffle the pieces of purple, green, and red print from the teller's hand into my pockets then hurry off again. Banks are the most unpleasant places. They have gone beyond the curtain of the horoscope. So solid are they in the eternity they allocate, the distance keeps their fingers cold. Their eyes and lips function from afar, rigidly remote, organs of some special tribe endowed with — Grace? Eternity? The final blessing? None of these. They are the priesthood without priestliness, vanguard of a new ice-age, and I run from them as soon as I get the exchange which will help me make Bobo happy.

On days like this when the sun is pale and sombre, it is no good passing time with the civil servants of my vintage who out of pity — or perhaps as antidote to their uneasy success — still tolerate my presence. They are decent people, for the most part. Well-meaning too. But they never know what to do when I start talking of the curtain which sometimes draws apart. They fidget, and go silent, and turn their eyes away, or steal surreptitious looks at each other. They wait. And when sufficient time has passed one of them would say Ahem! Well, yes. Now as to so-and-so . . . which has nothing at all to do with what I open before their eyes. Bobo is different.

Bobo is a drummer. Not just any kind of drummer, he's a Shango drummer. He knows the bata. He knows things. He sees, he hears, and when the powers call on him he knows how to give in, give himself up so they may speak, cavort, bring care and discipline for their sons and daughters. We are all their children. Many of us don't know it. Some who know reject it, but that's what we are. Bobo knows. When Obatala lights on him, his round black face shines. He grows tall and spare, cadaverous with wisdom. He reads the spirals of the snail, and in a drone like swarming bees reveals the messages surrounding the first womb where light and darkness did their work so we may see. Under Obatala trees tell when their fruit will ripen, chickens how their eggs will hatch. Disease if out of time comes forward to confess, and where in time answers clearly why life must end so. All secrets come out to defend themselves, petition us for their release. Secrets cannot stand secrecy. Obatala tells. Bobo knows.

Or again I've seen him seized by Ogun. Short, squat, with a round belly his cheeks puffed out like bellows, lips cracked from the blistering heat of the forge. Ogun makes everything tremble. Wherever he tramps the earth shakes. And all who never knew fear would know it then, a power that makes all things of blood fall under our hands, and drives us on. At the feast Ogun glares. Bobo drinks a full bottle of rum right down without stopping for breath. He calls the dead, and warns all hands against being raised to harm his children. Until dawn breaks, and exhausted, he must withdraw to sleep. Bobo is a store of what we wish to know. But he is a Shango-man, and it calls for courage to take him seriously.

Bobo is a gambler too, and when I found him at the club he had just ended an all night game of whapee. As they filed out of the back-room, his eyes were red from sleeplessness. The other gamblers moved grey and heavily with tiredness, and some lay down on benches around the wall to recover their sleep. Others, on momentum, sat in the open window. They looked out on the late school-girls passing by in their uniforms, the women on their way from market, and they talked about why they lost, what they would have done if the cards had fallen differently. But Bobo was happy. He was a winner that day, and I counted that as my good fortune.

He wanted to eat fried chicken and chips, but the Indian girl behind the counter said it was too early for that. Bobo settled for bread and cheese. He ordered two beers, and we sat down at one of the dusty tables. He spread yellow pepper on his cheese and asked "Wha happen to you? You look like dog bite you, Sport."

"Dreaming," I told him. "He's pale today, weak and yellow."

"Oh ho! I did feel the going down whole night, yes, but I didn't stop to follow. These fellas here like shark this dry season. So that is what! You're making your rounds already?"

"I stop by the bank, yes. You have time, I'll take a taxi with you up to the beach. . . . "

That's what we would do at a regular time like this. It is the one time when I would ride in car up to the eastern water and make the day go backwards. The canopy of trees that goes right down to the sea saves us from above, and by the time we're on the beach the sun's off to the side, and we could stare across the water without seeing our shadows. Sometimes we never went all the way to water, but stopped at the shaded shop in Marac, and over some bottles of beer and White Star finish the day talking between ourselves and with the villagers who know. But today Bobo could not go.

"I can't make that one today, boy," he said.

"I have money."

"I know that. I have money too. And that's especially why I can't make. You see them fellas in the window? Minute they catch their breath they're making a rounds and coming back for me. That's what I'd do too . . . you understand. . . . "

I understood. Though I never gamble, I know the code, and it's an honourable one. But I couldn't stand it being by myself on such a day. I waited.

"You want another beer?" Bobo asked.

We had another round, but I had guiness instead of beer. Bobo was tired, I could see that, but I couldn't bring myself to go away as yet and allow him to sleep.

"See those fellas leaving?" he said.

I looked up, and the gamblers who were in the windows were now walking through the door, cigarette smoke across their eyes, hands in their pockets, the saunter in their stride telling of their profligate mission, the unpredictable nature of their lives.

"You see them?" Bobo said. "When they come back here is war," he added, patting the roll of paper money in his shirt pocket.

"It's the dreaming," I said. "Four nights in a row. And then today. . . . "

"What kind of dreams?" Bobo asked.

"The same one."

"All four times?"

"Same one."

Bobo stood up. "Leh we go in the back-room," he said. He called to Marie, the girl behind the bar, "We're in the back-room. Bring more beer. Chicken and chips too, when you start up."

The back-room, a narrow walled-off section of the club without windows is always thick with the hang of stale cigarette smoke and dry dust. Bobo switched on the electric light hanging from the ceiling and closed the door behind us. He rocked a chair back against the wall and put his feet up on the scarred wooden table where money changes hands. I couldn't sit like that. I turned two chairs to face each other, and sat in one with my feet up on the other. In his pose, Bobo would sleep, I knew. But that didn't matter. "You have to tell me," he said. "Tell me this four time dream. I'm feeling it already. The sun wearing skirt today, so I know a woman in the whole thing. Tell me what happen."

I watched Bobo lean his head against the wall and close his eyes. His face went slack, and I could see the stubble coming grey and silent, row by row over the black skin, skirting around his chin, and searching for the boundary at his nostrils. We had neither trees nor open water and it would have been better if we had drums. Then Obatala would have come and restored everything. But the back-room was a quiet place except for the two of us breathing, and "Say what happen," Bobo commanded.

"It's a dream.

At night we walked past Big Hill and Frederick and walked all the way to Corosan. We crossed two cocoa estates that are now in teak, the five of us. I was in my youth again, and so were Harold, Johnny, Roy, and Alwyn. We were The Five. Healthy, tall, and handsome, we were the pride of our village, and its envy too. Show us the unspeakable and we said it. The unattainable, we do it. We were the heart of the village football team, we were the warlords on the cricket side. We knew how to dress and talk to girls, and when we danced even our worst rivals had to give us credit. We were the hunters who went at night into the deep forest and never came back empty-handed. Tatu, lappe, quenk, and when we didn't feel like pushing too hard we brought out manicou regularly.

Johnny held three dogs. Harold had the carbide reflector strapped to his head, and the tank tied at his waist. He carried the lance. The rest of us had our cutlasses. The moon was there before us, and in the dead of night it held the teak trees still and silent so we could hear the blood pounding in our veins. When the dogs scented manicou they tugged at Johnny, but he wouldn't let them go. He switched them with the small branch of shining bush he carried and drove them on. At a ravine where the grass grew up to our waist he stopped us. 'You hear that?' Johnny asked.

Moonlight glinted off the dewy grass and we waited. No sound came. Nothing moved in the bush behind us, and across the ravine things were just as quiet. Johnny was dead serious. We went on down through the grass, and Harold moved hard and slow like sliding stone. He was our finisher when we cornered animals. He came up to drive in the lance. He moved sly as listening stone, and when he came to the trickling water in the bottom he said, 'Something's out here tonight.'

We didn't answer. Johnny and the dogs splashed across, and we followed. We left the wild grass behind and were in the middle of a narrow open paddy when the scent came down strong on us. It was like ladies-of-the-night in bloom, stink-toe, and agouti musk all in one. On top of that a freshness came like snakes, and Roy whispered 'Mappipre!' The dogs were whining.

'Nah,' Alwyn answered. He was the skinniest and tallest of us. He put his nose up to the sky and added, 'That's not animal.'

'You have the matches?' Johnny asked.

'They're dry,' Harold answered.

Suddenly the dogs lunged. They broke loose. They bounded for the bush beyond the paddy, and we, our cutlasses to hand dashed out behind them. They charged across the muddy bank, out of the open moonlight and we followed them on into the thick brush. We scrambled up the hill, pulling ourselves up on balisier, sage, mosquito bush. At the crest our trail went down again, and we did too, sliding on our feet where we could, trying not to get too far behind the dogs. We could hear them. Down through the whipping underbrush and then more trees, until Harold called for us to stop.

'Johnny and Bobo go left,' he called. 'Roy, you and Alwyn together next side. We're going up. I in the middle. Don't let nothing pass!'

Harold knew hunting. He knew that quenk and agouti were masters at doubling back, so that while you're thinking they're infront of you they're already far behind.

We spread out. We could hear the dogs had stopped running, but from their bark it was hard to tell whether they had cornered something or had missed the trail. They barked as though they had lost interest. Johnny and I went left and picked our way toward the barking. We spread a little ways apart, and I knew he was listening. I was listening too. We could hear Harold calling, 'Hoo! hoo! hoo!' like a night owl, and if I didn't know where we had left him it would have been hard to tell what direction his voice came from. It came from behind and in front, as well as to the side where I knew he was advancing. I was trying to keep in a straight line with my eyes and ears open, when suddenly the dogs began to whimper.

Johnny dashed off. I could hear him hacking and crashing ahead, and I tried speeding up too. But the ground there had holes, besides being slippery. Harold called 'Hoo! hoo! hoo! All yuh hearing me?'

Everybody called back except Johnny, and I knew he was anxious for his dogs. I ran as best I could, and scrambled where I had to, and by the time I topped the rise the dogs went silent altogether. When I broke into the clearing under a silk cotton tree, my cutlass ready, I spot something light in the shadows. I stopped. And when it moved again I saw it wasn't anything but a jackass. I thought, 'Somebody's donkey got away,' and looked around for Johnny because he should have gotten there before me, but he wasn't anywhere in my vision.

Then the jackass turned. It came into a patch of light under the silk cotton and right there before I could say hoo! it turned into a lady dressed in white, tall and wearing full petticoats, and with a broad hat come down over her face. The scent almost knocked me down. Hot and sweet, like tar mixed with talcum powder, it made my throat dry. I couldn't move. I didn't know what to do. The tall woman turned as if to go away, then turned back to look at me. Only she wasn't looking at me at all. She was dancing. I opened my mouth to call Harold, but the voice stuck in my throat. Then, 'Come little darling. Don't be afraid,' I heard the words distinctly. The woman was still dancing.

Alwyn and Roy burst through into the clearing right then. Same time Harold did too. He walked in a straight line for the dancing lady, and when he crossed about half the clearing he struck match to the lamp. He kept the light on her and raised his lance. And right as he started charging forward to put it in her she turned into a massive deer and in one bound passed over us. Harold yelled and threw the lance. The rest of us turned to watch her passing. She flashed right through the trees, an arc of light, the lance lost behind her, then she dropped out of sight.

Roy, Alwyn and me, we caught up with Harold chasing into the bush. We rushed to where we knew she must have come down to the ground. We fought the branches, slashed right and left as we hurried, but when we got there all was silent. We stood, waiting, but all that came was our own breathing. No smell but our own mingled with the dewy leaves mashed down around us. Harold swept left and right with the reflector. He put his light into the trees. He turned it all around in every direction, but she was nowhere in sight and he cursed, 'Blasted diablesse! I catch you here tonight is poonyah in your ass!' he shouted. 'Wey mi lance?'

"You find it?" Bobo asked, as though stepping out of a light sleep.

"We turned to look for Johnny," I said.

"And where's the lance?"

"It lost. We're looking for Johnny now."

"You find him?"

"We find him. But something else happen before that."

"The dogs? . . . "

"Not the dogs. They're gone."

"What then?"

"We decided to turn back. It would have to be the first time we returned from a hunt empty-handed, but we decided not to go on. Harold called out Johnny's name. No answer. He called again, still no answer. He turned to me then and asked if Johnny went a different way.

'I don't know,' I said. Which I didn't, really.

'How you don't know? And the man went with you?'

'You're getting vex for nothing,' Alwyn said to Harold. 'Better to look around and call than to get vex over nothing.'

'You call this nothing?' Harold had the cutlass in his right hand, but with the lamp turned off all our faces were in shadow and I couldn't tell what he was thinking. 'The dogs gone! Mi lance gone! Johnny gone! You call that nothing?' He was hot all right.

'You vex because you ent get nothing to stab,' Roy said.

'Who say I ent have something to stab?' Harold was shouting.

I knew that he meant me, and I looked to the others. But they had already turned their backs and began walking off. I knew he was going to stab me. I could hear the cutlass come already whistling in the shadow, feel it drive me back and to the ground. I could tell already exactly how everything was going to happen, even to how I raise my hand and open my mouth to speak but couldn't get a word out. When suddenly a high wind passed. The ground upheaved. A clap of thunder greater than all I had ever heard put together burst out. The sky went dark, and the ground we were standing on rumbled. It caught us stock still, while whole trees broke off, bush and dirt blacked out the moon then fell back from the sky. Miraculously, none of us fell down, and nobody got hit with anything heavier than some dirt and light branches. With all the tree-tops around us gone we were standing bare under the open sky, and 'Volcano,' Alwyn said. We understood. When we found Johnny he was naked on his back in a nest of roseau, his clothes scattered back, his cutlass on the ground, and a big branch from the silk cotton tree across his chest down to the lower part of his body.

'You see that?' Harold was in tears. 'We ent do you nothing!' he screamed to the tall lady who was back, dancing in mid-air before us, spreading her scent of tar and blossoms everywhere across the night. 'You see that?'

Without a word she forced us to sit down. She came. She danced. Her petticoats billowed about our heads. She never showed her face. She danced. And when her light became too much for us, the dream ended."

When I looked across the table after talking, Bobo was fully asleep this time, his lower jaw slack, his hands interlaced comfortably across his stomach. The girl had brought beer, and there were three untouched bottles on the table. The other was halved infront of Bobo, although I never saw when he drank from it. I shifted my chair to stand up, and without opening his eye Bobo said, "I hear everything. Never mind it look like I'm sleeping, I hear everything. So what you want to do now, Sport?"

"What do you think to do?" I said.

"Well, your dream is a mixed up business, you know. There's fooling going on some place. Everybody know already that last part is the Devil's Woodyard, right?"

That was true. The story was well known in the villages that one night two Indian fellows who were stealing mora trees to make coal came to a clearing in the forest to rest and take a drink. What they didn't know is that they sat on an old volcano. Not a big one like Pele or Soufriere, just a little fellow that goes up every once in a long while. But when that happens, everything in sight shifts and trembles. The ground rumbles. An explosion hits the air taking all sound for miles out of the countryside, leaving raw fear alone for all who hear it. Huge trees fly about then land all broken up. And those who could control their gut from trembling bless God for sparing them another time, give thanks for the mercy which sheltered them that day from the devil at work in his big woodyard. But for the most part ours is a tame volcano. It put up little cold mud puddles which spread and dries like pure cement. That's why there was a clearing. In that mud nothing could grow. But the Indian fellows didn't know, and they sat there resting. One fellow had the bottle up to his head when the blast came, the story says. It blew him, several trees, and a shower of mud twenty feet up in the air. When his dazed partner recovered enough to search, he found him dead under the trunk of a huge mora. Everybody knows the story.

"So how that get mixed up in there?" It was like Bobo to quarrel with a dream.

"It's a dream, Bobo. Anything could happen."

"True. But not so. You had any drums? You hear any drums?"

"Not a drum," I said. "Just the five of us, and the tall lady who danced then disappeared without a word."

"You see? . . . " Bobo sat forward and took a long drink from his beer. "You see that? How you could have dance and no drumming?"

"I'm telling you, Bobo." My throat was dusty and dry and I reached for a beer. "I'm telling you, no drums."

"Well then I don't know what kind of a dream that is. You know the lady?"

"I couldn't see her face, but she didn't look like the one I know for sure."

"And how about those fellows — Harold and Alwyn and Roy and . . . who's the other one?"

"Johnny. Fellows from my boy days. Harold, Johnny . . . were my two brothers. Everyone of them dead now. Johnny trapped in a sawmill where he worked. Harold stabbed in a fight. Alwyn killed himself drinking, and Roy, he went out with a fishing crew off Manzanilla one day and none of them ever came back."

"I know. And you're sure you never see the lady?"

"How could I be sure? My lady comes in many forms. . . . "

With the heel of one hand and his fingers Bobo starts drumming on the table. He leaned his head to one side as though favouring his right ear, and drummed. He finished the beer, and drummed again. "You should've heard that," he said.

"What?"

"That is Oya," he shifted his left ear, then raised his chin to look at me. "She is the one who went to market with Shango. She is the one who has no love for hunters. She is the one who did not stay behind when the king went on his last journey of sorrow . . . Oya . . . Tell me for real," he finished, "you really had any volcano?"

"That was my addition," I said. "She danced a long time and we didn't know how to stop her from dancing."

Bobo drummed harder. Already a sweat was forming on his forehead. The shirt under his arms was wet, and little beads rolled down his throat and spread out along his collar-bones. "You should've heard this," he said, bending low over the table. "She danced with light, not so?"

"It was too much for us. The dream ended."

"She danced with light for you fellows and all you could do was think about hunting."

"It was too much, I said. Besides, look what it did to Johnny."

"So what you want to do, live life forever?"

"Our bones got tired," I remembered.

"And she laughed. Did she laugh?"

"Not in the dream, but I could hear her now inside my head hissing with a roar. . . . "

"She laughed. That's Oya." Bobo's eyes were closed now, and his head swung from side to side in time with his drumming. He reached inside his shirt and straightened his necklace. Then he said, "Gimme this," pounding a measure with both hands on the table.

I know it. It is the throb beneath my score. I did it. I picked it up, and we made the beer bottles dance around their stains on the dusty table.

"That's her," he said. "Oya . . . "

"Our bones were tired, and she left us scattered there without our clothes. We didn't know what to do," I said.

"That is Oya. Our lady who goes before the fire. . . . " Bobo drummed harder and looked straight at me. " . . . our virgin who brings the message of thunder . . . our lady of justice! She knows how to make all male things listen. And when they do, she'll teach them how to fly. And yet you ask me . . . you ask me why the sun's wearing his skirt today? Ha ha ha!" Bobo laughed.

I gave it back to him. I laughed too. I had to laugh with him. Bobo reared with laughter. The sweat ran down his throat and his skin gleamed. His eyes closed, and his whole body gave itself to the rhythm we were making. We did it to the table and we laughed. We let it come out harder, until we turned back the day. When we reached the irresistible crescendo the Indian girl came to the back-room door and peeped in, then shut it quickly and went away. After she left, one or two of the gamblers came. They hung in the doorway and watched us, then closing the door they too turned away. What did they see? Two grown men. One bare-headed in the rags of a former long-sleeved shirt drenched in sweat, the other in the flop-brim panama Bobo always wears to hide his head from electric lighting pounding the table, laughing. How insane, the looks on their faces say. But they wouldn't have seen our vision, the angle out of which Oya danced and beckoned.

When I thought on all they wouldn't see I began to get tired. Bobo saw, and he stopped it. The Indian girl came again with a plate of fried chicken pieces covered with pepper sauce. We ate.

We finished the chicken, and Bobo called for more beer. When she came with four fresh bottles on her little round tray the Indian girl was followed by two of the gamblers who came right in and sat down. One already had a deck of cards in his hands, flipping the faces down onto the table and gathering them up again. The other, a spare coal-black fellow with a scar crossing his right eye-lid said, "Yuh ready?"

Bobo did not answer immediately. "I hope yuh ent spend up that take and telling me how you send money for your sick mammy in Moruga," scar-face said, and the other two gamblers laughed.

These are a type of Bobo's friends I don't appreciate. They make me uncomfortable. Anyone who never looks up makes me uncomfortable.

"You get something to eat?" Bobo asked them.

"Long time," the one with the scar said. "What you two old fellas doing back here — calling Shango to help you?"

"With fish like you I don't have to do that," Bobo said. A change pass over him. His voice was still mellow and friendly, but a hardness crept in underneath. "I'll have one foot in the grave and all yuh young boys will still have to come to me for lessons."

"I like to hear old folks talk like that," said scar-face, reaching in his pocket and pulling out a roll of money which he dropped onto the table.

It was time for me to go. "Well Bobo," I said, "it's time for me to go."

"You all right?" he asked. His eyes were still red but had lost their tiredness. The stubble on his face was more firmly grey, and his forehead shined from the sweating.

"I'm good, man," I told him. "Good."

"You're walking which part now?"

I knew he would ask, and I said, "To my sister Marjorie. You know, she's living Manahambre side. . . . "

"Good. Good," Bobo said. "Take care with the motor-cars." And as I was leaving he reached in his shirt pocket to pull out his roll of money.

Outside, the sun was slanting for the west, pale and lonely. The mangoes and the sapodillas, I barely felt their shadows. The market was still open, but most of the stalls were unattended, covered with bags. The few mashuns holding open stations were taking something to eat and chatting quietly among themselves. It is just about a mile to Manahambre. The beef stall was closed, but a small flurry of shoppers around where fish is sold drew me. I went there. Two young Indian men were selling from a basket of carite, claiming the fish to be fresh that day, straight from Mayaro. But the old film across the dead fish eyes, the colourless gills, told that they were lying. Iced-fish. But with only a mile or so to go, I bought one. At the front, near the outside end of the market I bought a hand of sikiye figs, then started out.

With only a mile or so to go I started out for Manahambre. School children early out in their little uniforms were playing themselves along the way. The breeze, still fresh, carried a faint scent of the distant sea, and salt birds hovering in the air. I do not answer when they call me. The children love to tease, but I do not answer.

From overhead the sun pokes weakly at my face. There is no command in his presence. What else? What else to expect from the day
following a night's cavorting? I walk on.

Marjorie will cook. She will make a broth. She knows how to
do the fish with thyme and onions, shadow-beni and whole peppers.
She knows how to let the sikiye boil until their jackets split. And after
that, after a decent plate of food I'll wait until dark and walk again
to Moruga. I'll go to the beach where fishermen tell stories and mend
their nets by flambeaux. There I'll keep my back to the east and look
for sleep, perhaps dream with a different dancer. Oshun, Iemanja,
Elegba, Obatala — either one might visit. When morning comes I'll
awake with the stretch of clear open water behind me. I'll watch, and
wait, until the sun sends first light from behind the clouds. Then I'll
walk. As long as the little black spots don't dance before my eyes,
forcing me to look for shade beside the road, I'll walk. . . .

Who's Speaking Here?

The Politician

He was a regular village boy who came from a well-known family. He never went to college or law school, but he was a hard worker. From working around the courts he learned something about legal practice, and he developed a penchant for public advocacy. When party politics came, he joined the leading party. In 1971 he was nominated as the party candidate for his district, and won. He was a good man. A generous man. He held an open door to everybody, and worked his best at making life better for those who came to him. He was a moral man. An honourable man. But he had no flair. His term in the legislature, where he was a good party supporter, was quiet and undistinguished. He was not nominated for a second term. When he returned to the village and quietly resumed his life in the wooden cottage where he was born, some villagers couldn't help making the observation — 'He in government for so long, and couldn't even get a house built for his mother.' He was a good man, and they liked him, but he was a failure.

In the Field

Coming Home to Stick and Steel

All the young people
Many of the old
   the vision up in the distance

before their eyes
On a bump-itty-bump music
With union on the bumps alone.
The steelband is a cumbrous instrument
Lugu bri ous motion
Face to face: rump to rump
A mindful motion in the imitation of trance
Impossible trance in the gales of consequence
    deadened and cynical laughter.
Trinidad pain knows no neighbor
Is come drink your rum

Curry down, the promise of booty
Who can pay for whom
Who pays most for whom
Sai Baba, and other consequenceless religions.

Underneath this all is the drum
The drum that is no longer known in Europe
Drum of Africa India Amerindia
The people without drums are
Trinidad's worst enemies.
The people with false drums are
Trinidad's worst enemies
To give away the drum for
    an amplified guitar?
To give away the song for
    plastic imitations of woe
Give consciousness to ganja
As though the drum
    had never told about
The return of blood
The ritual passage!

At the Second Desk

Some townspeople asked in the wake of the 1983 invasion of Grenada, 'Who could stop America if a decision is taken in Washington to over-run Trinidad?' Just as, 'Who could stop the

Japanese from over-fishing the waters?' And, even, closer to home, when Venezuelan border patrols arrest and abuse Trinidadian fishermen for drifting into supposedly international waters, what does the Trinidadian government do beside "talk?"

On every side, internationally, nationally, and otherwise, Caribbean societies operate from a position of powerlessness that keeps them open to being moved by others, and poised to be hostile to each other in the pursuit of individual self-interest. Awareness of such vulnerability challenges any faith in the integrity of local cultural systems.

The balance between individual and community interests is not predicated on any immutable moral. It is contingent. It shifts back and forth in response to the current status of significant variables — chief among them, the economic variable. A good deal of cultural energy, then, is given to negotiating.

This state of affairs means dealing incessantly with questions of power and powerlessness. It means constant effort to locate and assert from one's high ground; or call up the fortitude for surviving the pressure of being on low ground; or be innovative, in translating or interpreting experience as empowerment. Reference as metaphor. Enchantment increasingly disappears as assertions of its presence stridently takes its place.

I Witness

So it was that night in council meeting when we start arguing about street lights for the village. First of all we had Teacher talking for one side, and Pharoh for the other — two people who naturally can't stand one another. Pharoh is our madman. He's crazy a lot of the time. And Teacher, he wasn't no ordinary person like you or me — no, no. He was brown-skinned, had dohgla hair and straight teeth, dressed everyday with white shirt and tie, because he was learning and knowledge, the better class and our future all tied up in one. He was flag carrier for what civilize mean, in his garbadines and flannels and Elite silk shirts, and couldn't stand the sight or smell of Pharoh.

To be truthful, Pharoh wasn't easy. Some of us stay on good terms with him because when he is in the mood he makes the best mountain dew anybody ever could taste, bar none. He is master at that, and so we drinkers don't take on his cursing much. That is his habit. He comes from a whole family that's like that. His old father, his brother and sisters, cousins and them, they all congregate on their family land near the pond and separate from the rest of the village by that lonesome stretch pass the church. They live a law unto themselves. They do everything church teaching say people mustn't do. Most of them never go to school for long, their children run about in rags, and though they make garden to feed themselves goat, pig, fowls, everything live in their yards as they please. No special living space for thing or people. Bold dog eat out of the same plate as babies sometimes, and if one of the women get hot and want a thing she's apt to deal with whoever's close at hand, and it's all the same. That's true. That's how they live.

Many more in the village beside Teacher couldn't stand the sight of that family. But give Pharoh his due, he tried to come out. While many of us rampant wicked with our boy days, Pharoh struggle to be acolyte in the church. But the particular priest he served was a madman himself going around trying to chase Shango from the village. Some people say it was he who made a mistake in one of his exercising rounds with Ogun that turn Pharoh crazy. All kinds of things happen to people who serve priests. They carry that fellow away from here in a van. And he leave Pharoh behind to walk the road. For years now Pharoh walk the road because he has to. On any given day, at any time or hour, when the power take him Pharoh has to get up and walk.

From the village to Princes Town, to San Fernando, and back again. So he goes. And only the Lord knows how some driver hasn't knocked him down yet, or how he isn't dead from the beatings he does get from people who don't know him. Because Pharoh has the dirtiest tongue, and he lash anybody with it. He has to preach while he's walking. He has a memory for the Bible that could put the Pope to shame, and he could preach the signs of Revelations or the inner teachings of the gospels. But from preaching one minute, he can turn to the worst kind of cursing the next. Nobody knows what makes him do that. He curse anybody happen to be passing by, he curse his father and mother, the sky, the breeze, airplanes, and other things and people he alone know. Pharoh isn't easy. But he's not all madness either.

He calls himself The Messenger and say he's a warning to this village. Whatever. But times now and again I feel cursing deep down inside of me miself. I want to curse everybody and everything to hell up, tell everything kiss-mi-ass, and go take a breeze by miself. That's true. Some of the other fellows too. We feel that. I don't do it, because somebody's got to keep up what respect is and show it to the young ones. Pharoh different from the rest of us not in kind, only in his open publicity and too much of it.

That's why Mack, Carter, me, Jo-Jo, and some others, we stand up for his right to enter when we have village council. He belongs here. Some others, especially the women, they want to put him out. We say no. If he wants to come into meeting he has a right to come, and plenty times he does have sensible things to say, and he does work too — when the mind take him. Like that time when we had to have somebody guard the cement at night when we were building the community center. He took the job. He guarded it day and night until all the building finish, and with not a cent pay. He was the only one say if we give a walking race from Princes Town to Moruga it would help us make money, and it did. I forget how much, but it did. So we say he must come to meeting if he want, but there are others who don't like him there. As for Teacher, he was for putting Pharoh and that whole clan in jail or the madhouse already. To him, they signify the lowest of the low, and he hated it whenever Pharoh contradicted him. Yet he was the one who started the arguing, first by agreeing the village should put in a request for street-lights, then going on to talk about where lights should go, and who light sould shine on.

He wanted light by the school, then by the church, at the center, and of course one planted so it shine on his yard. Plenty members want light shining in their yard, but everyone can't have it. He says that, and we know that. Then he goes on "But one territory which absolutely can no longer be left to the darkness is that denizen in the vicinity of our pond, where the reprobate and the diletante find succour in the criminal, immoral pursuit of their miscreant behaviour. . . . " High talk! "We must have a light or lights in that vicinity. Metropolitan scientific theory illustrates light mitigates the nefarious and the social radical. It is time we applied that theory in this village. . . . " Teacher in his glory. You don't have to understand every word he says to capture his meaning, and right away Pharoh interfered.

"Nobody enh ask for no light by no pond. You hear anybody ask for light there?"

"This is the village council!" Teacher's standing up now and looking around. "When we come to decisions we talk on behalf of the whole community. People, if they're not here . . . "

"I feel we good enough right now and ent asking for no light by no pond. Put light where you want but don't come saying you have to put where we don't want it."

"And we know why you don't want it. We know. That is why in my considered esteem. . . . "

Teacher had a point that pleased the staunch church members. They always liked to put up Pharoh's family and he himself as living example of the pure and easy way to damnation. To listen to them

you would think the devil himself made home in the quarter with
that family. But there were others of us who never took all that
damnation talk seriously, and in fact, some of the sweetest times I
miself pass is right there in that quarter. Others too. One of Pharoh's
sisters, Thelma, she has a parlor like, there where a man could eat
and play cards out of the rain, throw dice, and if you choose carry
on with one of the girl-friends she usually have visiting from Point
Fortin. There's always a little dew, and I don't think there is a single
grown man in this village who hasn't tasted a hand from that quarter,
quiet as it keep.

Plenty people too decent to be seen going there send their bottle
to get fill when they hear Pharoh's making. And if you know how to
look you could tell, because when dew is in at the quarter then
Singh's rumshop empty. Nobody enh drinking bad rum when the
cream there for the tasting. So while it's true Pharoh's sister wasn't
no cook, a man could find company there, have something nice to
drink, and have a laughing time night or day depending on who congregate. True again, they have fighting. And Pharoh's young brother
like to chase people every now and then with his cutlass. But he never
chop nobody yet. When fighting break out mostly it is between
family people themselves and all you have to do is keep your mouth
and hand out of the fracas. No big thing. As a matter of fact, that
quarter was the only liveliness in the village for those who didn't go
to church, and who liked little things Singh couldn't sell in his shop.
But there was another foot in the mud behind Teacher talking " . . .
we must call a halt to the disgraceness happening there and bring
our village out of the morass onto the map of developing communities. . . . "

"What disgraceness?" Pharoh shouting, jumping up and down
like bobbin in a basin of water. "What disgraceness you know carrying on in we quarter?"

"I mention no name . . . but if the shoe fit wear it. We all know
who in this village live like animals. We all know where some of our
lost young men gather to idle life away. They should be studying
books and thinking about trades instead it's lime and pass their pen-
nies around over card and dice while learning how to find women
to mind them. That is so. We all know where some of our fallen girls
get their belly. And if we are to come out of degradation and
backwardness. . . . "

"So where you want them to get it?" Pharoh ready to foam. "You want them get it under you? You red-nigger peacock! Cocksucker! With your high talk fuh we but yuh nose up Singh ass and all the first-class thief in his backshop. . . . "

"Pharoh! Pharoh!" Sam call. Carter, me and Jo-Jo, we get up to stop him before he goes too far. But we know the point he was bringing.

It wasn't no secret that Teacher who was too good to drink with us on the ground did his drinking in the backroom of Singh's shop. That's where he and the councillor and the inspector when they come to the village and their other high-class friends carry on their feting. That is good business for Singh, because they drink whisky. But he wants the rum trade too. He have those already who don't drink nothing but puncheon, and others again — mostly Indian — who wouldn't buy any place else. But he want it all. He jealous of the people making dew because by law his shop can't make nor sell it, and we had long since heard how he tried to bribe Pharoh's family into letting him buy all they make so he could color it with caramel and sell it for Portuguese rum the government license. That came out one time when Pharoh curse Singh so bad, the Indian had to close the door of his shop until Pharoh hit the road for Princes Town. And it wasn't no secret that if Singh couldn't bribe one, he would bribe the other. Same way if he couldn't take over something he would try his best to get rid of it. Business instinct, people like to say. So we know who Teacher talking for. We don't know what Singh give him or promise him, but we know who he's arguing to bring an end to traffic in the quarter. Yet this is council, and we can't let any and everything happen in council meeting.

"Yoh moderass!" Pharoh's saying, "talking 'bout girl getting belly! Somebody should put wood gi your stiff-assed wife. I have plenty. Bring she leh mi give she some disgraceness! And that moderass who put you up to this too. . . . "

Pharoh's gone totally out of hand, so Sam and Carter and me we hold him. He still cursing, calling Teacher all kind of things, but we're moving him, and he put his stick on his shoulder when we get him out the door, and start up the hill taking his direction toward Moruga.

"Well, that demonstration speak for itself," Teacher saying when we get back inside. His voice still cool, but you could see he's cut up inside. Plenty bad feeling. "There's a time and a place for everything, I always say," he carried on, "and everything in its place. Just like that madman don't belong anywhere in council meeting, it is time for this village to put such element out and march forward to become the number one village in this part of Trinidad. Plenty things we could do. We have picturesqueness here. We have the Devil's Woodyard — a natural tourist attraction. If we clean up our yards, plant more flowers, keep grass out of the roadside drains, that make it prettier for people to come here. We could build a guest-house near the volcano for tourist staying overnight which calls for a restaurant too, and you could see already not only we could make a name for ourselves but there'll be money coming into the village. . . . "

"What all this have to do with lighting and the pond?" Jo-Jo ask. And I was wondering too. All this business about tourist, we had that talk again and again in council. Wasn't nothing new. But tourist business had to start with government doing something. We all knew that. And I couldn' see the connection.

Teacher say, "Ahhh. . . . " and he look around just like he's dealing with a class full of children. By the time he finished explaining, we felt like a class too. Of course tourist like to go where they have recreation, and in the islands that mean they're coming for the water. So we're inland, away from the sea. But we still have our own water. With a little here and a little there we could make our pond so people could do their sunning and swimming, and even diving for things we put in the water if they want to. Makes sense.

"And you can't have any of that with a criminal element in the very place where you have to put your recreation," Teacher finished up. "We have to expose them. And if that doesn't make them go we'll have to use other means. But no tourist coming here to see what they have there in that quarter."

True. But what about we? Those of us who didn't mind Pharoh and his family, and in fact got our enjoyment out of passing time there?

"Well, look at it this way," Teacher said. "If tourists come and you have entertainment for them, it can't be only for them. Those of us who want entertainment, it's there for us too. And besides that, the pond is ours. We'll have it to enjoy, tourist or no tourist. We could enjoy ourselves swimming and diving. We could enjoy ourselves relaxing in a cool breeze on decent benches around the water. We're a nature loving people. A clean pond with nice grass around, electric lighting over all and pitch to walk on — we could fish nights if we want to. We'd have the sort of place that inspired the great poets like Wordsworth and Tennyson, who some of us recite still. We could bring in music for ourselves and expose our young people to culture. When it's time for church baptism, the pond's there ready. . . . "

The church people didn't like all the views on entertainment, but when he mentioned baptism they all said "Amen. . . . "

To tell the truth, he paint a nice picture. And people like Sam, Carter, Jo-Jo and me, we have to think what there was to lose, and what there was to gain in the package. With Pharoh gone, and all of us feeling a little bit tender for the way he treat Teacher, we forget him. We didn't have no idea what people living in the quarter want for themselves, but the question foremost was how to get tourist if they're coming, and at the same time not give up what we liked with things as they are.

"Is years before we get any electric light though, not so?" Ramdhanny who was secretary ask.

"Not at all," Teacher was quite sure. "I know the councillor. He happens to be a personal friend of mine, and he gave me his assurance that our representation for lights will be dealt with forthrightly. But we don't have to wait for lights. There are things we could begin to do even before we get lights."

There is a back game to all this. I know it, and others in the meeting know it too. What we don't know is who the game's for. Singh? The councillor? Two of them? Other people in government who already decide to do something in our village? We just didn't know. We let Teacher talk.

"This is my home. . . . " Now he's speechifying. He passed his palm over his hair and smoothed it back. "And as a man worth his salt, I intend to make the place I call home as good as any elsewhere in the world and better than most. Now, we village people as a rule don't fully appreciate the thing called environment. . . . " He's done that before. Come with something nobody ever heard of in our meetings. But like him or not, he was one for knowing what he was talking about. "Not only here, but all over Trinidad we don't think of where we're living as environment, but it is. Happily, those of us in touch with the times know from America that there's a movement stating people should save their environment. That means you and me, we have to stop destroying the land. . . . "

"How anybody go destroy land, boy?" Carter asked to know, but
we made him quiet so Teacher could go on.

" . . . And we have a start to make right here in reclaiming our
pond. When I was a boy I learned to swim in that pond. I remember
bringing water on my head from there to fill our barrel, and water
plants. Look at it now. . . . " Where people who make rum would get
their water then? I'm wondering. Where would they wash their
barrels? " . . . I am sure all of us here have some childhood memory
with that pond, and if we don't take steps now to save it the wild lillies
and the para grass going to dry it up and an important piece of environment with it. I don't have to tell you all it would take is our hands,
our backs, and a bent of mind to clean it up. We could do it, and
it would make a difference in all our lives. A healthy environment
is the basis for a healthy community, and what we have there now
sadly needs our attention. . . . " I had never thought of it that way.
True, there were black drains carrying waste from where people boil
their rum down in the water, and sometimes when the water went
low you could smell it. Grass and wild bush did have the other end
too, but I never thought of that. Pond was the last thing on my mind
when I'm in the quarter. " . . . clear out that pond and everyone of
us will feel good to see clear water again, and being able to bathe or
take a swim or fish if we feel like doing it. . . . "

"What about the mermaid and them?" Samlal, one of Singh's
cousins who didn't like him catch everyone with surprise. "You know,
say, they have mermaid in that water and them ent nothing to
play with."

The mermaids. Yes, the mermaids. We had forgotten clean
about the mermaids, taken up with Pharoh, and all the sweet talk
from Teacher. The mermaids. Wasn't Pharoh himself the one to
first say he saw them? And wasn't he the one who said they would
bring rain?

"We are not children of superstition here, Mr. Samlal," Teacher
said. "Mermaids are a thing of the past imagination. We're talking
environment now. Science and culture. God made the world in the
beginning, but it is mankind's trust. . . . "

"Yes, yes. But I remember dey that time when everything dry
up," Samlal made it clear he had no disrespect. But he had seen.
"Bhodi dead, ochro dead, all the plants and them dead, and animals

too. I lost one calf because the heifer couldn't give no milk. And I think Narine did loss some goats too. And it was that same fellow Pharoh who come and tell we about mermaid. . . . "

Which was true. I well remember the day. One of those days when the sun sting so, ants 'fraid to go crawling. Too hot to work garden or most anything else, and some of us sitting down in the shade at the corner when Pharoh comes up. Fresh from Moruga, he said, and telling everybody he had a message. What message could he have? Mermaid, he come out with. Mermaid. He personally had done ceremony and intercession — something to do with that time he spend with the priest, and all the walking he does walk in the sun — and mermaid was coming to the pond to bring water. That time, the pond dry. Big cracks in the bottom and everything dead there. So we say, What mermaid? Who believing in that stupidness? Mermaid happen where they have English people with long hair, but not in we village. Pharoh say, All who live will see. Rain tomorrow night. And it happened. Rain the next night, and two or three days after that. And we had no choice but to say Yes, the mermaid bring water.

I wondered how Samlal remembered that? Because for a time everybody talking mermaid. Everytime a new thing happen — it's mermaid. This time, nobody never see her. Some people call themselves camping out at night to catch her when she come to comb her hair, but nobody never see mermaid. When we ask Pharoh about that he said we looking for the wrong thing. Not all mermaid make like those come from England, he say, they have some come from Africa too. And so we figure out he was talking Shango business, and those of us who don't go in for that just leave it there. Yet it was a mystery how Samlal remembered, because mermaid business had already passed out of style for years that night when Teacher's telling us about environment.

"Well, Mr. Samlal," Teacher picked up where he left off, "when last did a mermaid do anything for you?"

"I'm not saying that . . . " Samlal was stubborn. But Teacher cut him off.

"Exactly to the point of my meaning. With the help of God, and only God, we have to do things for ourselves. And God has no fear of seeing us care for the environment that he gave us. We have a stewardship to fulfill. . . "

It took a while for the rest of us to say something, because most of us didn't know what to think. True, the pond was not like we remembered it. True, a lot of us had childhood memories there. I looked across at Madam Johnny and remembered the night when she was young Elfrida James and I new in my manhood. An old cardboard box on the ground, her eyes flashing up at me in the dark, and a cool breeze from the pond passing across my bare bamcee. She didn't have such a long face then, no lines around her mouth and high veins at her temple. Sweet memories.

"I don't know about that," Madam Johnny said finally. "Not only the pond, I see old people dying and some young ones too. That pond there is God's own to do what he please with. All of us meet that pond there, all of us will go and leave it. And if He says it's time for para grass and wild plant to take it over for a while, then so be it. Environment nor nothing else is to interfere with God's work."

"I didn't mean to talk about no God and no devil in this thing here," Samlal came to the fore again. "I just don't want no dry season bad like that one mermaid save we from. It's true that we don't like Pharoh and we put him out the meeting. It's true his family not nice. But he's got more than madness and I don't think he said everything he wanted to say here tonight."

"You're talking superstition, Mr. Samlal. I'm talking econo-political fact. But perhaps we all need to think this matter over in a quieter frame of mind and come again to consider. Madam President? . . . "

Madam Josephine was a school-mistress too, and from a quiet family. She ask, Anybody else have something to say? Everybody said it was all right to go ahead with getting street lights for all the junctions. Teacher was the man to talk to our councillor about lights, and he said he would do it. But we couldn't come to no certainty on what to do about the pond. Madam Josephine tell everyone to come prepared next week to make our decision, and meeting close.

All that week Pharoh gone from the village. I miself went to the quarter three times to see if I could find him and get a little decent something to drink, but he's not there. First time, Thelma had a little residue, so I sat in the parlour for a while with a petit-quart having intentions to make jolly like I usually do. But it wasn't the same. I watched the fellows on the gallery around a game of all-fours, and I hear the talk they're talking. I hear Manny slapping his men on the draughts board and trading with Jo-Jo what they're going to do with one another. I hear the women — Thelma, one of her cousins and two girl-friends — teasing the men, and making everybody laugh over what Malcolm couldn't do in the back room. I laugh too. But it doesn't feel the same. I keep thinking to one side of all that environment business. The voices in talk and the smell of fish Thelma's frying behind the counter, I look at the women and see them barefoot, Thelma dashing dirty water from her cooking out the window, the smell from their swamp coming up, all of that. I get to asking miself, what it is that I find nice about this place?

"Aie! That fish want seasoning," Jo-Jo call. And I could smell it fresh too, as Thelma's frying it in the pot.

"What you know 'bout cooking fish?" she call back.

"I cooking before you born," Jo-Jo call.

"Well cook for me nuh," Thelma say, coming to the counter with the big spoon in her hand dripping oil. "Come and cook for mi nuh. . . . " Thelma's a big woman. Her hair is not combed yet today, and while she's saying that there's a grin on her face so everybody can tell what's to follow.

"Why I must do that?" Jo-Jo trying to keep the talk from shifting.

"You ent man? Come gi me a little cooking. I waitin. . . . " Thelma said. And all the fellows laugh. The other women too, they laugh.

"It have too much cook in your kitchen already," Jo-Jo say. "You can't have room for no more."

"But you the one I waitin on," Thelma with her face sweaty, her breasts hang down low in the old dress she's wearing. "Come cook for me. I waitin. . . . "

"I ent taking you on," Jo-Jo said, trying to put all he had in a move on the draughts board. But nobody letting him. Everybody has something to add about how cooking should go, who could cook sweet and who can't cook at all, when the last time they cook. I get up and walk out in the yard.

It look the same, disorderly. Clumps of bush and grass where the ground's not scraped bare and hard. Tree roots where some of the children sitting down to shell peas, and a sow lying with little pigs around her teats on the other side. A half-built coop with no chickens and wire falling off, the slimy pool under the window black with

green water running down past the latrine without no door, down
between the tangled up bush and cane grass through where one of
the stills empty, and then in the pond. Anybody standing where I
was could smell it. And if I walked next door to where Pharoh's
brother had his house, same thing. The father too. All of them. No
potted plants, no little beds for cassava and cucumber vine. No
croton hedge with poinsietta, or stone-walk to save passing in the
mud. The petit-quart was gone, so I didn't bother going back inside
the parlour.

I went back twice during that week to find Pharoh and talk with
him about environment and what he had to say about mermaids.
Second time I didn't bother to stop by Thelma's. I pass her parlour
straight and take the little track right down to the pond. There wasn't
much to see of the water and if mermaid was there she really had
to do all her business under water because there wasn't any bank for
her to come up on. Grass almost tall as me everywhere. I make a
rounds to where Pharoh keep his still and fish out his leggings from
the little cave where he put them to stay dry, and I pulled them on.
The ground swampy black and spongy where Pharoh does empty his
boiler, but with leggings on I walk through that, looking for where
the bush stop and it come to open water. I want to come where I
could feel water-breeze in mi face, but the place is a jungle. I turn
back. Third time I went to the quarter I went straight to Pharoh's
own yard up hill from the pond where he live in a carat-topped hut.
I called and pushed the door because he never bother with latching
it. I look inside, but nobody there and I came back.

All that week nobody see Pharoh in the village. We hear he's on
the road, some saying they see him going to Moruga, others that
they pass him on the way to San Fernando. Jo-Jo, Sam, Carter, and
me, we hang by the shop on Friday. And when Samlal and his wife
come to make message we talk to him about how he did remember
mermaids in the pond. He wouldn't answer why he remembered, but
said again, "Everyday is not madness with Pharoh you know. And all
yuh shouldn't get so vexed with him all the time."

Nobody wasn't vex with Pharoh, I tell him. And then ask, "So
how're you voting come Monday night? Light and environment, or
no environment?"

"What I have to say?" he asked back. "I don't read no papers
from New York." And went on about his business.

Monday evening we see the Councillor come to the village, and he and Teacher gone to the back room in Singh's shop as usual. That night, the community center pack. Everybody want to hear what we decide on light, environment, and the mermaids. Madam Josephine open the meeting, and right away call on Teacher for his report. Teacher ready. He is wearing tan garbardine pants, a blue Elite shirt, and his bow-tie. He stand up and smooth back his hair. "Madam President," he said, "I am proud to announce Councillor Vigorat has assured me that we will have street lights in this village no later than Christmas-time this year!" People loud with their clapping. Everybody happy. This village going on the map, and from now on nobody can't stop we. I'm there listening.

"How much lights he say they sending?" secretary Ramdhanny wanted to know.

"Mr. Secretary, sir, I assure you on behalf of all the representations, made to me by the councillor, we will have lights at every junction on the main road, we will have light outside the church near the burial ground, we will have light outside the school, and we will have light marking the road to the Devil's Woodyard."

"And what about the pond?" Samlal asked. "What go happen with the pond?"

"Yes, the pond. . . . "

"That's right. What about we pond?"

"They bringing light to drive away the mermaid and them?"

We don't like to be first in starting contradiction, but once the question raise, everybody putting in their two-cent worth.

"That too," Teacher said. He still standing up, and his hair done smooth now so he has his handkerchief out and patting his jaw. "That too," he said, in quelling down the clamour. "But I believe Madam President has the preference to bring that determination before the meeting." And he sit down.

Madam Josephine is not a big woman. She's small-boned and has a little manicou face, and she hardly has a voice to raise. But she's talking now we're quiet. "As Mr. Ricardo said last meeting, there is a time and place for everything, and the wise ones know when the time has come. Ours is a rich country. And where our riches come from? The soil. Ours is a pretty country. Nature has blessed us with much to be proud of. And now we're no longer yoked to the days of labour isn't it meet and proper for us to give something back in helping nature? As Teacher Ricardo said, there is a world movement those of who read will know, bringing people back to the land, showing us to guard and cherish it because it gives us everything we have, and we here in this village will not be left behind out of this great movement. Councillor Vigorat therefore has agreed to support our whole package for development of a nature center and sight-seeing at our Devil's Woodyard, with a new road from there to our new recreation center which will be erected at the pond."

"Pharoh hear about this?" Samlal raised his voice and asked.

But Madam Josephine didn't stop to answer. "Government will be petitioned for the capital outlay for this model development of which we can all be proud. Our village will become known not only to other fellow citizens of Trinidad and Tobago, but citizens from abroad as well who no doubt will find great satisfaction in visiting our exotic community. . . . " And on, and on.

Before Madam Josephine is finished, everything's clear. We're headed for development, and that means light, environment, and to hell with any mermaid because she didn't mention mermaid once. And she's talking just like everything done fixed. We come to vote, but we're not hearing a call for no voting, so at last Boysie, Jo-Jo's next-door neighbour who is a quiet fellow until he get vex over something jump up and say "So what we voting on? What we here to vote on?"

"I'm coming to that," Madam Josephine says. "We have the choice before us to go forward and take our place in the modern world, or remain forever wrapped up in backwardness. I therefore urge you to give your vote to the development of our future by saying yes to the proposal so pleasantly received by our councillor at the presentation of our own Mr. Ricardo."

"What's the proposal?" I ask out. I already know, but I ask out so everybody could get a hearing because my mind's already made up and I feel if others sense what I sense we would all be voting together.

"Mr. Ramdhanny will give that to you."

And Ram read that it is proposed to take up the government gauntlet and build our village into an environment tourist center for sight-seeing, recreation, and other things, and in furtherance of this, roads, lights, and other commenities are now requested from government, so development from backwardness into the modern age may proceed.

I like the proposal. It sound good. Something in the move I find likeable, and when I look around I could tell most other people like it too. We didn't like hints that Teacher and Madam Josephine may have carried things too far in talking with the councillor, but we vote yes for the proposal, and right away Teacher jump up and say how happy he was to see that his confidence in our community has ramified, and he had one other thing to say before he sit down again. And that was, although Councillor as a rule does not intervene in village council discourse, the honourable representative who is here in our midst on this outstanding occasion would like a few words before the meeting break up.

Naturally. Who ever hear of politician coming and sitting down through a whole meeting then taking leave before he have something very important to say?

Councillor stand up and addressed us, then said, "Well, I have to let you know," we're waiting. "I have to let you know how impressed I am that you people showing initiative. When your president and your representative first bring this proposal to me I say to myself right away, people with foresight to make a proposal like this must have the backbone to undertake something right away for themselves. This proposal is long term. It will take months of hearing in the legislative council before a vote get passed although, you have my assurance, it will pass. So I say, what immediate work I can help them with to show my appreciation? Because I appreciate it when constituents take up challenge the way you have. What immediate work? I ask your representative. Is there anything immediate the village could start to do that I could help with, and he said Yes. What? I ask. And he says, We could clean out the pond and begin to get things ready. I liked that. A people who not sitting in wait for everything but ready to get up and make things prepare for when government's time to come in. And he don't know what I do, but I did it. I talked with the right people, I went to work right away, and I could tell you that whenever you get ready to begin that work on the pond I have support ready waiting for you. . . . " Some people clapping already. "I have support for you and I want to tell you the sooner you start the better it is because support is a thing doesn't always stay where you put it. Sometimes you put it up and when you go back to find it, it disappear. . . . " People laugh. "You think you could start Saturday? Let me hear you. What about Saturday? . . . "

We moved to say yes.

"I have already talked with the people in charge," Councillor carried on when we quieted down, "and Saturday when we come out in the morning — yes, we! because I like this so much I'm coming too." Councillor really going, now. His face shining. He has one hand in his jacket pocket, and the other going through his hair again and again. "When we come out Saturday morning it wouldn't be for a day of work and nothing else. This village has a vote for expenditure on food, on drinks, on entertainments for the whole day, to help this development plan so astutely prepared, to get started. . . ."

We like that. But it's not time to clap yet. You could hear a pin drop.

" . . . Government has authorized all the things we will need for a good fete. So it's not only work we're coming out to do. We'll have a steelband, and. . . . " And that's when people start clapping. We clap, and we clap so, you could hardly hear when councillor finish off saying " . . . Thank you . . . Thank you. . . . " People wouldn't let him sit down.

They glad too bad. The one way to make work easy is to bring a fete with it, and any fete the government give bound to be good. The more Councillor talk about the free fete government giving to go with cleaning the pond, the more people happy, saying Yes, the time for tourist development has come. I like mi little fete, and I'm pleased. But you can't fete without Pharoh. The thought must've struck Carter same time it strike me because he call out, "What about the people living in the quarter, Pharoh and his family them?"

I don't care about that family so much because in my feelings I've already made a break with that quarter. I don't have to be going there. But Pharoh! You can't have a good fete without dew from Pharoh.

Councillor turned to Teacher then for some help, and again Teacher stand up. "Anybody from that family here?" he asked.

Naturallly, not one of them there. The only one who ever would have been there was Pharoh, and he was on the road.

"Anybody see Pharoh?" Madam Josephine ask out.

"Pharoh gone Corosan," one voice said.

"Not Corosan, boy. Is Moruga he gone," another one contradicted.

"Nah! San Fernando!"

"I hear he gone quite Biche. . . . "

"What he does look for, boy?"

"He bringing food gi the mermaid. . . . "

And before everything break up in laughing, Madam Josephine rap the desk four or five times to let Teacher go on talking.

"We all know," he said, "we all know that family has the right to live where they're living, but the pond itself, that pond my friend — it belong to the whole village. Environment belong to everybody. They're welcome to come and share in all development undertaking. We shall not trespass, and neither shall they on the right of this community in carrying out our responsibility to nature. . . . "

"Here! Here!" some voices say, and so, no problem. Not to worry. If they want to come and fight, law and theory on our side, and besides, they had never stopped anybody from getting to the pond before. No problem. But Madam Johnny wanted to know details. "Who doing all that cooking for Saturday?" she wanted to know.

"All of that paid for" . . . Councillor said.

"But who doing it?" she insisted. "You bringing people from outside to cook?"

"No, no. People right here getting paid to do the cooking. And don't worry about drinks — that paid for too. The steelband coming from Port-of-Spain! . . . "

"Now that's the way to do things," Mack said.

"All yuh hearing that?" Ramdhanny kept saying. "All yuh hearing that? Leh me see who remembering this next time we have election."

"Don't worry about election," Councillor said. "Government has authorized all the things we will need for a good fete. So when we come out on Saturday . . . Yes, we! because I have to be there too. When we come out everything will be nice, and we'll have the newspapers here and the radio, and you see, this is only the beginning of the kind of thing this village can go forward to. . . . "

It took a while for the meeting to quiet down.

On Saturday, true to his word, Councillor had a steelband on the hill by the pond. They came quite from Port-of-Spain on a truck which they park respectfully off a little distance, and they're lining up with their pans while a few of us who get there on time watching. By half-past ten they tune up and they start to play. In the meantime Councillor and Teacher busy showing the ladies hired to cook where they want to put their tables, and showing Singh's brother-in-law where to park so he could pass out drinks of rum and beer from the back of his van.

With the noise and commotion, more and more people come out. And even more when the steelband start to play. Some ladies come in leggings and old skirt tie up around their waist. Some of the men wearing leggings too, and everybody carrying either a brushing cutlass and crook stick, a rake, or poonyah or something. And little by little, the cleaning begin. The Councillor went in with his leather shoes and rayon pants to pull para grass and came out soaked with mud up to his knees. Those who had head trays load the pulled grass to dump it on the low side of the pond between some black sage and mosquito bush where the roots wouldn't catch again. Some who didn't have trays carry bundles on their heads anyway, never mind the mud and water falling out on them. Mack, Ramdhanny, me, everybody happy with what's going on. There wasn't no newspaper nor radio, but we're working, and the steelband playing a nice leggo around we. Nice. People working and talking, helping one another. Madam Johnny and the other ladies wearing straw hats or with their heads tie up seeing to the food. They're busy, but they're joking and laughing too, and some even get bold enough to go up to the van for their drink just like men. Nobody en say a thing about mermaid.

In fact, everybody's beginning to feel that we're doing something good for people and nature. Teacher even. We see him going in the swamp-water pulling out wild plants, sweating and muddy, and then going up the hill to the van to take a drink with everybody. A stranger looking on never would be able to tell that he was Teacher and everybody else just ordinary people. Then somebody say "Aie, aie! Look Pharoh!"

When we look up the hill, there's Pharoh stoop down under the hog-plum tree like a driver. He's looking on. He's stooping down with his back straight, looking down on us, and it feels strange to see Pharoh there so still and quiet. Some of us hail, "Pharoh! Pharoh!" I feel glad to see him too, because although things already gone ahead without him he might still have something to bring for the finishing up. He stoop there, we don't know where he come from, nobody see when he enter, and he's looking on. He's not talking — which for him is more than strange. Mack tells Jo-Jo he should go and bring him, but Jo-Jo tell Mack he should go, and nobody went. Those who didn't stop continue working, and the rest of us join back because nothing else to do anyhow, and we could deal with Pharoh later.

When the work finish, and everybody's eating roti and pelau the ladies make, we send some up the hill for him, but he wouldn't have nothing. Anyway, forget Pharoh. We have all the grass and wild plant pulled out of the pond, and the bank brush back, and while we're taking time to eat, the swampy's settling down so pretty soon there's water there where it used to be, beginning to look clear and nice. When we look out at the water, the whole thing seemed new. It covered more ground than some of us remembered, with the breeze playing little waves right across from bank to bank. The whole place look so fresh and nice, till I feel like taking off mi clothes and just going in. This is we water.

Before long, some of the steelband boys who finish with their resting and eating did just that. They take off their clothes down to their under shorts and they go in the water. Some of our village boys go in too, with people laughing and calling jokes. The boys swim out to the middle and show off their little diving. Ramdhanny, Samlal, all of us start remembering how it used to be in the days when we had a barge there, and Samlal with a few drinks under his belt and excitement from the working said, "Leh we put back a barge, nuh. . . . " and before you knew it he and Ram and some of their family nearby gone off to make a barge. They come back. They bring everything. And just like that, in two-two's box build, barrels cork up and lashed together, and the little barge floating in the water with fellow's poling it out, taking some of the ladies and girls for ride as far as the rope it tie up to would let it go. When I was young I would've done the same thing, and the sight of our young people enjoying themselves make my heart feel glad.

All that time Pharoh's stooping under his tree without a word, and nobody else from his family anywhere in sight. We could see the spots where dead branches cover their stills around the pond, but not one of them came down to give a hand, or challenge, or even just to see what was going on. Pharoh the only one there from his family, and suddenly his voice cut through everything. "All yuh ent see she out there? All yuh ent see she out there looking at all yuh? Mermaid don't forget. She know everyone o' all yuh bitches. . . . " The after-noon breeze so quiet you could hear him all around. "She's waiting. All yuh playing all yuh can't see she's waiting. . . . " Some of the village boys begin to laugh, but that didn't stop him from going on, " . . . Look at your handiwork! Look at it well. If you think all that big-shot talk on environment guh save you from she. . . . "

The Port-of-Spain boys, when they find out Pharoh's talking about mermaid in the pond, some of them start edging out of the water.

Some of the women get vex. They say, "Why you don't go back Corosan or where you come from with your walking?" They call out, "Why all yuh mad people always trying to spoil things for everybody? Go way!" They want the men to rush him, because by now Pharoh's standing up in his true style, his voice peeling down on everybody like he's giving sinners a sermon or something.

"Yuh're going to find out. Everybody gunh find out. Mermaid don't forget, mermaid don't forget. A watery grave is her command for all yuh. . . . "

The women want us to rush him, but we know he would soon run out of wind, and the best way to treat Pharoh is not bother with him unless you have to.

I look over at Councillor where he's sitting on the ground eating a plate of pelau with his fingers. His back's turned to the hog-plum tree and "The work went nice . . . " he's saying. "You know how long it is since I eat a nice pelau? You can't beat village people when they really want to do something."

"That's our due," said Teacher, looking proper even in his muddy clothes. "Look at us! With direction and incentive there's nothing we can't do. And thankfully we're in touch with that place they call America. America! . . . You can't beat them when it come to how people must take the world, and make it through a vi-sion. . . . "

"That's right," Councillor agree without looking up.

"You see this environment thing they started? It's going to take the whole world. And we're the ones getting it off the ground here in Trinidad. . . . "

"When the Prime Minister hear about this," Councillor add on, "people will come to this village from all directions for sight and inspiration. This calls for being proud. . . . "

We did feel proud. Even though we didn't know everything there was to know about environment we could see what happen when it bring us together. Look how we cleaned up the water in that little space of time! Look how we put back a barge. If we could do that . . . I begin to have visions.

I could see the hills of wild cane and bamboo grass around the pond turn smooth green like where the estate people have their golf course. I could see a concrete wall going around the pond — nothing tall — paint white, going all around, and little benches for old people to sit down when they want to take a breeze. Past that we have a smooth pitch road taking you back to the center, and everybody have nice yards and gardens mark off with white fencing, and the houses painted in colours. I'm seeing all that. I don't care much about any tourist visitor coming to see what we have, I'm seeing us, the people, change. We are wearing good clothes, nobody limping from back-pain, and when we meet one another we're talking in quiet voices about good things what happen to us, and in parting this land leave behind a happy place for the young people to take over. I vision all that. And I wondered if Councillor, Teacher, Mack and the others vision that too. But I don't say nothing.

I have a feeling I wasn't the only one, though. Plenty of us there must have gotten filled with that vision, because though we didn't talk much we had a nice common feeling around those of us sitting there on the ground. The pelau was good. Nobody even bother to criticize the roti. Some of us don't like shop rum, but today the White Star's no problem. We're mellow. It would take a whole lot to bother we — not even Pharoh who we could still hear preaching in the background. Calamity is coming down on us he's saying, and to sit there hearing his voice coming all by itself in the wind, some of us feel sorry his mind mix up so, and Mack ask Councillor if environment could do something for Pharoh.

Teacher was the one to answer, "Only one thing to do for Pharoh. He should be in the madhouse. In America they wouldn't have somebody like that on the outside walking around with other people. One of these days he will get dangerous, and nobody knows what he will do."

"Pharoh don' trouble nobody," Mack said.

"That's for now," Teacher nodding his head in wisdom. "That's for now. But when a body's gone mad you never can tell. His family, if they had any ambition would put Pharoh in the madhouse and get him off the road."

"They can't do that," Carter said. "All he does do is walk about and talk. They can't lock him up for that."

"I'm not talking about lock-up," Teacher bringing down his tone to Carter's level. "That is jail. I'm saying the madhouse. St. Ann's."

"Same thing here in Trinidad," Mack said. "St. Ann's, Carrera — only difference is inside the madhouse they don't give you hard labour."

"We only have that from hearsay," Ram put in. "None of us never went there. And I incline to think Teacher right about Pharoh."

"That's cause he not your family," Carter point it back at them.

"I never been to St. Ann's," Mack said, "but when I was a boy I spend time at the Y.O.D.I. and we used to hear. They used to frighten us with St. Ann's back there. If you didn't behave, was straight to the madhouse. Sometimes they say Carerra, but St. Ann's was the thing that frighten everybody."

"That's long time," Teacher say. "Things change now. . . . "

"Change where?" Carter ask to the breeze. "Here in Trinidad? All yuh must be dreaming."

But Teacher went on. "We can't put too much sentiment in the past," he says, "nor blind our eyes with what used to be. In America they have a theory for madness. When people mad, first thing they do is separate them from regular people. Next thing they try is electric training where they put wires on and if you behave good it's all right, but when you behave bad, it's zap! If that don't work, they go to operation. They open the brain and cut away the part that's spoiled. And if that still don't work then there's no hope for you and they just keep you where you can't bother nobody till you die. We're going to get that theory here in Trinidad too. It's coming. And meantime, people like Pharoh should be where they won't cause trouble."

"What they call that theory in America?" I ask. It sound so to the point and manly.

"Behaviour modification," Teacher answer. "Everybody who do studies in psychology learn that."

Behaviour modification. "And you learn that when you come to be teacher too?"

"On my own I have learned a lot of things. When you have get-up-and-go sometimes you learn things that master teaching won't tell you," he said with a laugh at Councillor. They both laughed. And people join them, and more drinks pass.

Behaviour modification . . . it sound something nice — just like environment. With those two together, it cross my mind, what couldn't we do to make life sweeter in the village? With order and tidiness on the land, then smoothen out Pharoh and one or two others I could think of would make our place final. Finish. What else could a people ask for? Behaviour modification . . . I look at Councillor sitting there, and Teacher, and the others shaking their heads to the talk, even Carter. They feel it too. And the time level back again.

Some of us lay down on the bank we just cleared to let the afternoon pass away. The steelband boys and them play one or two more tunes time the sun's going down, and some of the ladies shake their waist a little with the music. The boys making merry again diving in the pond from the barge, and Pharoh — we didn't even notice when he stopped preaching and went away.

Just before the sun slip out altogether Councillor stood up as though he want to make a speech. He hitched up his pants and cleared his throat one or two times, but by then the women are busy packing their baskets and trays, and the steelband truck has pulled up with the boys loading their drums, and nobody much stop to give him any hearing. We older ones are feeling fine. What else could he say today? And we didn't want any speech to close things because we didn't have the feel for any closing. The day brought a big promise opened up, and nothing could feel better than just keeping things that way. So why not make a treat for Councillor? He gave us a fete, we could give him back one too, and we say You can't leave without the boys buying you one by the shop. He agreed. And until ten o'clock that night we're still in Singh's shop drinking. Every man put his hand in his pocket and it's whiskey and gin for everybody pack in the back room around Teacher and Councillor who're the only ones accustom to being there, and Singh even put in a bottle of Black and White himself to show he's in the swing too.

Councillor telling stories about how he is a hero with the government party in Port-of-Spain, and Teacher's talking too about his forays in the halls of various ministries where the clerks and them have to bend back and beg pardon when he finish with them. At first, they take him light and treat him like he was a nobody. We're listening, meanwhile rum, beer, everything flowing, to these two telling we how little piece, little piece, a big change starting to spread through the whole country with village people getting cognizance. It sweet. I never thought we could find a spree so sweet, with nothing but mostly talk about things most of us didn't know. But we did. And when time to break up, Teacher said Councillor shouldn't drive the narrow road to town that night, and we walk both of them back to his house where Councillor should sleep and leave for town in the morning.

That night I dreamed the vision of environment again, only it didn't stop with our village. It spread out like a new light all the way to Moruga, Mayaro, then back the other way cleaning up all of Princes Town through Manahambre, and turning San Fernando into a place anybody in the world could be proud of. And again I wasn't the only one. Sunday morning when I meet up with Mack, Jo-Jo and the others to take a morning sip at Mack's gallery, they're already talking about yesterday — the kind of feel cleaning up the pond bring, and Sam says "You have to give it to Teacher. He sure bring something good this time."

"Councillor too. Teacher talk, but Councillor's the work man," Jo-Jo added.

"All two of them. Everybody," Sam said. "Teacher with his psychology, and Councillor know when and how to make fete, but we handle it too. We back do the work. . . . "

"Everybody," Jo-Jo agreed. "The things we could do with all them theory from America. . . . " He let his voice trail off, and nobody didn't argue because we agree.

We pass the bottle. It wasn't first-class, but nothing to start the day off like an early sip of even half-way good dew. By the time we finish that, the sun still coming from behind Gran-Gran chanet tree. The morning breeze cool. And in a mellow just like the night before we decide a walk to the pond would be a nice thing. Just to go and see it and see the change, and feel close again with everything environment could make happen. Nobody even had a thought about Pharoh.

But when we get to the pond, before we quite get there, we could hear Pharoh preaching " . . . Mermaid carry the harvest and all bounty in her hand. . . . " his voice coming up the hill from where his hut is. "When hard time come it is she who ease all sorrow she who take away all suffering. No devil can't make it right for you to turn your back on mermaid. No, no, no! Where they live man passing in mortal danger but not to confuse mermaid with diablesse! . . . And who is man? . . . To claim in might the fortress and abode of power that succour him? . . . "

Pharoh was posed as usual, on his feet before the door-way of his cabin facing down to the pond. When he caught sight of us coming down the track to pass under his hog-plum tree he called, "So what all yuh come for? There are those with power to desecrate and those who know how to supplicate the divine powers in this land. What all yuh come for? The desecrators hath forfeit all rights to the beneficiaries of the most mighty. . . . "

Then turning his back on us, but just the same talking to us, "What all yuh come for? I want to know. . . . "

Mack called as though Pharoh hadn't talked, "Pharoh! What's happening? You have anything there?"

"Rum drinkers!" Pharoh say, as though we're something low. "Yuh don' even know why yuh're rum drinkers. And rum make all yuh do that yesterday. Is only rum. Anybody set out rum for yuh throat and food for your belly, and all yuh following them like puppy dog. . . . "

"Bring it out nuh man," Mack say, as though he hear something altogether different from what Pharoh saying. "Bring out a whole bottle because today we feel like drinking dew! We have to make up for yesterday, man. . . . "

"All yuh drinking? . . . All yuh ready to drink dew? . . . Look down there and see what all yuh do, look!"

I had already looked and the pond was still there clear and cool in the morning light. But I didn't like what Pharoh was saying. Most times, when you're accustomed, you don't take him on, because you know after he cool down from his talk you're getting some of the best dew made by god or man. But I didn't like his talk, and I didn't feel that I had to have his dew. I didn't like what I see in the pond either. Councillor was there, and Singh, and Teacher with his whole family. We never knew him to be out so early on a Sunday morning, but there he was, he, his wife, their son and daughter, in swimming trunks and bathing suits, and Councillor in swimming trunks too.

And if they weren't hanging on to the barge they're swimming around it, or climbing up to dive off again in the middle of the water. They have a spread on the ground with food basket on it just like they're on an excursion, and a big red and white balloon floating between them on the water.

It was a strange sight, only because we didn't expect it. The wife and children out in bath suits diving up and down in we pond. They're swimming and diving and splashing water just like they belong there. And while in a way I was glad to see it, I still had some mixed feelings about them playing in we pond. "What dem doing there?" Carter mutter.

We're settling down now, and Pharoh still standing up like Captain Nelson at Trafalgar looking at us in a way I don't like. But I don't have any hard feelings for him. At least, I'm forcing miself not to have any hard feelings for him. Maybe he and his family, they really lost something. That wasn't for me to tell. "Is beach party they're making, or what?" Carter still muttering, and from the tone of his voice you could tell he didn't like it. He wasn't one to hide his feelings.

"Let them play, man," Mack said. "The man bring his family, and it wasn't for he we wouldna have back we pond no how. Let them enjoy theirself man. . . . "

"And what happen to them yesterday?" Sam asked.

"That's what I'm saying," Carter's tone turned caustic. "Time for work they're not there, but time for play. . . . "

Maybe Carter's going too far, and "Have reason, man," I said. "Teacher was the one to bring environment, and he pulled para grass with everybody yesterday. Is his family enjoying theirself, not strangers."

Which was true. We all knew it. But we didn't expect to see them, or anybody, there and that interfered with whatever it was we had come to the pond to see and feel.

After a while Pharoh stopped standing up on his stick like John the Baptist. He goes inside his cabin and comes out with a full bottle of dew and his glass. Good dew. We pass it around. Even though I didn't have to have it, good dew. While we're sitting on the ground there, Councillor look up from the pond waving and calling out, "How're you boys this morning? I see you wake up with the same thought as we. . . . "

We wave back to him but we don't say nothing.

Teacher's wife stop her swimming to look up at we but she didn't say a thing. She goes back to the water with a stiffness in her body. You could see she's feeling her sport done spoil. Teacher and the children pay us no mind.

"All yuh have breakfast already?" Councillor calling out.

"We having it now," Sam raise up the glass and we all laugh.

"All yuh fellows too good, man," Councillor laugh back too. "We have things to eat here if all yuh get ready. . . . " And he dive off into the water again.

"So Pharoh," Mack says, his voice teasing, "you don' like environment, eh?"

Pharoh is back to stooping there in his ragged khaki pants, his big toes pointing inwards and the little grey beard against his black face. "What I have to like that for?" His voice telling us that not because he brought our rum we shouldn't think he was with us. "Mermaid don' forget, mermaid don' forgive."

"But who ever see this mermaid you're talking about?" Carter was still caustic.

"You see."

"Not me," Carter says sharp. "I never see nothing of the kind so don' say that 'bout me."

"You see what mermaid do for this village. You was there when we had dry weather make the ground crack open. You was there when I followed mi vision and plant shrine in the pond. All yuh like to say I crazy, but it's not me. You see what happen before three days when I put that shrine there? Rain. Plenty rain. And this village never want for water since."

"How you know that was any mermaid?" Mack teased again. "It have god too, you know, and all the Baptist people was praying."

"Pray!" Pharoh got heated again. "Pray all yuh pray. All yuh mash up she shrine now and we'll see what happen. All yuh tell mermaid all yuh enh have no more use for she and we'll see what's gunh happen."

"What shrine, Pharoh?" I ask. "What shrine? We're in that water whole day yesterday, and nobody enh see nothing like no shrine. Whole day."

"Yuh can't expect for all yuh to see. What all yuh could see? Things happening all around all yuh don' know, all yuh could see something? But I'm saying, we all gunh see when mermaid take retribution. Mermaid don' forget, mermaid don' forgive."

"Anybody ever talk to you about going to St. Ann's?" Carter said with cold.

That stopped Pharoh short. He sit back on his heels. He wrap his fingers around his shin bones and drop his chin on one knee with his eyes staring wide open.

"Why yuh have to do that, man?" Mack says to Carter. "Why you have to do that?"

"Do what? You only worried he ent bringing no more rum."

"The man didn't troubling nobody."

"I didn't trouble he neither," Carter said maliciously. "All I do is say if anybody mention St. Ann's to he lately. What in that? . . . "

"You know. . . . "

Right then Pharoh fell over. His eyes gone pure white, and he's on his side, his hands still round his knees, wrap up like a ball. I rush up, and Sam too, and we try to stretch him out but couldn't even get his arms unlocked. Pharoh wrapped up tight like steel, and old people like me don't have much strength. I hold one hand and Sam take the other. Mack take his heels, as we stretch him. But before we could get him straightened out Pharoh start to flutter and froth coming from his mouth. He's fluttering and beating up on the ground so hard all three of us catching hell to hold him down. We knock down the rum. And still Pharoh have everybody tossing. What a time! Carter's the only one didn't move an inch. He still sitting on his heels watching us toss with Pharoh, and in the glimpse I catch of his face I could see he's calling us stupid for not letting Pharoh beat about where the fits throw him. But all we have to do is hold on for a while longer until Pharoh pacify, then prop his head up and let him sleep. We know that, so we hold on.

By the time Pharoh quiet down and lay on the ground snoring in his deep after sleep, I'm wringing wet with sweat. Mi back tired, and mi body feel like I just finish hoing one of those long estate tasks.

"This man sick no ass," Jo-Jo said, sitting back against the plum tree.

We're all tired out, except Carter, and nobody else say nothing. After a while, "You think they would take him at hospital?" Mack ask.

"What hospital?" Carter was in a separate mood by himself. "The man mad. Why government must waste money on hospital for people like he?"

"Yuh're drinking the man dew and that's how yuh're talking about him?" I feel the edge in Mack's voice too.

"I paying for it," Carter cut back. "I drinking the rum, yes, but I paying for it. That don't make me have to lie about what should happen or not happen for Pharoh."

"So they should put him in jail!" I shoot out.

"I ent saying that," Carter back off. "All I saying is I don't have to lie."

"Well if you ent lying then, well what're yuh doing?" There's a heavy feeling in mi chest and I have to let it out. "What're yuh saying? By law Pharoh and all his family shouldn't be making no rum. By law you, me, all ah we here shouldn't be drinking what they make. If so, we should all go to jail. . . . "

"What that have to do with anybody sickness?" There's strong vexation in Jo-Jo's voice as he cut me off. "This man sick! He walking about sick! That's what I'm saying. All the shitting talk about worship for mermaid and Shango god put on he, we're not dealing with facts. The man damn sick and we should do something about it."

"Why me?" Mack want to know. "He have family. They should be the ones put him in hospital."

But I wasn't finished. "All ah we sick!" burst out of mi mouth. I don't know where it come from but once I say it I have to back it up. "Look at we!" I say. And I want to mean everything. I want to mean Pharoh there on the ground, Teacher and his half-naked wife in the pond bathing, the five of us old heads barking at one another. I want to mean how we have to have our dew and would break any law to get it. I want to mean how easy we could change things! Look at the pond. And yet we don't. I want to mean this story about tourist coming to see Devil's Woodyard — since I was a child I used to hear the same story but I never see one tourist come yet. I want to mean us talking about mermaid and Shango not really believing mermaid and Shango but going behind the high things we feel's for us some place and taking whatever short-cut we could to get there. Even madness. Or environment. Who's to say who is the sick? I want to mean all this, and by the time I get through spouting, the others quiet.

Same time, I hear Singh calling from the pond, "Aie, aie! All yuh come quick!" And right next to that Teacher's wife screeching "Louie! Louie! You have him? You have to go down Louie! Don't tell me you can't find him!" I wonder who is Louie? Find who?

"Like their boy drowning," Carter said, looking off coolly down on the pond. "Why Teacher don' dive for him?"

"Jesus Christ!" Sam let go Pharoh and take off down the hill. I let go Pharoh and stand up. Mack and Jo-Jo, too, but Sam gone down way ahead, and by time we get there he's already in the pond.

The water near the bank turning cloudy. It's no use me going in. I never was no diver. I could swim a stroke if I have to, but I never like going underneath no water. Teacher's little girl crouch up on the barge looking down in the water, and Singh there holding onto her. Teacher holding onto the barge itself with one hand catching breath, and feeling around with his body in the water. Coucillor, the boy, nor the mother nowhere to be seen, but pretty soon the mother comes up blowing water out her nose, and back down again. Councillor pop up too, with Sam right behind him. Sam's old as me, but he was always a good diver. He catch his breath, and back down again. Councillor holding to the barge. His eyes red, and he so short out of breath that when Mark call "What happen?" Councillor's face twist up in a knot before he could tell us "The boy swimming good, good . . . Then all of a sudden. . . ." He dive back in the water again. As the water turn brown and cloudy Singh says "They not finding him in that now."

They kept going up and down a while longer, until Sam came out and stretch himself on the bank, his chest heaving. Councillor come out too, and start with vomiting. "He gone. . . . " Sam says between breaths. "He gone."

"This ent no sea, it's just a little pond," Mack says. "How he could gone? All yuh can't find him? . . . "

"Sam don't mean like that," I said. "He mean the boy. . . . "

"Oh he dead!" Mack understood. "But if he dead why they can't find him?"

"Gone . . . " Sam saying again and again, talking about more than the boy now, his head lay back on the ground, and it wasn't nice to hear him say what I was feeling.

They didn't find the boy for another hour. It was Singh who went to get Samlal after Sam stretch out on the bank. When Samlal come, he take off to his shorts and walk in the water. When he get up to the barge he duck under and came out right away with the boy. Anybody with sense would've known to do that, he said afterwards. The boy's foot was tangled up in some rope hanging from around the barrels that tied together to make the barge.

People hearing the news, a lot of them flock to the pond. Some of the women in little more than their night clothes, others again who were going to church early in their Sunday best. They all flock to see. But nobody couldn't do nothing but stand there. Some of the ladies trying to console the mother. Her face in knots, and water running from her eye. Teacher holding her hand. He had caught himself, time they found the boy, and though his eye full too, he's saying thanks to Singh and Samlal and everybody who standing there watching and talking to them.

It was too much to go back home right away when everything settle. Mack, Jo-Jo, and me, we stray back up the hill to Pharoh's yard. Sam's there already, with his clothes hanging up to dry, a piece of old cloth around his waist. He's stooping down a little ways off from Carter who hadn't even moved his back from the plum tree. Pharoh awake now, and sitting against his doorpost time we get there looking like he's come from far and weary. Mack and Jo-Jo sit back on the ground as they were before, but I can't bring miself to go down.

I look back at the pond. The water's clearing, and everybody gone except Samlal and Singh who're sitting on the barge, not bathing. The place look quiet and peaceful, as though nothing bad could never happen there. It look like a place where man could settle with peace if he wanted. I look at the water. . . .

"Yuh have anything left there?" Mack was half-hearted at first. But when Pharoh didn't change his stare, didn't answer, he said in vehemence "Come nuh man! Bring something for we to wet we throat. If is money yuh want, I paying. . . . "

But Pharoh sat dead still.

I look at the others, Jo-Jo and Sam and Carter. I've known them all my life and never thought the time would come when there was no sweetness in their company. They're watching Pharoh too. "What the ass!" Mack burst out. "Yuh playing dead? We have a real one here already this morning you know. . . . "

"Yuh enh see the man tired?" Sam said. "Yuh have to have understanding what fits make people go through."

Then suddenly Pharoh spoke, as though quietly explaining to somebody with patience, "I ent never went to no St. Ann's yet. . . . Nobody can't send me there. That is a place for mad people. . . . "

Mack look at me and Jo-Jo, we look at one another, and now somebody had to move. Sam was the one to get up. He walked inside Pharoh's cabin like he's going in his own house, then come back with a half bottle of dew. The glass was still on the ground. He pick it up and rinse it in Pharoh's bucket. The bottle pass around.

"Well, it was a good start," Sam says, looking off at the pond. "We can't let nothing prevent we from keeping it up."

"Yeah," Jo-Jo says. "With help from government we bound to finish putting this village on the map."

I'm standing face to the pond. It's still there, the clear water bristling with little waves, the barge swinging on the end of its rope. Samlal and Singh talking. Everything look nice. If everybody could keep serious about it, who knows? . . . I take my drink with the boys. I take a sizeable one, and the dew feels good going down behind mi chest. It spread out warm and nice. "We should've had some of this for Teacher," I said.

"Since when he does drink this? . . . " Sam say.

"Since when he does drink with we? . . . " Jo-Jo was even more emphatic.

"You forget yesterday?" I ask. "Everybody drink with everybody yesterday. And when a man have sorrow. . . . "

"I ent talking about that," Sam say.

I want to argue with him. I want to remind him and everybody that Teacher's man just like we, but I get a better idea right away. "Why we don't take Teacher a gallon or so for tonight? They bound to want some. . . . "

"You crazy?" Jo-Jo say. "You know how much policeman coming to that wake? Sergeant and officer? You forget them is big shot? . . . "

"Police's been at wakes before where they had dew."

"That's with family," Jo-Jo shout back.

But Carter remembered a time I was talking about. Sam remembered one too. I get down on the ground, and we're arguing because it seem to me it was a time to put aside bias of all kind.

Jo-Jo tell me I sound like I want to join high society. "Them people don't have no use for you and me, you know," he's saying. "All this talk about work together and that, you think them people don't have plan? You're stupid. Where's we plan? What plan we got? . . . "

Then Mack cut through the arguing with a heavy, serious, "But what the ass . . . " and jumped up bawling out "Aie! Aie! You can't do that. . . . "

We all turn to see what he's bawling at with his gaze down over the pond. At first I don't see nothing but the water with a little shine to it in the sunlight. But when I raise mi eyes I see one of Pharoh's sisters standing just in the bush on the other side where there's a track going back up to her yard. She's one of the older ones. Older than Pharoh but thin and hard just as he. She's wearing an old working dress, and on top of the felt hat she's wearing she's carrying a half-drum on her head. We all know what's in it.

"You can't throw that there!" Mack bawl out at her.

She stand up, and her face turn in our direction, but she don't say nothing. From below, Singh and Samlal staring at her too, but they don't say nothing. Mack stand up. We all stand up, except Carter. "Carry that somewhere in the bush!" Mack's voice is steaming.

Pharoh's sister still stand there, looking as though she turned dotish and didn't know what to do. Mack start down to the water with Jo-Jo and me following. "Carry that back! Get away from here!" he's bawling.

And by the time we reach the water we could hear her answering " . . . who the hell is you? You the owner of this pond?"

"This all ah we pond," Jo-Jo call out. "We break we back cleaning it yesterday, so don't come with that shit to be dumping here again. . . . "

She's standing just inside the bush looking raggedy and dotish, but one hand on her hip and the voice coming strong. "This who pond?" She's staring straight at us. "All yuh talking this and all yuh talking that. . . . " And quickly she finish walking to the water edge. " . . . Any of all yuh put pond here? . . . " Then with that, she started lifting the half-drum off her head.

"Aie! Aie! If you throw that there. . . . "

She let the drum down to the ground while we're bawling at her. Then as if to shut us off, she pulled it backward a ways almost into the bush, but where we could still see her bend and turn it over.

Right away the stench came. The left-behind from a strike when it sit down for days in the sun doesn't smell good. The same breeze

bringing little ripples into the bank where we're standing bringing
the stench too.

"How yuh gunh stop that?" Mack had the question for everybody. "Yuh see that? What happen now when rain come?"

"What happen everytime they make?" I'm saying. "They have to
clean their barrel and throw that left-behind some place. . . . "

Mack looked at me as though there were things I didn't understand, and said, "Them is nasty people."

By that time Singh and Samlal come off the barge, and Singh's
saying "Somebody have to put an end to this nonsense. . . . "

And Samlal, "Who gunh stop that? All yuh have to build a wall
if all yuh want the pond stay clean."

But Singh, with vengeance in his voice say "The only way to
deal with them is police. Somebody have to talk to that commissioner
in Port-of-Spain."

"Who gon talk to him, you?"

"Well what we have Councillor there for? . . . "

I look at Singh, and I listen to everybody because by now
Mack's telling Singh the only reason he want police is so he could
break Pharoh's family and get all the rum business for himself.
Everybody knows police love bribe! And who could pay bigger bribe
than Singh in the village? And Sam saying, Yes, that's true. And
Jo-Jo saying everybody's too hasty . . . I listen, and my mind's going
around on the whole thing. Teacher, the dead boy — it wasn't like
he was really one of we, but still . . . Councillor, police, the council
and environment. I never live nowhere else. Mi heart's in this village.
People. I end up feeling strongly how I don't like. People I don't like.
Things I don't like. And when after a while Jo-Jo say "What we standing here in the sun carrying on like this for? Leh we go up by
Thelma. . . . " I knew I didn't want to go there.

Mack and Sam agree. They look up the hill, calling Carter who
still sitting down in Pharoh's yard, telling him to meet we across by
Thelma. I don't want to go there. Then Sam remember he have to
go back by Pharoh to put on his clothes. By this time Samlal and
Singh taking another track up to the road where Singh have his car
parked, and we start out. But while Jo-Jo and Mack make for
Thelma's parlour I branch off to make mi way home.

"What happen to he?" I hear Jo-Jo say, but I don't worry with
looking back or saying nothing.

As I make mi way back to the junction mi feet take me right past Teacher's house, and I see people there. People who never before crossed Teacher's yard sitting in his gallery quiet and respectful like. One or two standing up in the front yard and road. Councillor car's gone. By time I come abreast, the police car comes, and the inspector get out with the D.M.O. carrying his black bag right behind him. The boy still inside.

I see Teacher come out his door between the people on the gallery. He's changed clothes now, wearing white shirt and bow-tie, his hair combed and parted, and a quiet serious look on his face. He shake hands with his friend the inspector. He's not laughing, but from the way he do it you could tell they're going inside and will have a drink while the D.M.O. take care of his business. I go on.

Later that evening, when I couldn't stand being inside the house no more, I walk back out to take a breeze and see what's going on. I start up to the junction, the thought in my mind that when I see the others maybe we could pass a quiet game of all-fours for the time. But just before I get there I could hear him. As I come up to the last two houses before the shop I could hear him. Pharoh is in the road. He's there, talking like his regular self, and I hear him " . . . all yuh think all yuh know about pond. . . . All yuh talking 'bout tourist in the Devil's Woodyard. . . . All yuh know who put any of that there? . . . "

I turn back. I have to take mi breeze in another direction.

At the Desk

Metaphors, to do what they do must, along with everything else, be elusive. That is, they must have the capability of mesmerizing us with a dance on meanings. When we manage to put them in their places, assign them, fix them permanently, they lose their potence.

From the infant-stage chanting of nursery rhymes through the philosophic study of literary masterpieces, imaginative literature functions as a medium that opens passages between our own and the subjective world of others. It does so by detailing patterns of congruence and incongruity in the interior world we share, and at the same time organizing our acceptance or rejection of such patterns.

If a people wanted to understand us well, they could do much worse than go to our imaginative masterpieces. Such works have, for generations, carried the burden of instructing us in what it is to be

217

characteristically whatever we are. If entering the "native" subjective world is desirable, and standard ethnographic texts do not take us there, why not the literary text based on as thorough a knowledge of "native" culture as field-work makes possible?

Afterword

I began field work with the wish to document a criticism of the theory of social and cultural pluralism as applied to Caribbean society. Not that plural elements and the problems to which they give rise are absent from the Caribbean: they are all too painfully evident, and quite dominant in some cases. The idea was to shift emphasis in the application of the pluralism thesis. Given the recent and artificial origin of Caribbean society, pluralism seemed best understood not as an explanation for existing social-cultural dynamics, but the description of an historical condition — a stage — out of which Caribbean society was necessarily groping. The problem then was to seek out patterns in the cultural strategies — syncretism, accommodation, acculturation, etc. — people use to transcend the pluralist heritage. I write of this with much more understanding and clarity now than I did at that time, and with the benefit of a later awareness that conception of the problem was incomplete.

Overlooked was the circumstance that cultural and social choices in plural situations are dominated not only by pragmatic exigencies, but by aesthetic imperatives as well. The aesthetic we may understand here as a composite sensory-intellectual value exchange between ourselves and our environment, with satisfaction linked to the ideals of an interiorly ordered world. Aesthetic imperatives condition the experiencing of life as a satisfactory or unsatisfactory combination of achievements in time, consequently all relations are subject to aesthetic valuation.

In the development of modern Trinidadian culture, for instance, antipathy between "the elite" and "the ordinary," "black" and "non-black," "creole" and "Indian" is grounded in a mutual distaste between opposing categories as networks of values, distinct from the biological affiliation or economic status of particular people. "Indian," "creole," "black," "elite," etc. in this context stand not only for distinct social groups of different historical and biological origins, but for different aesthetic attitudes as well, particularly in respect to what constitutes the best quality in human relations, the best value for which life in general might be exchanged. The Trinidadian cultural heritage, then, is heavily marked by conflicting aesthetic categories, and integrating or mediating oppositional categories tends to be a source of tension. Mediating this tension is a common objective in the personal narratives that people tell about themselves and others with whom they are familiar.

Personal narratives reflect or report directly various meanings and attitudes associated with everyday life, and many of those in the first person which I have collected cast the principal in the role of handicapped hero, with the handicap being a moral or altruistic decision taken by the hero. An ironic sensibility helps to make sense of this and the real incongruities it reflects. Thus hero figures in personal narratives may also be the ones whose failures precipitate ridicule and laughter.

Laughter is important. Humor is very important. In the social sphere the aesthetic is experienced in the enactment of relations. Here, in Trinidadian culture, the comic makes its appearance as an ever ready antidote to uncomfortable meanings in the incongruous associations in history, or those evoked in argument and other disputatious discourse. Often, misunderstandings of history, and differences in cultural orientation constitute the root of argument and dispute. James Fernandez makes the point that the mission of argument is "to preserve our place and our gratifying performances and hence the world in which these things are lodged and to persuade others to recognize that place, that performance, and that world." [viii]. But here, where argument is as patent an activity as conversation, so too is humor, and probably for a balancing reason. If argument preserves our presence, laughter controls its value. There are very few instances in which the cost of laughter will be prohibitive enough to enjoin it.

What we have then is an everyday world in which the aesthetic sensibility plays a grand role. Maquet (1971) asserts that "Aesethetic perception is a manifestation of one of the few fundamental ways" in which we relate ourselves to the world. Even as one agrees with Maquet, it still needs to be noted that aesethetic activity extends much beyond the specialized work of "artists" and the "works of art" they make, and expression consequent upon aesthetic perception is not always of the pleasantly enchanted variety. In our aesthetic world, the intrusion of unlikeable situations and others are experienced as disturbances. In multi-cultural situations there is ample room for such disturbances, and depending on their intensity they may stimulate a range of expressions from mild statements of disgust, to segregation, to the active elimination of the other. Explorations in the aesthetic dimension, then, becomes necessary to a full understanding of any situation in which cultural pluralism is a salient factor.

In regard to ethnographic presentation, the restoration of the subject to the text involves more than the brief and fragmented delineation of individuals who are substantively treated as elementary factors in the intellectual puzzles through which we take ourselves. I think it is important for us to understand the people among whom we do research as palpitant contemporaries and to convey such an understanding to the audience. In the ethnographic field situation their puzzles and ours come into direct contact. The ethnographer initiates the contact, gives significant focus to the encounter, and thereby undertakes the responsibility of elaborating a universe in which their puzzle becomes comprehensible, as a rule, in terms of ours. In general, this has been approached through the re-contextualization of their experience in terms of an expository statement of our intellectual interests. Alternatively, by integrating their participation in its construction, the dramatic account permits an enhanced achievement of the imaginary universe in which we come to understand them.

On two counts, then, both as a way of addressing a serious problem in the understanding of plural situations, and as a way of generating an enhanced text, the dramatic (or dramatized) account seems to me arguably preferable to the expository. The proof of that rests, of course, with the narratives themselves.

One other question — how do we integrate the ethnographer as conscious participant in the text? As ethnographer, there is a part of me that spends a lot of time looking on, contemplating the meaning and relevance of the moment, even when I am involved in it actively. I also regularly re-deploy experiential details in my imagination to garner a sense of their extensionality, relationality, and their reflexive carrying power. This, it is probably fair to say, is an aesthetic exercise. It is also important — although perhaps unnecessary — that we be reminded aesthetic exercises do not occur in isolation from the intellect. In the aesthetic process, what is considered are those factors that take into account the laws (rules) of the phenomenal and the conditions of the epiphenomenal simultaneously. Both are aspects of the aesthetic world which is continuous, replete with its own insights and conclusions, and through which we guide ourselves by submission to certain conventions. The conventions in the case of the narrative medium are widely familiar.

The summary passages between narratives are intended to convey a sense of how my choices of situation and theme were stimulated. Although the instances of contemplation and the substantive materials called up in these passages are not categorically different one from the other, they were conceived at different levels of remove from the actual field. The perception of certain meanings and relations literally occurred during moments when I was actively involved in fieldwork. Others occurred while I was secluded but still in the village, and still others while I was back at my academic desk. The choric 'we' is a device that is well known in literature — from classical works to the fiction of George Lamming and Roger Mais — and one that is suited to the situation in which the ethnographer is among his chief informants.

Glossary of Trinidadian Terms

bata	drums used in African religious ceremony
bhagwat	East Indian religious ceremony in which the holy scriptures are read and neighbors feasted over several days
bhodi	a long string bean, similar to green black-eyed peas
crapaud	a large toad, commonly evoked as a reference for ugliness in appearance and foul behavior
dhalpurie	flat bread cooked with ground peas (dahl) on the inside, served around a curry stew of meat and potatoes
hice	to raise up or lift
kaiso	old-time calypso
kalinda	also calinda, or calenda — song and dance form associated with the performance of Orisa ceremonies, and ritual stick-fighting
lavwe	tunes and lyrics of stick-fighting songs
liming	equivalent to convivial "hanging-out" in small, reasonably intimate groups that are generally age-graded, and based on neighborhood, school, occupa-

223

tional, or other social affiliation. Groups may be mixed, sexually, but frequently are not. The sharing of food and drink, and intense verbal exchange mark liming behavior.

mashun	creole form for marchande — tradeswoman
mountain dew	illegal home-made rum
pelau	a spicy dish, similar to the Spanish paella, made of diced chicken or beef with pickled pork, rice and pigeon peas cooked together
poonyah	a medium-length, pointed, and very sharp cutlass, originally used in cocoa and coconut cultivation. To be distinguished from the heavier, curved "gilpin" used in cane cultivation. The poonyah is also a general gardening tool, and sometimes weapon
poui	a hard-wood tree noted for its beautiful blossoms and heavy, durable wood. A "poui" is also a fighting stick made from this wood, or a blow from such a stick
pyol	term for those who are of local Spanish ethnicity
qua qua	two flat strips of bamboo (sometimes other kinds of wood) which are slapped together in rhythmic accompaniment during the bongo dance
quenk	local wild pig
roti	soft flat bread served with curry stew. An East Indian contribution to local cuisine
rounders	one of the English games from which baseball was synthesized. Resembles softball.
sadhu	East Indian holy man
schupse	to suck one's teeth in disgust or derision

shadow-beni   an herb which grows uncultivated around yards and gardens. Used for spicing meats, and for medicinal purposes.

sikiye figs   the smallest variety of banana; usually cooked before full ripening in soups or as a side dish

souccouyant   female vampire

tampi   another name for marijuana

whe whe   an informal and illegal game of chance, similar to "the numbers" in North American cities and "bolita" in Spanish speaking Caribbean communities.

References

Asad, Talal
   1975   *Anthropology and the Colonial Encounter*. London and Atlantic
          Highlands, NJ: Ithaca Press and Humanities Press.

Armstrong, Robert Plant
   1971   *The Affecting Presence*. Urbana, IL: University of Illinois Press.

Bandelier, Adolf F.
   1916   *The Delight Makers*. New York: Dodd, Mead and Company.

Borenstein, Audrey
   1978   *Redeeming the Sin: Social Science and Literature*. New York: Columbia
          University Press.

Brathwaite, Lloyd
   1953   "Social stratification in Trinidad." Social and Economic Studies
          2:5–175.

Burroway, Janet
   1982   *Writing Fiction*. Boston: Little, Brown and Company.

Casagrande, Joseph
   1964   *In the Company of Man: Twenty Portraits of Anthropological Informants*.
          New York: Harper and Row.

Clifford, James and George E. Marcus (eds.)
   1986   *Writing Culture: The Poetics and Politics of Ethnography*. Berkeley:
          University of California Press.

Crapanzano, Vincent
   1980   *Tuhami: Portrait of a Moroccan*. Chicago: The University of Chicago
          Press.

Crowley, Daniel J.
   1957   "Plural and differential acculturation in Trinidad." American
          Anthropologist 59: 817–824.

Dumont, Jean-Paul
1978   *The Headman and I.* Austin: University of Texas Press.

Elder, Jacob D.
1969   "The Yoruba ancestor cult in Gasparillo." Trinidad: Institute of Social and Economic Research, University of the West Indies.

Fernandez, J. W.
1974   "The mission of metaphor in expressive culture." Current Anthropology 15: 119–45.
1985   *Persuasions and Performances.* Bloomington, IN: Indiana U. Press.

Gleason, Judith
1971   *Orisha: The Gods of Yorubaland.* New York: Atheneum.

Geertz, Clifford
1973   *The Interpretation of Cultures.* New York: Basic Books.
1983   *Local Knowledge.* New York: Basic Books.

Goldschmidt, Walter
1986   "Clan fission among the Ygoloporthna: A study in dysfunction." American Anthropologist 88: 172–175.

Herskovits, Melville J. and Frances S.
1947   *Trinidad Village.* New York: Knopf.

Hymes, Dell (ed.)
1974   *Reinventing Anthropology.* New York: Vintage Books.

Jones, Delmos J.
1970   "Towards a native anthropology." Human Organization 29: 251–259.

Josipovici, Gabriel
1972   "Mobius the stripper." Reprinted in Burroway 1982: 323–337.

Klass, Morton
1961   *East Indians in Trinidad.* New York: Columbia University Press.

Levi-Strauss, Claude
1966   "Anthropology: Its achievements and future." Current Anthropology 7: 124–127.

Lewis, Diane
1973   "Anthropology and colonialism." Current Anthropology 14: 581–591.

Lieber, Michael
1981   *Street Scenes: Afro-American Culture in Urban Trinidad.* Cambridge, MA: Schenkman Publishing Company.

Maquet, Jacques
1971   *Introduction to Aesthetic Anthropology.* Reading, MA: Addison-Wesley Publishing Company, Inc.

Marcus, George E. and Dick Cushman
1982   "Ethnographies as texts." Annual Review of Anthropology 11: 25–69.

Niehoff, Arthur and Juanita
1960   *East Indians in the West Indies.* Milwaukee: The Olsen Publishing Company.

Oxaal, Ivar
1965   *Black Intellectuals Come to Power.* Cambridge, MA: Schenkman Publishing Company, Inc.

Parsons, Elsie Clews (ed.)
1967   *American Indian Life.* Lincoln: University of Nebraska Press. (Originally published in 1922)

Price, Richard
1983   *First-Time: The Historical Vision of an Afro-American People.* Baltimore: The Johns Hopkins University Press.

Rodman, Hyman
1971   *Lower-Class Families: The culture of poverty in Negro Trinidad.* London: Oxford University Press.

Rosaldo, Renato
1980   *Ilongot Headhunting.* Stanford, CA: Stanford University Press.

Schmidt, Nancy J.
1981   "The nature of ethnographic fiction: A further inquiry." Anthropology and Humanism Quarterly 6: 8–18.

Schwartz, Barton M.
1963   *The dissolution of caste in Trinidad.* Unpublished dissertation: University of California at Los Angeles.

Shore, Bradd
1982   *A Samoan Mystery.* New York: Columbia University Press.

Simpson, George
  1965   *The Shango Cult in Trinidad*. San Juan: Institute of Caribbean
         Studies.

Tyler, Stephen A.
  1986   "Post-modern ethnography: From document of the occult to
         occult document." In Clifford and Marcus 1986: 122–140.

Valentine, Bettylou
  1978   *Hustling and Other Hard Work*. New York: The Free Press.

Valentine, Charles A.
  1968   *Culture and Poverty*. Chicago: The University of Chicago Press.
  1972   Black Studies and Anthropology: Scholarly and political interests
         in Afro-American culture. Reading, MA: Addison-Wesley
         Publishing Company, Inc.

Willis, Paul E.
  1980   *Learning to Labour*. Hampshire: Gower Publishing Company.

Willis, William S. Jr.
  1974   "Skeletons in the anthropological closet." *In* Hymes 1974: 121–152.

Wood, Donald
  1968   *Trinidad in Transition*. London, Oxford University Press.